THE TYRANNY OF
NICENESS

To Katherine V. Sommers

THE
TYRANNY
OF
NICENESS

UNMASKING THE NEED FOR APPROVAL

by Evelyn K. Sommers, Ph.D.

THE DUNDURN GROUP
TORONTO

Copy-Editor: Jennifer Gallant
Design: Andrew Roberts
Printer: Webcom

Library and Archives Canada Cataloguing in Publication

Sommers, Evelyn K. (Evelyn Kathleen)
   The tyranny of niceness : unmasking the need for approval /
Evelyn K. Sommers.

ISBN-10: 1-55002-558-9
ISBN-13: 978-1-55002-558-3

   1. Self-actualization (Psychology)   2. Social acceptance.   I. Title.

BF637.S4S655 2005   158.1   C2005-901764-3

Conseil des Arts du Canada   Canada Council for the Arts   Canadä   ONTARIO ARTS COUNCIL / CONSEIL DES ARTS DE L'ONTARIO

We acknowledge the support of the Canada Council for the Arts and the Ontario Arts Council for our publishing program. We also acknowledge the financial support of the Government of Canada through the Book Publishing Industry Development Program and The Association for the Export of Canadian Books, and the Government of Ontario through the Ontario Book Publishers Tax Credit program, and the Ontario Media Development Corporation.

Care has been taken to trace the ownership of copyright material used in this book. The author and the publisher welcome any information enabling them to rectify any references or credit in subsequent editions.

J. Kirk Howard, President

Printed and bound in Canada.
Printed on recycled paper.

www.dundurn.com

Dundurn Press	Gazelle Book Services Limited	Dundurn Press
8 Market Street, Suite 200	White Cross Mills	2250 Military Road
Toronto, Ontario, Canada	Hightown, Lancaster, England	Tonawanda NY
M5E 1M6	LA1 4X5	U.S.A. 14150

THE TYRANNY OF

NICENESS

CONTENTS

ACKNOWLEDGMENTS   9

INTRODUCTION   11

CHAPTER 1
THE IMAGE OF NICENESS   15

CHAPTER 2
HOW TO BE NICE   36

CHAPTER 3
SILENCED INTO NICENESS:
FROM THE BEGINNING   56

CHAPTER 4
CONSPIRACY OR COINCIDENCE?
REINFORCING SILENCE EN MASSE   83

CHAPTER 5
NICENESS AS PROTECTION;
NICENESS AS MASK   117

CHAPTER 6
THE HIGH COST OF BEING NICE   145

CHAPTER 7
TRANSFORMATION BEGINS INSIDE   176

CHAPTER 8
LETTING GO OF NICENESS   199

BIBLIOGRAPHY   235

ACKNOWLEDGMENTS

IT HAS BEEN my good fortune to have many people in my life who have helped bring this book to fruition. All have been important in their own ways, whether they have provided emotional support, critical feedback, enthusiasm for my ideas, or hands-on editing. Family, friends, and associates have contributed to the production of this book. They have encouraged me in direct and indirect ways, often when they said "you must have written it about me!" when I shared my ideas with them. These moments have been galvanizing for me, reinforcing again and again the relevance of the topic.

To my clients I say a special thank you. I am grateful to all who gave permission to include their stories, and to others who provided me with a reason for writing this book as they engaged in their individual struggles with niceness.

There are several more people whom I wish to thank by name.

For their continuing support and love, and for reading and commenting on the manuscript, I thank family members Lauren Shuster, Bobbie Sommers, and my mother, Katherine Sommers. My son, Adam Revesz, gave all of the above and also listened to my evolving ideas, dialoguing with me throughout the process, from its beginning to conclusion. Wendy McNamara and Jennifer Bamberry-Sommers have been enthusiastic supporters.

For their influence on this project, especially in its beginning stages, I thank Cindy Stone for her belief in the importance of the topic and her feedback and M.T. Kelly for suggesting I should be writing a book, not an essay. To Tom Allan, I am grateful for his affirming response to my ideas with the phrase "tyranny of niceness." Margaret Malone, Bruce Etches, Joanna Holt, and Carole Anne Armstrong have been encouraging presences and sounding boards.

Thank you to Joanne Duma and Dave Graham for their careful reading and thoughtful comments on the entire manuscript and to Paula Caplan, Sam Minsky, and Astrid Stec for feedback on parts of the manuscript at different stages along the way.

Thank you to Tony Hawke of The Dundurn Group for his enthusiastic response to the ideas and to Jennifer Gallant for her careful copyediting.

Finally, I am especially grateful to Larry Hoffman: He has been steadfast in his belief in the book and in my ability to write it, and he helped me define the kind of book I was writing — a clarity I needed in order to continue to completion. He enriched the text with his knowledge of history, lent his skills as a researcher and editor, and found a publisher. His energy and enthusiasm have been contagious. When I was struck with critical illness at one stage of the writing, he helped manage the details of my life, kept my spirits up, and took care of my dog and her puppies. He always believed I would survive and that the book would become a reality. His emotional support has been fortifying and inspiring.

INTRODUCTION

I WAS CROSSING the street in a small town one day, walking towards the entrance to a restaurant. A lone man was standing in front of the restaurant, between me and the door but at least five feet away from it. There was plenty of room for me to pass by him. Nonetheless, as I approached the area where he stood, he stepped away and said "Sorry" as I passed by. I cannot imagine why he was sorry unless he judged from my facial expression or demeanour that I was suffering in some way because of something he had done. There were at least three body widths between us and he had not been blocking my path. He was being neither unpleasant nor threatening, nor was he disturbing me in any way, so he had no reason to excuse himself. Yet this nice man not only moved but also apologized as he did so. If he had been unpleasant, blocked my way, or called me names I would have wished for him to be nice, but that was not the case. The man apologized simply for being there.

You may find yourself behaving in just the same way from time to time. Perhaps you are the one who apologizes to the person who steps backward onto your toes in the checkout line. Even though your apology leaves you feeling a bit uncomfortable, you think no more about it, except that you recognize yourself as someone who says "I'm sorry" far too often.

Fifteen years of hearing stories, in my practice of psychotherapy and counselling, from clients who have struggled with their own niceness have convinced me that being nice is not always a good thing, nor is it harmless or something to ignore. On the contrary, it is a troubling and complex phenomenon with a variety of implications. To be nice means to silence ourselves in some way, and in doing so, we compromise our authenticity and give up freedom to act and speak. On the other hand, niceness may facilitate the shedding of responsibility. When we teach children to be nice we may put them at risk. Trusting others who are nice, or appear to be nice, may not always be in our best interests.

This book is an exploration of what it means when we are "being nice." My starting point was my own experience of niceness, inspired by my own disappointments, regrets for those times that I did not act and speak authentically, and some stories that I wanted to tell. I have drawn from case examples and everyday observations, all of which have been disguised to respect the privacy of the people involved. Some of the case examples are composites of stories I have heard from many people, although most are actual cases.

In this book, I dig below the surface of niceness to show you the ways we learn it, how it is reinforced, how it is used, the impact it has on us, and what can happen when we teach our children to be this way. My analysis is cultural, political, and psychological. I pull together the contextual and the internal, the outer world of the people you and I live with and encounter every day, and our individual psyches. As you read on you will see the profound manner in which behaviour is affected by context, including the expectations and actions of family, teachers, friends, doctors, employers, clergy, lawmakers, and law enforcers. We need these people in our lives, but as you read you will learn why it is important to make our own voices heard with them.

My hope is that this book will be an awakening, that it will generate discussion, confirm feelings you experience and knowledge you already possess but have never voiced, and provide options for transforming what has become traditional niceness into behaviour that is vibrant and authentic.

Readers will be at different life stages when they pick up this book. Some will be young, just starting out in adult life, choosing careers to follow and deciding whether to live with someone as a couple or chart a solo path. Some will have young families and be immersed in the sea of children and work. Some will have completed careers and child-raising and be in a reflective phase of life with less emphasis on what they will do and become.

As we look back it is not always comfortable to see with the clarity of hindsight the results of our actions and decisions. It is not always comfortable to gain insight into our personalities and the emotional impact that we have had on family members, friends, and colleagues. We may feel good about our accomplishments but we may also have regrets.

At any point in time we have limited information — about ourselves, the people in our lives, the world outside us, and how they function in relation to each other. We have limited understanding of our own behaviours and we act on the basis of that information. There are many instances where we do not have complete control over our behaviour even though we may have certain intentions and understanding. As we look back at our past behaviour, we can stand in harsh judgment or we can understand that we have always been limited. At best, we can accept our limitations and our responsibility, congratulate ourselves when we are pleased with what we have done, and forgive ourselves when we are not. We can endeavour to learn from the past and live with integrity in the present and future.

If, as you begin to read, you believe that being nice is nothing to be concerned about, I suggest you think about giving it up. What would replace it? How would you teach your children to conduct themselves? Would the dissolution of niceness lead to a decline of our culture as we know it — to anarchy — and if so, why? Can you imagine living in a world without niceness?

In the chapters ahead I cover the functions of niceness, our ways of producing it, the reasons we hold on to it, and the impact it has on ourselves and other people. In the final two chapters I present elements that are necessary for transformation. The comment I have most frequently heard people make about the usefulness of self-help books is that they see themselves in the book. It is the "aha" of self-recognition that means the most to the reader. Less useful are the prescriptive exercises that are meant to assist change but often lead to still another failed attempt. Therefore, instead of offering a step-by-step program for change, I provide suggestions for activating seeds of transformation that will encourage a new way of thinking about yourself and the world in which you live and assist movement towards a more authentic, freer way of living. Reading about and identifying with niceness can be illuminating, enlightening, and frightening. Finding balance among these responses to the subject matter is the challenge.

In his January 6, 1941, address to Congress, Franklin Delano Roosevelt named four essential human freedoms: the freedom of speech and expression, the freedom to worship God in one's own way, the freedom from want, and the freedom from fear. Most people would say they want as much freedom as possible, to live their lives the way they desire. Yet we give up freedoms that are ripe for the picking every day when we suppress our thoughts and comply with others in ways that leave us feeling disappointed, unsatisfied, and alienated from ourselves. What wish for freedom is this, that we forfeit it so readily?

CHAPTER 1
THE IMAGE OF NICENESS

A WOMAN AND her six-year-old daughter were found dead in their neat, orange brick suburban home. The husband and father had murdered them and attempted to take his own life. He was found unconscious alongside his family. Quoted in the newspaper report, a neighbour commented, "They were a really nice family — they were a happy family…."

The news that the man killed his wife and daughter, then attempted suicide, drops uneasily into the slot beside the image of this "nice" family. How could both the perception and the event possibly be true? It seems illogical and frightening that a nice family could come to such a horrible end.

This family was like millions of others who present one face to the public and keep a very different one hidden. They present an image of niceness, maintaining a false connection to the outside world while living lives of anguish and disconnection from each other, and themselves, in private. Sometimes the bubble of niceness bursts, as it did with this family, and then the extent of the superficiality is revealed. More often, people resign themselves to living undramatic lives, which Thoreau described as "quiet desperation," lives that result in compromises to their health, safety, and happiness. Although we are healthier when we live authentic, open lives, we hide because we think we must in order to be considered nice. We have learned to be nice in order to be accepted by others. The price of such acceptance can be a sense of alienation from oneself.

The news of the family in the orange bungalow is stunning, and yet it is everyday news. With rare exceptions, the daily newspapers and news broadcasts carry horror stories involving nice people. Children are molested by priests, voters are disappointed by politicians who renege on promises, and pensioners are swindled out of their life savings. In these stories, the perpetrators are people the victims thought they could trust. The victims, who have good reasons to believe the culprits are nice people, are ultimately disappointed and hurt.

Dylan Klebold and Eric Harris, the teenagers who went on a shooting rampage at Columbine High School in Littleton, Colorado, in 1999, were portrayed by the news media as boys from nice families. They lived in a nice community made up of nice people living in well-kept homes, people who went to church on Sundays and attended their children's little league baseball games, whose anti-social behaviour went no further than an occasional traffic ticket. People move to places like Littleton to avoid acts of violence such as these youths committed. Yet Dylan Klebold and Eric Harris had lived in that community. It was in the wake of the fatal eruption of violence that their neighbours discovered the extent to which the youths had been living lives of profound conflict.

In the small community of Woodbridge, a suburb of Toronto, neighbours were surprised at the arrest of an unassuming family man who, it turned out, was Alfonso Caruana, a drug lord with links to the mafia. He was one of the world's most wanted men, yet neighbours knew him as a family man living a quiet life with his wife and children in the suburbs.

You may have felt the sting of such deceptions yourself. Although you may not have experienced anything so dramatic as being physically injured or bilked out of your life savings, maybe you have been jilted by someone you thought was the nicest person you'd ever met, someone you loved. Maybe you asked a friend for an honest opinion about the new suit you planned to buy or a colleague about work you were doing, but all you heard were stock comments that felt meaningless or seemed untruthful. Although not quite convinced, you accepted the feedback because you are a nice person who doesn't probe too deeply even when you are in doubt. On those occasions when you have felt deceived, you may have wondered how someone you thought was nice could hurt you.

Maybe you have heard people struggling with the contradictions of niceness — my husband is a nice person when he's not drinking, my wife was wonderful until she walked out on me for another man. How could someone so nice be so cruel? The contradictions of niceness are so imbued in our culture that we have clichés to describe them: "nice guys finish last," "no more Mr. Nice Guy," and "too darned nice." In my psychotherapy practice I hear, on a regular basis, "I've got to stop being so nice," as clients struggle to honour their own needs and desires rather than sell out in order to be or say or do what they believe people want of them.

Maybe you have noticed your own contradictions in your interactions with people, expressed in the interests of being nice. Any or all of the following examples may apply: You remain silent when you might have spoken out and expressed authentic feelings. You conform to styles of dress and furnish your home according to the advice of self-proclaimed experts or your neighbours rather than according to your own values, tastes, and financial capabilities. You are less than honest in giving your opinion and repeat clichés as if they were meaningful statements. You rarely express so-called negative emotions such as sadness or outrage, preferring to blot out or rationalize events that set off such feelings. In order to appease others you do things you either regret or simply wish you had not done that you cannot bring yourself to undo. You say nothing rather than risk confrontation even when an issue arises about which you have strong feelings. You avoid telling people, especially authority figures, that they have offended you or that you disagree with their opinions or suggestions. You lie rather than tell the truth when you simply do not feel like attending a social engagement or meeting. You keep your different opinions to yourself in order to hold on to your job even though the management's positions are ethically and philosophically different than your own. You pretend you can afford to buy whatever is being sold or fabricate reasons for not buying rather than simply refusing. You agree to get together with an acquaintance who is attempting to strike up a friendship, then cancel and hope the person will not call again rather than say you believe there is not enough common ground for a relationship. You use your telephone caller identification to hide from people rather than telling them that they have called at an inconvenient time. You contribute more work in your workplace or volunteer situation than you can and still be able to maintain some balance in your life. You suppress your exuberance when you are happy about some success you have had.

Your niceness grates against your true feelings and thoughts, causing an ongoing internal friction. You feel you are betraying yourself and feel stuck. Still, you have spent a lifetime learning that niceness is good, and as far as you can see, niceness *is* good, so you carry on and try to ignore the grating.

All his life Max tried to be nice. He came to me for counselling because his marriage was in trouble. He told me that on his wedding day, ten years earlier, the voice of inner wisdom in his head said, "You shouldn't be doing this, it's not right." The message was clear, but at the time, Max found himself in a dilemma of overwhelming proportions. He could either cancel the wedding or go ahead with it, consigning the quiet but distinct voice inside him to the emotional scrap heap labelled pre-wedding jitters. If he cancelled he would lose the woman he professed to love and he would disappoint his parents, siblings, and friends, who had put a great deal of time and money into the wedding. He would be unable to explain why he had waited so long to announce his doubts or the exact reason for backing out. He would incur the wrath of his fiancée's parents and siblings, who would never speak to him again. When the deed was done he would feel aimless, because the entire previous year had been dedicated to planning the wedding and preparing to be married. The prospect of facing these important people with such a decision was too much for him. He also admitted that he had not wanted to lose the buffer against loneliness that marriage promised. He could not let his small voice of inner wisdom guide him. At the eleventh hour he could not face the consequences of heeding the voice he heard so clearly.

He went ahead and got married that day, instead of listening to the voice. Being an honourable — and, above all, nice — man, he continued to live in the marriage and be a faithful spouse, though one who was often distracted by thoughts of other women. Ten years later Max was sitting in my office, unable to endure any longer what had felt wrong to him all those years before. The problems he saw back then — his wife's religious views were much different than his own, they shared few common interests, and his wife had been ambivalent about having children — had taken on mammoth proportions over the years. He could still appreciate some of the qualities that had attracted him to his wife, but he could not let himself give to her in a way that would have been fulfilling to him and to her because he felt at a great emotional distance from her. They argued constantly and seldom had satisfying time together. The guilt he had accumulated along the way was enormous and growing. He wanted children, but as her career interests grew her interest in children waned even more.

Despite all these problems, he could not speak up and end the marriage. Although his intention on his wedding day had been rooted in a wish to be noble, his decision to go ahead had serious repercussions for him and his wife. Through his inability to act on what he felt to be right, out of fear of personal losses, he deeply affected the woman he married as well as both their families. Acting on his need to be seen as nice hurt him and others in a much deeper way than if he had been honest — but not nice — on his wedding day.

Max kept silent. He ignored his inner voice of wisdom that told him to step out of his commitment to marry before it happened. At the time all he could see was the embarrassment of changing his mind at the last minute. He imagined that people would think he was an unkind cad, leading his fiancée on to humiliation. Unable to imagine the much greater agony a decision to wed would initiate and believing that he had the strength to overcome whatever obstacles his decision might create, he went ahead with a marriage that was doomed. He maintained a facade for years, trying to convince others and himself that the marriage he had entered into was a solid one. Until the moment came when he could no longer abide the conflict he felt inside, he held onto the image of niceness, silencing the voice that knew better, that urged Max to act in his best interests despite the risks. In the end, he divorced his wife and they started new lives, but they had both paid a ten-year price for his niceness.

Another client, Brad, told me about a weekend away with his lover, Jane. At her invitation he had flown to Washington where she had business. Although she had work to do, they planned to spend a full day together visiting the Smithsonian Institute during the weekend. By Sunday, the last day of their three-day weekend, they had spent almost no time together and Jane had another appointment that morning. As she left the hotel room she said she would be back in two hours and they would go then to the Smithsonian. Brad waited. And waited. He ate breakfast and read a newspaper in the hotel lobby. He ate lunch and continued to wait. Jane called after she'd been away three hours to say she'd be another half-hour. The bellman and Brad were beginning to establish a relationship. "Brad," said the bellman, "you are one patient dude."

An hour later Jane called saying, again, that she would be there in a half-hour. Brad weighed the possibility of going to the museum alone and meeting her there, but the logistics were too complicated and he continued to wait. When Jane finally arrived there was no possibility of going to the museum because they had only two hours before heading to the airport. Jane was apologetic and Brad was forgiving, but later that week he told her he felt he needed the freedom to see other women. As he told me the story and we explored the feelings he was having while he waited for Jane that day, Brad commented, "I've got to stop being Mr. Nice Guy. People just walk all over me. I should have gone on my own when she didn't arrive at the time she originally promised."

Brad was full of anger at Jane but wanted to preserve the relationship, and so he covered his anger by being silent. Unfortunately, his behaviour did not achieve the intended goal. The relationship ended soon after this incident, and Brad never told Jane that he had been angered by her failure either to keep her promise to him or to let him know that she could not keep her promise. If it had been the first time she had kept him waiting it might not have been so upsetting, but this was part of the pattern of their relationship. Brad could have released himself from the bondage of waiting had he not been such a "nice guy." It is worth noting that his niceness did not save the relationship.

Both Max and Brad were motivated by fear. Max was afraid that if he did not go through with the wedding he would lose the respect of his fiancée and her family and his connection with them. He was afraid his own family and friends would not understand. Brad was afraid of losing Jane, as he had been afraid to lose others before her.

Brad and Max remained silent by choice, but there are also instances when people do not make the choice themselves. In her book *Gone to an Aunt's*, Anne Petrie describes, with great sensitivity, cases of unmarried teenage girls in the decades of the fifties and sixties who were silenced about their pregnancies. These young women had slipped across the line dividing "nice girls" from "bad girls" through the single act of having an egg fertilized. They were removed from their family homes under the guise of an extended visit to an aunt's home and forced to wait out their pregnancies in hiding, in group homes set up to shelter these "outcasts." The parents of these women, and perhaps the women themselves, also acted out of fear. They were afraid of being judged and ridiculed by their relatives and community.

As a society we have outgrown the silencing of unmarried pregnant women, one segment of society's powerless, but we still silence ourselves and others in the interests of being nice and expecting niceness. We do this with the best of intentions, but too often the silencing results in troubled or wrecked relationships, stifled children, botched or uncomfortable friendships, or a sense of alienation from ourselves.

NICENESS   MEANS   SILENCE

The word *nice* was derived from the Latin *nescius*, meaning "ignorant," and the French *nescire*, meaning "not to know." It is the notion of silence and silencing that links current use of *nice* to these Latin and French derivatives. When we fail to express our thoughts and opinions or refuse to hear what others say, we are colluding with "ignorance" or "not knowing." There is a shutting down — or silencing — of oneself or the other. In this way silence, in some form or degree, is the essential characteristic of being nice. The silence of niceness means deference and obedience to the authority or mere presence of others, without question. Such silence is the equivalent of self-denial: denial of the need to speak, to form opinions and share them with other people, denial of the ability to think critically, denial of honest human interaction. Since we know ourselves better if we think critically, practise speaking out, and interact with honesty toward others, the nicer — more silenced and obedient — we become, the less we know ourselves.

When we agree with someone while stifling a different opinion we comply with the questionable bit of advice we have heard since childhood: "If you can't say something nice, don't say anything at all." When we compromise ourselves in this way in order to be thought nice or to avoid confrontation we silence ourselves. To accept prevailing opinions rather than think about the implications of a situation or issue and then express our own conclusions is to silence ourselves. When the words we speak are only to reinforce the view of the other person even if we have different views, we are silencing ourselves. Silencing can take the form of restraint in behaviour or strict conformity in your choice of clothing or lifestyle. It can be a censoring of speech, withholding an opinion we believe others would not want to hear. Nice people don't ruffle the feathers of others.

In the precarious world of human interaction the silence of niceness can take many forms. It can mean running errands for people when we do not have the time or when we know favours will not be returned. We cannot say no, so we say we are able to run an errand and then drive across town to pick up packages for family members who serve themselves with the assumption that it would be no trouble for us to do it. Or the silencing may take the form of volunteering on yet another church or school committee because we have an hour of uncommitted time and everyone else seems so busy. We watch the neighbours' children when we would rather not have the added responsibility, and the fact that they never reciprocate or contribute to the endless snacks we feed their children remains unmentioned. We feel unable to express a difference of opinion when the family doctor offers us a medication or other treatment that we do not want. We assume our child's teacher knows best rather than challenge her methods even though our child complains. We do not question the opinions expressed by the minister in his sermons, even though they leave us squirming in the pew. We feel emotionally coerced when these things happen, yet we say nothing that we think might offend. On the contrary, we may say something to convince ourselves that we are in agreement. Perhaps we convince ourselves that the errand or favour was really a benefit to us in some way. We choose to believe it was our idea so we can remain nice and reduce the discomfort we experience when we feel exploited. Perhaps we find it easier to dismiss a child's complaints or listen less closely to the minister's words than to act on what we hear, which might mean confrontation.

We rationalize our silence: we do not want to risk offending or confronting someone or denying another person's request or authority.

As nice people we pursue passivity, paradoxically expending a great deal of effort holding onto feelings, words, and actions that, it is believed, would be expressed at our peril. The hard-won passivity reveals itself physically in a stiff smile, strained conversation, and tightness inside the chest. In the extreme, the *really* nice person is a chameleon, saying nothing even as others behave offensively or express outrageous disturbing opinions. The disciple of niceness is identified by the absence of expressed opinions. Using rationalization we add weight to the emotional silencing. We equate stating our thoughts with rejecting or judging. Rather than do this we silence our honest opinions.

In contrast, think what it would be like to be outspoken and opinionated. Think about pushing the limits of conversation and behaviour, refusing to grant favours out of a sense of obligation, expressing your preferences, and making your dissatisfaction known in a clear and respectful way when something or someone fails to deliver promised goods or service. Think about complaining when a meal or service does not please you. Think about telling the parent down the street that he can hire a good sitter from the local agency rather than call on you. Think about telling your physician that you have questions about his or her suggested treatment and want something different, or a second opinion. Think about telling your child's teacher that he needs to encourage your child to express her opinions and then to validate her for speaking.

This directness does not have to be rude or unkind but rather straightforward statements of opinion or information. Think about being honest all the time and maintaining allegiance to your own beliefs even when you feel you may not be accepted because of them. Think about the freedom and the excitement of saying what you feel and think. Think about telling your friends that you like — even love — them rather than letting them assume it. Think about resurrecting some of the exuberance and enthusiasm you felt as a child. This honesty is as noisy as niceness is silent.

A wonderful by-product of such honesty is the lack of resentment when you agree to fulfill a request for someone because you *want* to do it. You agree with someone because you have weighed the options and believe in that agreement. You bestow sincere and unequivocal compliments and bask in the reflected glow of the recipients' pleasure.

The difference between being nice and not-nice lies in degrees of silence. Niceness requires a stifling of opinions, preferences, and behaviours, conforming in real or superficial ways to some standard that is never defined. So, if both the payoff for giving up niceness and the cost of being nice are so great, why do we behave this way? The answer is both simple and complex: there is risk involved. People who are not-nice according to this definition risk confrontation because their directness may be misunderstood in cultures where niceness is cultivated. We are so unaccustomed to speaking our minds that when someone does, we find it shocking, even in situations of relative insignificance. I was in a restaurant with my partner, Larry, and two friends. The three had ordered starter courses, but only two plates were delivered to the table. When the server failed to reappear and it became clear that an order had been forgotten, Larry signalled, as soon as possible, to the server and reminded him. The soup was delivered ten minutes later by the server, who offered a perfunctory apology. As Larry was sipping the last mouthful the server stopped by to whisk away the bowl and inquire, "Was it worth waiting for?" Of course, we all knew the expected answer was "yes." Larry chose to respond, in a respectful tone, with "no," which for him was the honest answer. The soup was not worth the wait. It was not good enough to eradicate his annoyance at having to eat it alone after the others had finished their first courses and at having to rush because the main courses arrived before he could finish it. Everyone, especially the server, was surprised at the answer. But why? Larry was answering the question with honesty and directness, and the server should have expected nothing more than that.

The hallmark of nice people is that they rarely, if ever, take even the small risk Larry took at dinner, to speak with candour. While there are many causes and good reasons for occasionally silencing ourselves, it is important not to underestimate the power of a culture in which being nice is accepted, without question, and promoted as a desirable quality. Niceness as a way of life is typified by passivity, obedience, denial, avoidance, and fear of making a direct, honest statement.

NICENESS:
THE "DISEASE" TO PLEASE?

By now you understand that I believe niceness is a problem. Like me, others have noticed the problem and some have attempted to both describe it and offer solutions, sometimes under the heading of people-pleasing.

In keeping with a growing tendency to medicalize behavioural problems, people-pleasing, or niceness, has been designated by some as a "disease." In her book *The Disease to Please*, psychologist Harriet Braiker presents a battery of questionnaires for readers to self-diagnose the so-called disease, along with a twenty-one-day action program. Her program was designed to aid the "recovery" of the ill persons whom she describes, using the language of psychological pathology, as having a "compulsive need to please."

Oprah Winfrey has made much of the people-pleasing phenomenon in her popular magazine, *O*, offering stories about celebrities such as Jane Fonda who have been afflicted with the "disease" from which Oprah herself professes to be suffering. Both Oprah's and Braiker's identification and description of the problem validate the feelings of inferiority that many people feel, especially those of their target audience, women. For that alone the work is valuable. However, while they mean to help people with such problems, they form part of a cycle that fosters the phenomenon in the first place and that keeps women rooted to a spurious causality. Dr. Braiker quotes Eleanor Roosevelt: "No one can make you feel inferior without your permission." This quote implies that the fault is our own if we feel inferior and therefore cannot speak on our own behalf, even though the culture in which we live sends out the message that we must not speak with candour. This is a small example of the cultural context in which niceness is expected and reinforced.

Applying a disease model to a psychosocial phenomenon is troublesome because it roots both problem and solution in the individual. This approach ignores the fact that humans are social creatures who need interactions with others for their physical and mental development and are thus affected by environment. Implicit in the notion of niceness is relationship, which is ignored in conceptualizing niceness as a disease. If we could survive alone we would never have to think about being nice or not-nice, we would simply be. But niceness is a problem of relating, and the solutions can be worked out only between people, not exclusive of other people.

The disease approach fails to produce options for change beyond individual behaviour management. It provides no context for understanding how the problem is generated in a social context and therefore leaves the sufferer alone with her problem. Readers of self-help books may identify with the described behaviours and try to practise the exercises, but most often they fail to change for more than a brief period. When this happens, the reader feels even more blameworthy, for she is so "sick" that she cannot stop the undesirable behaviour even after receiving all the instructions in the book and listening to Oprah's or some other celebrity's confession and learning about their road to recovery — after receiving help from experts. I have heard it from clients: they feel worse than when they were pleasing people and as a result give up the self-help program and return to their beginning level of compliance, or worse. As an added bonus for this exercise in futility, many acquire a heightened sense of failure. This result is similar to short-term treatment programs that aim to repair problems of character that have been resilient and resistant to "fixing" for years of a person's life. Although not the intention, the programs may ensure a person's ultimate failure, because once the novelty has worn off and the person is left alone without support, old behaviours, tried, familiar, and therefore much easier to carry out, quickly resurface. There is no easy solution to such problems, no foolproof cookbook method of changing one's character. Still, in this age of instant gratification, people continue to search for an easy, prescribed fix, and many others are willing to provide brief hope that it is possible.

Dr. Braiker notes that pleasing equals niceness, and, consistent with a portion of my analysis, identifies the self-deceiving expectations of self-protection as a basis for the behaviour. However, her explanation of the origin of the "disease-to-please" is limited primarily to the omnipresent blame-alls, abuse and parental alcoholism. Like a multitude of other self-help books, her analysis focuses mainly on the family. The social context within which the dynamics under discussion occur may be given a nod, but it is not probed. The question — what is it in our culture that leads to the parental abusiveness and alcoholism that turn people into pleasers — is not addressed. Although she touches on some real and contributing problems to people-pleasing, she fails to provide a broader and deeper understanding for her readers, one that may give them a more profound and contextual view of themselves.

BEYOND DISEASE

By the time you read this, you have probably claimed the niceness problem as your own. It is entrenched in your thinking and behaviour, and there may be good reasons for staying in the trench. However, since you are reading this book you are probably not at peace with your niceness and you are seeking a way to change. Freeing yourself begins by understanding the problem in its complexity, determining how you came to be so nice, the impact it has on you and people whose lives you touch, and the reasons you stay that way. It also requires a course of supported analysis of the catalysts for its reoccurrence, which takes time. You may wish to hold on to some aspects of niceness, but you can make a wise decision about that only if you know what you are keeping and what you are giving up. A dedicated "pleaser" will feel uncomfortable trying to become someone very different but will become happier by relinquishing some habits that feel like clear sellouts.

Although the problem is not something you asked for, you cannot simply give it back. No one can make change for you. Even worse, change is hard when it means relinquishing some of the comforting aspects of niceness and colliding with the context that fosters it. The changes you make may not always be received kindly. Although others may help along the way, they may also thwart your progress, however unintentionally, because they, too, are caught in the trap of niceness. This might not seem fair or appealing, but it is the reality that confronts you in your quest to undo your niceness. The starting gate for your marathon of change is a new understanding of the context you live in and how you function, or do not function well, within it. Grappling with the problem means looking inside at yourself, looking at your family relations, and understanding how you and your family are affected by the world, including its people, beyond your front door. Change can be initiated and carried out only by you, but to do it effectively you must understand the impact the world in which you live has on you and your struggles to achieve that change.

All institutions, groups, clubs, and organizations have membership requirements. In formal institutions they form the exclusion criteria. That is, you cannot belong if you do not donate a required sum of money, if you do not follow the code of conduct, or if your beliefs oppose those of the group. Formal organizations set out the requirements explicitly in a written document. Informal organizations or groups agree on a standard through an unwritten, unspoken code. In day-to-day interactions many people adhere to the standard of "being nice," which is not formalized or articulated in a methodical or concrete way but is nonetheless embedded in an understanding of how to relate to others. The standard is never discussed as a standard, but it exists as surely as if it had been designed as a requirement for membership in an exclusive club, and people may be excluded if they do not meet it.

As an individual, you struggle to meet these requirements without knowing what they really are. All you know for sure is that what you say, what you wear, and how you behave in public are all determined by the expectation of niceness.

ISN'T IT GOOD TO BE NICE?

Some niceness is good, the type in which people act from their deepest ability to be kind and forthcoming with compassion. In this book I examine the instances that are beneficial neither to the people who are nice nor to the people they affect.

Even though we feel stressed by our niceness, we do not question that it is a standard that brings out the best in us and works on our behalf in our relations with others. Underlying our dedication to niceness are intentions about which we neither speak nor think except perhaps in an offhanded way. We believe that being nice will:

- ease the beginning of relationships,
- endear us to people,
- hold relationships together,
- prevent emotional pain for ourselves and others,
- cover up our flaws or unkind thoughts,
- mask our true motives,
- spare us from having to say things that are hard to say, and
- provide us with a peaceful existence.

Stories about people who hold or held beliefs such as these are sprinkled throughout this book. Although there may be moments when any one of these expectations are realized, if being nice means silencing important thoughts or feelings the outcome cannot be positive in the long run.

For certain, there are times when we wish other people were nice when they are not, if they are loud with anger, say hurtful or spiteful things, treat others badly, or refuse to hear another point of view. There are many reasons for wanting people to be nice, to silence the things they might say that we find offensive, confrontational, or more direct than we can tolerate because it means we have to think more about an issue. We may not want to alter our thinking about this because we would then have to face our own contradictions and change some of our own behaviours.

We want others to be nice because it makes us feel safer. We do not want people to disagree with us or be too honest when their opinions and feelings are different than ours because it makes us feel threatened or uncomfortable or it may mean that we must think harder about our own position and how to explain it. I suspect this inclination is an arti-fact of the human condition, of people's tendency to herd. People are gregarious and need to have others in their lives. We crave the company of others, and this is not a frivolous desire. Just as other primates need physical contact in order to survive, we need other people if we are to survive. It is much easier to be with others who see everything our way than with people whose thoughts, behaviours, and opinions are different. It is easier to hang together as a group if everyone shares the same opinions. When people do not agree they can still coexist if they silence their dissonant voices to the extent needed to maintain stability or find another way to be together. It is unlikely those relationships will be satisfying at any more than a superficial level.

Exposure of differences between people can lead to difficulties. Nations are built and distinguish themselves from other nations by emphasizing distinct features such as dress, diet, language, and religion. Wars and divisions within and between countries occur when people cling to different beliefs. Although people need to be free to choose their own belief systems, the fundamental similarities in religions, such as fostering goodwill to all, are often lost in the struggle to emphasize distinctions. Men and women are further apart emotionally than need be because small differences between them are exaggerated. Gender relations, as they exist, would be challenged if men were candid about their feelings of dependence and fear and women exhibited their strengths in public and refused to act coy or helpless — subordinate — in the presence of men. People have not learned how to express their differences peacefully without creating huge rifts. They either dig in their heels and fight in order to dominate, or subordinate themselves to the other. Both postures stunt or distort the growth of all parties concerned.

We feel safer with niceness because the reassurance that others approve protects us from our harsh feelings about ourselves. When someone is "nice" to us, we can think of ourselves as acceptable and good. If they are not nice we can defend ourselves. When they are straightforward and respectful we are left to struggle with our own evaluation of ourselves. Nice people may have thoughts very different from the ones we think they have, and yet we silence ourselves, withholding our own true feelings to live up to our perception of their opinions. Seldom do we consider the high price we pay to gain acceptance in this way.

Niceness fosters a culture of aloneness. Nice people exist in separate worlds, rarely or never revealing themselves to others in their lives. They may have lots of superficial communication with other people but little real connection. They fear aloneness, but their niceness perpetuates it.

FAR-REACHING EFFECTS OF THE SILENCE OF NICENESS

Some time ago I went to visit an elderly woman, Louise, who was dying of liver cancer. I had not seen her since the onset of her illness several months earlier. When I arrived, her two daughters, present to help their mother, greeted me. We had been chatting together for a few minutes when Louise suddenly asked me, "How do I look?" I was stunned for a moment. She looked deathly ill. Her abdomen was distended and her skin was yellow. Without waiting for my reply Louise said, with a look of disdain at her daughters, "They keep telling me I look good." She paused. Her daughters looked at me with uneasy half-smiles. "Why don't they just tell me how I really look?" she continued. "My seven-year-old grandson did. 'Granny,' he said, 'you don't look very good.'" She laughed. "So why do they have to lie to me?"

She shot her daughters a look of scorn that told me more than any words could about the pain she experienced from this rift with them. She knew very well that she was dying. The anger she was expressing could have been related to their failure to respond as she had hoped, to her condition or to other aspects of her situation, but asking them how she looked was Louise's way of inviting her daughters to talk with her. The rift developed because she had no better way of asking them and they were too nice to discuss the obvious. Their own discomfort with her approaching death or their sadness at the prospect of losing their mother kept them silent. To the world they would say they did not want to hurt her feelings.

Even though her daughters' niceness may well have been something Louise, like millions of other parents, unwittingly helped to foster in them as children, believing she was doing her best for them, she found it frustrating and dishonest. If they had been able to express, with kindness, that her appearance had indeed been affected by the illness she was suffering, that she no longer looked the petite bundle of energy they used to know, they might have cried together. They might have touched moments of pure intimacy instead of letting anger and silence deepen the split that already separated them at the end of Louise's life.

Although niceness is often intended to bridge difficult relationship problems and smooth over troubling issues, more often it creates fissures and leaves people feeling hurt and alienated. For one young man, the niceness of a lover who spurned him culminated in damage to his self-esteem. Richard fell in love with Heather, who took pride in being a nice person, always smiling, soft-spoken, and agreeable. Her friends recognized this quality in her and told Richard that he must be sure to appreciate her and take good care of her because she was so nice. Richard, who was attracted to Heather's niceness, took the advice, felt lucky to have her, and treated her with care. For a while, everything went well and they looked like a couple in love, but in a few months Richard began to feel uneasy, sensing some change between them though unable to put his finger on what it was. When he asked her, she denied anything was wrong.

Soon Heather announced that she was going to take a vacation with a friend who happened to be a man — many of Heather's friends were men, as Richard knew. Richard was alarmed about the trip and they had arguments about it. Heather accused Richard of being too jealous, of making her feel hemmed in. She introduced the friend to Richard, who felt somewhat reassured by the meeting. Heather went away for a week and telephoned Richard twice while she was gone. She returned, they got together, and she was just as nice as ever to him. Nonetheless, Richard's uneasiness, which had never completely dissipated, became stronger. When he asked her, Heather maintained there was no problem, and he could do nothing but take her word for it.

One day a few weeks later Richard called Heather as he routinely did. She wasn't home so he left a message. Evening came and she had not returned his call, which was unusual. Richard waited and rationalized that she was busy with work, catching up after the holiday. The next day came and went and still he received no return call. Richard reasoned that she was busy with work and friends, and since she knew his schedule was waiting until she was sure she could catch him at home. When Heather still had not returned Richard's call after a week he could no longer find excuses for her.

Some time later Richard came to understand, after struggling with disbelief, that the relationship was over. He was stunned, trying to take in and understand how a person who prided herself on being so nice could end the relationship without telling him. To him, it was an unfeeling act, and he was devastated, left in pain and deep humiliation. He reviewed, again and again, events of the past few months, questioning what he did that was so horrible as to render him unworthy of a respectful goodbye or explanation.

By chance, they met six months later. Heather was pleasant and congenial, acting as though nothing had happened. Richard, having become disillusioned about nice women but being a nice person himself, suppressed his hurt and anger, played along with her friendliness, but kept the interaction to a minimum.

This story has two endings: Richard's and Heather's. Richard's self-esteem suffered a severe blow. He was hurt and embarrassed and felt unable to trust or to evaluate other people's trustworthiness — or for that matter to evaluate his own behaviour in relationships with women. Heather walked away knowing she was a nice person. After all, she had said nothing mean to Richard.

Like Richard did at the onset of his relationship with Heather, most people accept the niceness of another person as a good thing. Like Heather, most feel that being nice is a good thing. Yet, for Richard, the relationship became mired in emotional pain.

Attempts to be nice in these cases resulted in disruptions in relationships and blows to one person's self-esteem. None of the nice people intended to cause such harm, but it happened despite their intentions.

HOW SERIOUS CAN IT BE?

When I am face to face with clients in my office each working day, I see the extent of damage sustained when people silence themselves. Women and men come to me hurting because they cannot say to people in their lives what is in their hearts and on their minds. Many have lived by the code of self-censorship for so long that their feelings and opinions have become fleeting glimpses, even to themselves. They struggle to find words for their feelings and deepest thoughts even in my office, where no feelings, thoughts, or words are off limits. Many have been so numbed that they have trouble knowing what feelings they are having even as tears stream down their faces.

A story on the Internet describing a couple's chicken-eating habits zeroes in on the miscommunication that can occur when people do not say what they think and feel. The wife said she always gave her husband breast meat because she thought he preferred it, though she herself preferred it. The husband accepted the white meat without question, thinking she was giving it to him because she preferred the thigh and drumstick, which was what he preferred. Although each thought they were putting the other's wishes ahead of their own they were actually projecting their own wishes onto the other. A casual onlooker might consider such people to be selfless and thoughtful, but neither was satisfied and neither had stopped to do the obvious — tell the other about their own preferences.

These two are like many couples who attempt to give what they think the other wants and, in the process, hide themselves from each other. They become familiar strangers, arguing day after day in vain and unconscious attempts to find the real person in the other. After years of living inauthentic lives together they do not know each other. And neither can speak the necessary words to break out of inauthentic relating and into taking the risk of exposing their deepest thoughts, feelings, and wishes to each other.

You may agree that subduing opinions and emotions in the service of being nice can be damaging, but you may wonder how serious it can be. You might wonder what possible harm can be done by encouraging your children to be nice. After all, something that has gained a widespread cultural following can't be all bad, can it?

In fact, the effects are wide-ranging and profound. Being nice can create an internal rift. It has the power to invalidate people's experiences, leaving them in a state of angst, waiting to be heard and understood by someone. Being nice can put children in physical danger if they are afraid to speak out against authority figures who might do them harm. It can create long-term emotional problems if they feel they must be nice to win their parents' approval.

Brad, who waited hours for his partner to show up, is now in his mid-thirties and working in therapy to resolve a lifetime of pleasing people at great emotional costs to himself. He tells a story from his childhood that etched itself into his psyche. One day, when he was five years old, his mother brought him a colouring book as a gift. Brad was thrilled until he opened it up and saw that it was a colour-by-number book.

"I don't like this book," he declared. "The numbers make the pictures look bad."

Upon hearing his words, his mother became upset, started to cry, and left the room. His father, who had witnessed the scene, scolded him.

"Look what you've done now," the father chided. Horrified, Brad picked up his crayons and began to colour furiously. After a time his mother returned to the room. "Look, Mommy," he said, holding his work up for her to see, "I really like this book now."

Brad's devastation at his mother's reaction was heightened by his father's stern reprimand. What could this little boy do to calm the powerful feelings of anxiety inside himself but that which was so clearly expected? He coloured in the book he did not like, hoping that the hurt he had inflicted on his mother would be healed. He needed his mother and panicked when she left him in tears without reassuring him. He regretted that by telling her what he thought, he had hurt her and chased her out of the room where she was not available to him.

Brad had learned one lesson in being nice — to silence his opinion about a gift. At a deeper level, he learned that his words might chase away someone he needs and that he must suppress his words to keep the person with him. He was too young to know that the problem was his parents', not his. Had they been more able, they would have encouraged him to express his preferences without fear of recrimination or driving them away. As it was, he learned the silencing lesson and many other such lessons thoroughly and has struggled with his niceness throughout his life.

People are happiest when they have some sense of being true to themselves. "Being nice" has invaded the culture and people's psyches in ways that endanger their relationships and sometimes their lives when they are rendered incapable of speaking up for themselves or acting on their own behalf in a critical situation. This book is an awakening of the parts of you that have been deadened through silence, and it is permission to break the silence, to liberate your authenticity.

CHAPTER 2
HOW TO BE NICE

As ADULTS, WE are able to call up niceness as needed, without conscious effort. We are able to say or do the nice thing as if it were our nature to do so. The behaviour is automatic.

Reduced to its lowest terms, niceness is behaving or talking in ways designed to make us compatible with people and situations. Often when we feel insecure we shore ourselves up by silencing the behaviours and words that we believe might make us less acceptable to others. Silencing may seem innocent enough, but in reality it often means that we compromise ourselves, that we are not honest with our thoughts and feelings. We think of ourselves as honest, honourable people, and yet the very nature of being nice, by silencing ourselves, contradicts that perception.

Such is the culture of niceness that we are able to believe one thing and do another. We cherish the ideal of honesty even while we speak and behave in dishonest ways by hiding our thoughts and feelings or lying about them.

THE LANGUAGE OF NICENESS

The word *nice*, itself, is often used in an ambiguous way when the speaker does not wish to commit to a certainty. When someone says "Thank you for the nice meal," the compliment lacks enthusiasm and specificity. Compare it with "The lamb was roasted just the way I like it," "The sauce was a savoury complement to the meat," or "The grilled vegetables were perfectly cooked to a slight crunch." Specific

HOW TO BE NICE

comments such as these are much more meaningful to the cook who worked hard to produce an enjoyable meal. Even a simple phrase such as "I enjoyed dinner" is more enthusiastic and honest (if it is true). To say that a meal was "nice" reduces a meaningful sentiment to insignificance. On the other hand, it may mean dinner was nothing special. Using the word *nice* leaves the diner uncommitted. In other words, saying dinner was nice can be misleading, a white lie. The word is used as a form of lukewarm compliment that may or may not mean that the speaker truly admires the cut of a new garment, your new haircut, or your artwork. The recipient of the apparent compliment cannot know from the speaker's words whether he is sincere, fudging the truth, or envious.

As a further complication, people can often judge from inflections and facial expressions what the speaker means, but it is also possible for the speaker to hide behind a suggestion of inflection. The speaker need not be direct or honest. He or she can offer some non-verbal cue — a smile, shrug, wink, nod, raised eyebrow — to imbue the lazy words with meaning. The listener then has the option to hear what he or she wants to hear, and the speaker can abdicate responsibility.

There is another side to the repeated and inappropriate use of the word: it is a lazy form of expression demanding nothing of the speaker. No mental energy is spent, no passion is felt or commitment made. After making love you have a choice of telling your partner "That was nice," "That was not unpleasant," or "The earth moved." Which do you choose? If your partner said either of the first two you might feel at least mildly let down for there has been no real investment in the comment. You are left feeling placated and wanting a more definite response. So it is in all "nice" interactions. They leave you feeling empty, whether you are the giver or the receiver.

A counterpart to this lazy language is the double negative, mentioned above. No passion is evident in the expression of a positive as a double negative. Thus, telling your friend that you are not unhappy that he arrived unexpectedly saves you. You have to make neither a direct statement of welcome, if you are worried that this will become a habit, nor a reprimand, if you are miffed that he did not call first.

NICE WHITE LIES

White lies, or fibs, are accepted forms of blurred truth. I am calling them white lies here because that is the way most people would describe them, but there is no difference between them and any other lie in the sense that they are not truth. They exist in a grey area of our understanding of truth and are present in many conversations. They appeal because they seem easier than saying what is really on our minds.

Jeff Hancock of Cornell University carried out research with thirty students. The students kept a communications diary for a week in which they documented the email, telephone, and face-to-face conversations they had lasting more than ten minutes and the number of lies they told each time. Hancock worked out the percentage of lies per conversation for each medium. The results showed that 14 percent of emails, 21 percent of instant messages, 27 percent of face-to-face exchanges, and 37 percent of phone conversations involved some deception. It seems that people lie less when they think they could be held accountable, that is, when the words are written.

Many lies in Hancock's study were spontaneous responses to questions such as "Do you like my new shirt?" Although the equivocal response to such a question might often be "It's nice," there are many ways of telling fibs to maintain niceness without using the word. We may concoct a story of heavy traffic or delayed public transit to explain our lateness to an event. There may be a hair's breadth of truth in the story, so we convince ourselves it was not really lying because it could have happened. We may say we've been too busy to telephone a person with whom we have not wanted to continue a friendship. We may say we have a previous commitment rather than tell a friend we would prefer to go to an event alone or do not feel like going out on a particular night.

Who among us has not been asked to give our name to the receptionist answering the telephone, only to have him come back on the line and tell us that Mary Smith is in a meeting or has just stepped out of the office? While it could be that either of those possibilities is true, we are so accustomed to hearing them as lies that we have learned to disbelieve them.

Consider this common scene: Joe and Sam met at work where Joe is a high achiever. Sam would like to accomplish what Joe has and feels pleased that Joe is spending time, outside of work, with him. They have just finished dinner in a restaurant suggested by Joe. The check arrives and Joe says, "We might as well just split this down the middle." Sam blanches. Joe has consumed two single malts, a dozen fresh oysters, filet mignon, salad, a half-litre of merlot, cheesecake, and a cappuccino to Sam's pasta, greens, and Perrier. But Sam does not want to appear cheap or financially constrained, so he agrees to Joe's suggestion with feigned cheerfulness. He lies, even though Joe's suggestion was not in his best interests. At the outset of dinner, Sam probably would have called Joe a nice guy. As they left the restaurant he may still have said so — because he is nice — but he may now feel otherwise.

White lies such as "I'm not feeling well" are used to avoid work, appointments, or social functions. This lie seems permissible to the nice person because the need to avoid may be so great that, in the moment, the person may believe it. In a mind-body collusion, the person's body produces just enough tiny aches and pains at the right moment to add substance to the story.

When my son, Adam, was five years old, I took him to visit a friend, Jody, and a disturbing situation arose. Jody told his mother he wanted to watch television. Preferring that the children play outside, the mother replied, "The television is broken," even though it had been on when we arrived. Her words were contrived to elicit her son's compliance while maintaining a perception of herself as nice. Sensing something amiss, my son asked me if it was true. Perhaps he noticed the change of expression on my face when I heard the woman's words. In that moment I had a choice between supporting the woman's deception in order to remain non-confrontational or being honest with my son. There was no contest. I said the television was not broken. Adam's puzzled look disappeared. Jody glanced inquiringly at his mother, who did not disagree with my response. I then suggested, in support of the other mother, that the boys play outside. They complied with no further hesitation because, I believe, they were conflicted by this troubling exchange and attempted to steady their emotional states by accepting direction.

We have come to expect and accept that people will talk in white lies and we may participate in this lie-telling. We tell the housepainter the work is fine even though we are upset because he splattered paint on the baseboards, all the while consoling ourselves with the thought that the rest of the job was just fine. We tell our friends it is not too late to call when they telephone just as we are crawling into bed. We accept substandard services rather than risk being labelled a nitpicker. We do not expect the truth when we ask an opinion. In fact, we are shocked to hear it if someone speaks it. "What do you think of my new suit?" may seem an innocent question, but few people dare to answer it with anything that might suggest a critical evaluation. Moreover, the person asking does not expect criticism. At the same time, we feel vaguely disappointed and disbelieving when we get the answer of someone who is being nice by being less than honest with us. We have learned to expect white lies and we accept them. But they rob us of authentic connection.

Lies are not always told directly. Sometimes lies are told by *omitting* information. Perhaps someone asks another for her opinion and instead of answering she diverts the conversation. Another may maintain his image by leaving out essential bits of information and garnishing other details when chronicling his life to someone he wants to impress.

Niceness takes other forms. While they all smack of dishonesty, the untruths that lie at the base are greyed down and mutated into recognizable behaviours such as accepting responsibility that is not yours, giving too much, saying yes when you feel like saying no. You may not think that giving too much is dishonest until you understand that you cannot be true to yourself or others if you do not honour your own needs and recognize your limitations. Knowing what these are is one way of beginning to unwind from the clutches of niceness, and they will be discussed in later chapters.

SAYING YES, FEELING NO

One of the most common ways of being nice is to say yes when you mean no. Saying yes to something when you would prefer to say no means you are complying with the wishes of others at some cost to your integrity.

"Frank" is a composite of many people I have known, a person who often says yes, especially at work. He works overtime without pay, staying long hours to complete jobs on time while other members of his team leave at their official workday end to go home to their spouses and children. Frank explains, "I have no children so it's not as important for me to get home early. If there's work left to be done at the end of the day, it's easier for me to stay and do it." His colleagues are appreciative. They thank him and let him know that no one else can do the job as well as he can. Frank is flattered but uneasy. He feels a vague sense of discomfort that he is always the person left working late but cannot rationalize leaving the office when work remains to be done. He has a wife but no children and therefore feels he cannot assert his right to go home at the same time as his colleagues. In the office building next door works his counterpart, Jim, who, like Frank, says yes to working late. Jim, however, has a wife and three children but feels that he has no reason not to stay because his wife is home full-time with the children, who therefore always have a parent in attendance. The fact that Jim is missing their childhood has not occurred to him despite his wife's protestations.

Frank and Jim share with Sam the tendency to say yes to requests made of them despite their deeper wish to say no. Sam paid a price for his "yes." His first mistake was to agree to go to The Big Steak when he wanted to eat at Café de Provence, and his second mistake was to remain silent when Joe proposed to split the bill. Sam paid in money, spending much more than he intended. But the price of Sam's "yes" pales in comparison to that being paid by Frank and Jim, whose health and relationships are suffering as they continue to plug away at the office for needlessly long hours.

Saying yes may mean agreeing with opinions you do not share. Thus, some people solve the problem of disagreeing with contentious opinions by declaring a moratorium on topics such as politics, religion, and sex in the interest of maintaining peace. What a bland and deceptive peace it is when these vital topics are abandoned! More importantly, the silence of those who do not speak may be misinterpreted as agreement with those who continue to speak.

Even parents can be compliant, bowing to pressure to let their children do things when they would rather not say yes because they do not want to be seen as depriving their children, or because they have trouble saying no. Ironically, the children do not always want what they ask for anyway. One day a friend of Adam telephoned and asked him to play.

Ten-year-old Adam had been outside all day, had just finished dinner, and wanted to stay in the house for the evening. Into the receiver he said, "Just a minute, I'll ask." Without covering the receiver he said to me, "Mom, can I go out to play?" all the while looking at me and shaking his head no. Picking up his not-so-subtle cue I said, rather loudly, "No, not tonight." Adam spoke back into the telephone, "Mom says I can't play tonight," said goodbye, and hung up. If I had complied with his spoken request I would have placed him in a position of having to do something he did not want to do. At that time in his life he did not feel equipped to say no when that is what he felt. He needed me to do it for him. He needed me to be the inner strength he could not yet honour without help. In this instance Adam was able to ask me for the help he needed, but usually children's requests are not so clear and parents must learn to read subtle clues so they can meet needs of which their children may not consciously be aware. Situations such as this one provide parents with the opportunity to model behaviour that discourages niceness, or saying yes when feeling no.

For a young child it is hard to stand firm and speak one's mind, even to peers. Speaking up to elders can be a formidable task indeed, and growing older does not necessarily mean that we can shed silence and emerge strongly verbal. For a friend, Martin, being nice took the form of living out a dream his father had for him since he was an infant. Martin was never able to say no to his father. He was a talented artist, but his father, who had always wanted to be a lawyer himself, encouraged him to pursue a profession in law or medicine. Sensitive to his father's needs, Martin complied and became a lawyer. He was moderately successful in financial terms, but unhappy. His dissatisfaction showed up in many ways, including a failed first marriage. Disturbed at the course his life was taking and his inability to be happy despite fulfilling his role as a good son, Martin began dabbling in art again. Increasingly, he found himself conflicted, believing he owed loyalty to the profession that had supported him over the years and not wanting to disappoint his father, but feeling the tug of his art. Two decades later he resolved his conflict by giving up his practice to pursue sculpting full time. He reasoned that he had given enough of his life over to his father's dream. Only then did he feel fulfilled. He further felt validated by a measure of financial success as a sculptor and basked in the satisfaction of bringing beauty to the world.

Often I hear stories from women who have become romantically involved with men who initially are quite charming but whose charm wears thin after the women commit to them. The women may soon sense that the man's charm is superficial but they say yes to him instead of heeding their own cautionary notes. It doesn't matter if the man is married, has a history of abusing women or of drug or alcohol abuse, has earned his living in questionable ways, or left behind him a series of broken hearts and empty bank accounts. They say yes to him and to the part of themselves that craves intimacy and a fairy-tale relationship like the ones portrayed in movies and books. They say yes to the part of themselves that fancies they can be the one to turn the man around and make him be who he says or implies he is. At the same time they say no to the part of themselves that knows the relationship will end in disaster. They make themselves vulnerable by refusing to honour their own wisdom.

On my wedding day at the tender age of nearly twenty-one I said yes to a traditional life. As I walked up the aisle to be bound in marriage tears welled up in my eyes. I could not then explain why I cried on my way to the altar, but in hindsight I know I was ignoring my need to explore other places and ways of life. For reasons I could not explain at the time, I chose a path that ultimately did not suit me. It was an about-face for someone who dreamed different dreams and only a short time earlier had voiced a wish to travel and work over- seas. Perhaps I feared being alone or different. Most of my friends had already married or were about to be married. I wanted to belong to that group, which I imagined to have greater maturity. Even at that time, in the midst of the social revolution of the sixties, few were bold enough to buck tradition — including the insidious message that a woman must get married — at least where I came from. My inner wisdom nudged me to spread my wings and fly solo. Lacking confidence and mentors I chose the tamer path.

For someone else my choice may have been perfect; for some peo- ple a traditional lifestyle is exactly the adventure they crave. Even for me it had its moments, especially parenting my son, which was the greatest adventure, one for which I am forever grateful. Nonetheless, the urge to chart my own course remained my constant companion for many years, until I finally heeded its call. When I did follow my path to higher education and a career as a psychologist I acquired a sense of contentment, despite the hard work along the way, and felt happier, stimulated, and healthier. I became more present, honest, and fulfilled in relationships.

Saying yes while feeling no can lead to other kinds of self-sabotage. A client, Warren, and his wife were hiking with another couple. The four were spending a long weekend at a northern lodge. Warren usually loved to tramp along wooded trails but on this day was still tired from the previous day's activities. He had not wanted to hike again but had succumbed when his meek suggestion to participate in activities at the lodge was vetoed by the others. After a strenuous segment of the trail Warren felt tired and wanted to turn back. The other couple preferred to continue and Warren's wife was indifferent. After some discussion Warren again complied. He agreed to continue rather than disappoint the other couple. Inside, however, he felt angry and resentful. A short distance along the trail Warren noticed a rock jutting out and knew he would cut his leg on it. He did not take precautions to avoid it and injured himself. The cut was deep and painful. He was unable to continue with the hike and after some perfunctory first aid he and his wife turned back while the other couple stayed on the trail.

Warren knew the cut to his leg was no accident. He had experienced similar incidents before and spent time reflecting on his behaviour. He understood that whenever he did not act on his own needs he found some way to hurt himself. As in this instance, the injury sometimes provided him with a reason to act on his own needs. It may be that Warren felt the cut on his leg was a legitimate reason to turn back, whereas turning back merely because he did not want to continue seemed selfish, self-indulgent, and confrontational. As he told me the story he resolved to honour and act from his own needs and preferences.

Warren's work in therapy moved ahead with the insight he gleaned from this incident. He began to see the patterns in his life that he had adopted for protection but that riveted him to an unhappy state of being and relating. He became stronger and found that he was able to ward off return bouts of the depression that had brought him to therapy.

Saying yes while meaning no sometimes means living a conditional life. The agreeable person says yes to every request, never follows through, and winds up with a lot of unfinished projects and unfulfilled promises. As well as angering the people to whom promises were made, Mr. and Ms. Nice never feel a sense of completion and are caught up in constant cycles of self-deception in which they tell themselves the promises will be kept right after _____, or as soon as _____, or "when I'm freed up." Keeping their word is always conditional on something else happening, but if that something else happens another thing pops up to interfere with keeping the troublesome promise.

Parents, too, often say yes when they feel and mean no, when they are pulled in too many directions. Their child makes a request that becomes one more thing to do on a list that already burdens them, but not wanting to disappoint, they agree. Other times they make promises in haste that they never intend to honour, hoping the child will forget. The parents may want their children to believe they are good or generous or "cool," and so make promises they are unable to keep. They may believe the promises they make but break them when something more compelling comes up. They may not realize that when a parent says, "Maybe we'll go to the beach tomorrow," to the child it means, "We *are going* to the beach tomorrow." Parents who say yes but mean no act as if they believe children are not affected by broken promises. In my fifteen years of work in the field I have heard scores of clients say this is not so. Promises matter.

SAYING NO, FEELING YES

Of all the ways of being nice, saying no when you would rather say yes has the greatest potential to restrict the range of behaviour.

An acquaintance, Martha, always regretted that she was not able to pursue a university degree. Her family was poor and needed the income she could bring in. A secondary school education had been all the privilege her parents could afford her. As a way of focusing on her own life rather than that of her parents, Martha married early and gave birth to several children in quick succession. Family took her time for many years. Now, at fifty-seven, she believes she is too old to go back to school. She forfeited the satisfaction of getting something she wants, of satisfying her lifelong desire for the stimulation of an educational challenge, because she holds to the outdated belief that education is for the young. She believes that a return to school at her age would be a challenge to propriety. How sad that she will miss out on the dream she has had since childhood, that she cannot follow her heart, that she may die with regret.

People learn to behave according to cultural standards for age-appropriateness, denying themselves the expression of a wide range of feelings and behaviours that are common at any age. People who meet the Dalai Lama report their surprise that he is childlike in his deportment. Gloria Steinem expressed it best when she said, in response to a comment that — on her fortieth birthday — she did not look forty. "This," she said, "is what forty looks like." While she was referring to her appearance, the same can be said about behaviour. Being playful at sixty is part of what being sixty is about. Being sad at ten is part of what being ten is about. Being nice means denying ourselves the experience of a wide range of feelings and behaviour and losing out on these potentialities in our lives.

People may say no, instead of the "yes" they feel, because they think others will be disapproving. Couples may fail to pursue relationships that feel promising because family members disapprove. A rewarding career opportunity may be forfeited in order to comply with someone else's needs or ideas of the kind of employment they should be pursuing. Others may say no when they feel the best course would be yes because some religious imperative would not be upheld if they were to go ahead. Women may feel pressured to say no to birth control alternatives and have children they cannot manage emotionally or practically, or they may be pressured by their partners who do not believe in birth control. Sometimes this produces tragic results. Andrea Yates, a Texas woman whose husband did not believe in birth control, was emotionally unstable and unable to bear the emotional and physical demands of raising her young children. One day, after she had given birth to their fourth child, her husband, Russell, found her holding a knife to her own throat. She was admitted to mental hospitals four times, diagnosed with psychotic depression, and treated with antidepressant medication. Against the advice of doctors who treated his wife, Russell impregnated her with child number five. Andrea gave birth to this child, like the others, without medication for pain. One day, unable to continue with life as it was, she systematically drowned all her children, telling herself they had to die to be saved.

Russell Yates was, according to news reports, a nice man who meant well. Yet his religious dedication ranked ahead of his wife's mental health and the advice he received from professionals who treated her. She was either unable to decide for herself to use birth control or overpowered by him and his religious beliefs. He would not see her desperation and say yes to birth control on her behalf. The results were tragic.

Perhaps the Yates's case seems a few steps beyond what you might consider an argument against niceness, but when one considers, as we are here, the impact of a culture that promotes silence and obedience at the expense of one's own needs and wishes, perhaps it is not. People silenced are people oppressed, and oppression can produce despair and hopelessness. There are few acts more silencing than the act of controlling another's body and choices.

One common way of saying no when you are feeling yes is to deny that you have feelings about someone or something when in fact you do. Count among them people mentioned earlier who restrict topics of conversation when they do have feelings and opinions, though they may have denied them for so long they would be hard-pressed to put their thoughts together and speak. Denying feelings in a dispute means nothing gets resolved; it is like adding another log to a pile of smouldering embers.

ACCEPTING RESPONSIBILITY OR BLAME THAT ISN'T YOURS

Lara, a client, was driving home from work one day when the back end of a car suddenly appeared in her lane. It was too close and she was unable to stop. The sickening crunch of metal on metal confirmed the accident that, in the split second after seeing the car, she knew would happen. Shaken, Lara's first concern was whether anyone in the other car was hurt. She climbed out of her car and walked up to the driver, who was by then emerging from his vehicle. He was upset but contained. Without further analysis of the situation Lara reasoned that since she had hit his car the accident was her fault. She apologized, he accepted, and they discussed restitution. Since there was no physical injury the man suggested they not call police. He said, further, that he would call her with an estimate of the costs. He did, within two days, saying the total cost of repairing his car would be $4,000. Knowing the implications for her insurance premiums if her company were to pay such a claim, Lara decided to pay out of pocket. She went to her bank, arranged for a line of credit, and was close to paying the man when she told me what had happened.

Alarmed at her hasty acceptance of responsibility I urged her to hold off payment and instead call her insurance company and the police to determine legal responsibility. Lara was hesitant. The man would be very upset, she believed, if, after leading him to believe she would pay damages, she did not come through with the money. With a great deal of urging Lara was finally convinced that there was no point in accepting responsibility if the man was at fault. I was convinced that he was in fact at fault and that he must have felt he had committed his error in judgment, backing into traffic, on a lucky day. Sure enough, Lara found out that he, not she, was at fault, and she informed the man that she would not pay for the damage to his car. If not for our conversation, she would have continued to accept responsibility and be out of pocket by $4,000 plus interest. The man was not happy, but Lara felt empowered and wiser. It was the first significant instance of many in which she began to turn her focus from responsibility for others to responsibility for herself.

Both Frank, who works overtime when he'd rather not, and Lara, who accepts culpability for things she did not do, respond to requests or accusations with what is assumed to be the correct answer, taking on responsibility when it truly belongs to someone else.

Sometimes when people take on responsibility that does not belong to them it is not because of an outright request from someone for them to do so. More often, the request is implied by one and/or inferred by the other. A husband may say his day is hectic and that he is feeling stressed. His comment may be innocent of any expectation of his wife or it may contain the grain of a request that she relieve him of some of his responsibilities. Tuned in to his responsibilities and his moods, and inferring the request, his wife may simply go ahead and cut the grass, pick up his shirts at the cleaner's, or do his household chores for him, saying nothing, but building up resentment.

I often hear people who are the eldest child in their family talk about accepting responsibility for their younger siblings. This may come at the actual request of overburdened parents or it may be a product of a malfunctioning family in which parents are too addicted or engaged in abusive dynamics to care adequately for their children. By default, the task then falls to the eldest, who carries with him for life the practice of taking on responsibilities that aren't his.

GIVING AWAY RESPONSIBILITY THAT IS YOURS

Denial is the most common form of eschewing your responsibility. It may be that a child turns up at your house with bruises on his legs that seem to be more serious than the usual child-at-play variety. You become alarmed and wonder about the possibility of abuse. You also weigh the implications of acting on your alarm. You've met the parents and you rationalize that they did not seem like the kind of people who would beat their child. You feel something is wrong but do not act on it because you do not want to risk insulting them. An underlying motive may be that you do not want to get involved in what might be a lengthy and difficult process. You tell yourself that if you see such bruises again you will do something about it.

Denial of responsibility can also appear in the form of outright statements, such as "I wouldn't do that," in order to distinguish oneself from the behaviour of others. If the behaviour in question is troubling it would seem that either it must be confronted or the offending party must be rejected. When the denial is made but association continues unchecked the speaker denies a part of his own reality that he would rather disown than confront.

Denial of responsibility can have disastrous results. Derran, a medical professional, approached a woman, Nora, from his condominium building for a date. She accepted, but only after asking about his relationship with a woman she had seen him with a few weeks earlier. Derran informed her that he had had a long-term relationship with the woman but that they were now just friends. Happy to hear this — because she felt attracted to him — Nora began to date him. They found they were compatible and the relationship sped along.

Soon the relationship became intimate, and it was not until then that Derran advised Nora that he loved the woman he'd said was just a friend and, further, when they parted as lovers he had specified conditions under which a reconciliation might be effected. As he told this to Nora he reassured her that it was unlikely the woman would ever meet those conditions but that if she did he would have to take her efforts into consideration, and he could not predict what might happen then. Shocked, Nora listened as he reassured her that he felt they hit it off really well and he felt very comfortable with and understood by her. Believing, again, what he said — that the woman would not meet his conditions — she continued in the relationship and fell in love with him. He helped her along with this, talking about what their future together might look like, telling her he loved her, and making tentative plans to be together.

The relationship was passionate, but the other woman crept into his conversation with increasing frequency and he spent hours of his time with Nora ruminating about wasting the years of the previous relationship if it came to nothing. In the end, the inevitable happened. Derran told Nora the woman had proposed a reconciliation and agreed to meet his conditions. Derran's feeling, shared with Nora on their first date, that the other woman did not understand him, that he had been frustrated with her because he had to repeat everything he said to her, that the relationship was over, seemed to fall by the wayside. Derran announced that he and the woman would reconcile. But he told Nora he wanted to keep her in his life because it was important to have someone who understood him so instinctively. Nora was devastated at the ending, by his self-centredness and lack of compassion for her. Despite the brevity of the relationship the pain was extreme, reflecting the intensity with which she had involved herself with him. She pointed out to Derran that he had pursued her dishonestly because he told her he and the woman were just friends. When he did give her more details it was not until they had become intimate and then he had assured Nora that he did not expect the woman to meet his conditions.

Derran had not been free to pursue a relationship with anyone, but he had led Nora to believe he was, trying on and disposing of the relationship as if she had no feelings. Derran chose to remember only that he had told Nora there was a chance of reconciliation and said she knew this could happen. He accepted no responsibility for the pain he caused her, even though he had also assured her that he felt a reconciliation would never happen. To Nora he was anything but a nice guy in the end, but because he was following through with the other woman and he believed he had warned Nora, in his mind he remained beyond reproach. In such cases of the heart, behaviour should be determined by empathy for the other person, and Derran had none. Empathy would have meant that he would have been clear of his other relationship before pursuing Nora.

Derran's striking lack of empathy is characteristic of people who dump responsibility on their unwitting victims and move on to the next. There are variations in the degrees of seriousness of this problem. Sometimes the victim, like Nora, suffers emotionally for a while, but sometimes the damage is much more serious.

Pedophiles provide the most shocking example of the phenomenon of giving away responsibility. Many seem very pleasant and helpful when they are stalking potential victims. Indeed, some are respected members of their communities. Then, when they are caught and confronted about their abusive behaviour, they blame the children they molest. Their stories are replete with comments about children coming on to them or being seductive with them. They try to avoid responsibility for their actions by blaming the least powerful among us, the children they befriend and abuse, or by believing that their victims enjoyed the molestation. They see themselves as victims of their own pasts or the innocents they harm, not the perpetrators of others' pain.

MAKING ONESELF SMALL

Marny lives next door to neighbours who monopolized the communal air space, hosting non-stop get-togethers with friends, playing rock music, bantering about baseball scores, and engaging in loud card games, long into each weekend night, all summer long. Marny considers her home a refuge, loves outdoor living in the summertime, and enjoys gardening, quiet chats, and Vivaldi. When a friend visits she prefers to entertain on her patio but often found the noise from next door made conversation outside impossible. Even so, she said nothing to her neighbours, unwilling to risk confrontation, fearing reprisal if she dared complain to them. She feared they would become even louder or damage her property. She found herself shrinking into her home and noticed that she was spending less and less time in her backyard. Instead of entertaining at home she began to meet friends in public places and she ignored her garden, knowing it was impossible to enjoy weekends quietly digging in the earth. Still, she said nothing while her anger and resentment built up. It took her years before she worked up the courage to speak to them. When she did, they turned down their volume some of the time, and Marny now wonders what took her so long.

Verna works at a computer near several other women in her office. At the next desk sits a woman who talks all day long. Verna spends her days doing a slow burn, willing and wishing the woman to be quiet. She makes herself small, hoping the woman will stop talking, but her wish never comes true and her tactic does not work.

People who make themselves small by minimizing their needs and desires do not want to appear self-serving, or they may not feel entitled to take care of their own needs and desires. People make themselves small rather than trying to convince another of a point of view or a course of action because they believe they are ineffectual. Sometimes they rationalize that they believe the other person has already made up his or her mind so it won't matter what they say anyway.

Sometimes people make themselves small by withholding information about their own problems or experiences. A friend, Joan, is a good listener. She is the one friends and family go to with their troubles. She never limits the length of time they take to talk to her unless she has a commitment to still another person. Rarely does she volunteer information about her own life. She doesn't feel she can confide in her friends about the deep depression she sometimes feels, believing she must present a strong front in order to be available for them.

Making oneself small may take a dangerous form. While in hospital I shared a room with an older woman who, among other ailments, had diabetes. Although she loved desserts she ordinarily did not eat them. However, she talked about the difficulty of being a guest in someone's house and being presented with dessert. She was often too embarrassed to tell the host that her sugar levels were high and she could not eat dessert. Instead, she would eat the dessert and then get to her glucometer and insulin supply at the earliest opportunity. The potential for her to pay a very high price for her niceness was astounding, and yet she let her fear of potential embarrassment override it.

Many times in life you may feel pressured to be with people when you would rather not because you do not want to hurt anyone's feelings, you do not want to compromise a work situation, or you feel obligated for other reasons. You may deny your social consciousness in order to fit in with the group, failing to speak up when friends express opinions or behave in ways that you find unfathomable. You may have strong feelings about racial prejudice, sexism, or religious persecution or simply see a particular situation in a different way than your friends. But in situations where yours is the unpopular opinion in the group you remain silent. You quietly protect your position in the group, though you might not describe your silence in those terms. Perhaps you would say the others could not be convinced to change their opinions anyway, or you might rationalize that a challenge to them would not be respectful on their turf, but fear lies at the bottom of your reluctance to speak, fear of ridicule or loss of companionship. Strong voices can be intimidating, so you keep your opinions silent unless you are with like-minded folks.

Keeping oneself small sometimes has less to do with expressing your opinions and more to do with group process. If you have ever sat on a volunteer board of directors you will know that there are always domi-nant personalities in the group. If the board is the overseer for a special interest group such as a car club or, more formally, a small charitable organization, and one person has borne most of the responsibility for putting it together, that person may feel entitled to be the reigning chair. More often than not, members are happy to let someone else take on the role that is most demanding of time and energy, but since the boards are to be run according to formal bylaws they must go through the process of asking for nominations for executive positions. Whether they want to or not, people do not volunteer to take over the dominant person's role. These are the positions that are acclaimed, year after year, while members make themselves small.

OFFERING TOO MUCH

Many community groups could not survive without the people who offer too much of their time. They are the people who volunteer to stuff envelopes, visit people in hospital, walk dogs, assist teachers in school, and sit on boards of directors for charitable organizations (which means a great deal of responsibility without pay). These are all worthy causes, but it is often the same people who volunteer, time and again, while others sit back and let them. Most volunteers find gratification in the work, but when they are the same people who do too much at home and at work, who do not know when to stop giving, they risk becoming resentful and burnt out.

Many individuals, too, rely on those who offer too much, who agree to do too much. Risa, at fifty-eight, was one upon whom many, especially the members of her family, relied on. As her son and daughter-in-law added to their brood of rambunctious offspring Risa became busier and busier. While their parents worked outside the home, she babysat the two preschoolers every day and chauffeured the older two to school, fetching them again at the end of the day. She visited her mother in the seniors' residence at least twice weekly, taking along homemade meals to supplement the food her mother received — and disliked — there. She typed letters for her husband's service club in the evenings, and at least twice a week, including weekends, she prepared and hosted dinners for her extended family. On Tuesday evenings she volunteered time at the church. On weekends she caught up on yard work and shopping. It was no surprise to anyone who knew her that Risa suffered from hypertension with warnings from her doctor to slow down before her heart gave out. It might have been more of a surprise for them to learn that she also had a drinking problem, unwinding each evening with a martini or two, and more on weekends.

Giving time to help with worthy causes is an honourable thing to do but must always be tempered by a consideration of what can be given reasonably. The giver must also satisfy something in herself through the giving. When people see only what they can give and not what they need they risk becoming needy or ill themselves.

A C T S   O F   K I N D N E S S

Niceness has another face. At times, people perform acts of genuine kindness or voice their support or approval without hedging. These honest acts and words also can be labelled nice, and they form the core of the transformation I discuss in the final two chapters. As you read through this book the difference between acts of kindness and undesirable types of niceness will become clear. Many adults are generous, kind, and peaceful. People are capable of such behaviour and happier that way. All too often, however, these qualities are buried in the struggle for emotional survival or distorted by a belief that our existence depends upon competing rather than co-operating. Nelson Mandela said, "Deep down in every human heart, there is mercy and generosity." It is these qualities that I wish to release in you as you read through this book.

In an ideal world, people say what they think and feel in an open and direct manner. They attempt to make themselves understood and to understand others. They have no need to pretend they are anything but who they are.

CHAPTER 3
SILENCED INTO NICENESS: FROM THE BEGINNING

SOME YEARS AGO I took a self-defence course for women and to my great surprise discovered that the Big Yell was one of the most difficult acts for participants in the class. Feeble cries squeaked from the throats of the women, including my own, even though we all appeared confident until we opened our mouths. The contrast between appearance and volume was startling. At the beginning of life, children have no difficulty raising their voices, yet all these accomplished women who once were infants had been silenced.

These women grew up in the same world as you and I, a world of families, acquaintances, and institutions of various types. All of these entities affect our perception of ourselves, the ways we interact with other people, the ways we express ourselves in the world at large, and our ability to get our needs met. We live within a social order that has evolved to ensure the silence and obedience of most people, to ensure that they obey authority, squelch dissension, and deny the need to speak out. We have freedoms, to be sure, but with limits that become obvious only when we wander outside the narrow pathways of culturally ordered lives. Obedience training begins early and is reinforced throughout life in one form or another. The obvious first teachers are parents and other caregivers, but they are merely instruments of a culture in which self-enforced compliance to official, as well as informal, standards is a primary method of maintaining social order. They have learned to enforce their own compliance and to teach their children.

Compliance can be characterized as movement into passivity. We force ourselves onto paths that our culture affirms as the norm. These paths are laden with social or financial implications, so even though we may privately question the wisdom of the path we believe we have no choice but to continue. We fail to challenge ourselves to see the reality of the world we live in and how we contribute to its good health or its demise. To take the edge off our silenced wish not to comply we dumb ourselves down with excesses of food, drink, drugs, and electronic diversions.

There are some real benefits, to its members, of maintaining a culture of self-enforced compliance. People co-operate to the extent that they can feed, shelter, and clothe themselves. People have company. Streets remain safe. But the same culture can be dangerous and unhealthy if obedience and silencing of dissension are taken beyond co-operation into the realm of shutting down individuals' thoughts and feelings. The social ethic that is being served may not be in the best interests of all or even most of its members and may serve some members of society better than others, usually the wealthiest.

Economist Jane Jacobs wrote a brilliant book, *Systems of Survival: A Dialogue on the Moral Foundations of Commerce and Politics*, in which she describes the two moral and value systems within which we live. People working within these systems, which she conceptualizes as commercial and guardianship, aim to be both loyal and honest. In our culture, these systems often conflict, leaving the individual to decide which path to follow. The police officer working as guardian must decide whether to satisfy her quota by stretching a charge on a traffic ticket or to remain honest and fall short in her supervisor's eyes. The officer has a difficult choice to make. Too many missed quotas might mean her job, and she needs to work to feed her kids. Her mood that day, the stresses she is feeling at home or at work, rather than the realities of the situation, may determine the outcome, especially if she is unaware of outside influences on her. The way each of us chooses to answer similar challenges in our lives affects the culture as a whole. This, in part, is our contribution to the direction the system goes. But that isn't the largest problem. The problem lies in a system that is inherently conflicted, which paves the way for those who would abuse it and manipulate people for selfish gain. When most remain silent and obedient, who will oppose them?

Infants are not nice. They are as loud and demanding as nice people are passive and at least superficially compliant. It is a long, oppressive journey from the first demanding wails of infancy to the muted niceness of adulthood. The silencing begins early and occurs throughout life within the structure of families, the workplace, and educational, religious, and governmental institutions. The lessons of obedience apply in different ways based on gender, sexual orientation, and financial position.

INFLUENCE OF FAMILY

To illustrate the early stages of learning to be nice I present a composite of childhood based on my observations, a baby whom I call Kendal, a rambunctious, creeping, typical ten-month-old. He is well-nurtured, attended by doting parents who begin to expose him to other babies with the explicit intention of socializing him. They want him to "play" with other babies, but soon it is not enough to encourage the children to interact and discourage exchanges that might result in harm. The parents require Kendal to learn to share toys, one of the main keys to socialization during the first years of life.

What must it be like for a baby to be told to share? Put yourself in his position. Imagine that you have been given something special — a car, for instance. You are the only person who drives it and you have reason to believe it is yours alone, given for your exclusive use. No one mentioned, when the car was given, that you might have to give it up. Now imagine being told to share your car and having the keys wrenched from your hand. You do not know what "share" means because you are still learning language. You have no understanding that you will get the keys and the car back. Not surprisingly, you protest. You may better be able to share if you had been given a list of terms and conditions when you received the car, or if you had been allowed to come to your own conclusions about sharing it. In the absence of understanding, you protest, and so does Kendal when his caregivers tell him to share his toys.

In the blinking of an eye Kendal is two years old and he is still resistant to sharing, still doesn't grasp the concept his parents try to convey at every opportunity. He cannot understand what possible benefit might accrue by giving up his toys, especially when he, as an observer of his parents, notices that they do not always share their things. They do not let him tramp around the house in his mother's good shoes or drag the sheets off their bed to build a tent. Kendal is speaking by this time, so exchanges that occur during these moments have become more than requests from a parent followed by cries of protest. The dialogue is familiar:

"Kendal," his mother entreats sweetly, "let Emily have your dump truck. She wants to play with it for a while."

"No! Mine!" he retorts, squeezing his truck as if his life depended on it.

"Kendal, be a good boy and share your toys with the other children."

"Mine!" Kendal shouts back as he strikes out at his mother with a tiny, defiant fist and tries to run away with his truck.

"Kendal!" says Mom in a more demanding tone. "Be nice! Share your truck with Emily!"

Mother is in a place of no return, having to force Kendal to give up his dump truck, retract her command, or remove him from the scene. The intention to teach sharing has become a battle of wills, and Kendal understands only that his truck will be taken away. Kendal protests, Mother silences, imploring him to "be nice," equating niceness with goodness and acquiescence.

It is impossible to explain adult terms and conditions that are sometimes contradictory to infants and toddlers, and it is impossible for them to understand why Mommy, Daddy, or the daycare worker is taking their belongings and giving them to someone else. These people are supposed to be children's defenders. For young children, belongings are extensions of themselves, so they cannot conceive of giving them up and must be mystified when the adults in their world, whose function is to ensure their well-being, urge them to do so. Instead of being supported they are ordered to be nice and obedient, to deny the need to keep their toys to themselves. What's more, they are expected to be quiet about it. Movement out of the self-involved world of infancy into the confusing world of toddlerhood with all its accompanying expectations is jarring. In order to win the approval of caregivers, children must stifle feelings and give up belongings, which are as important to them as they are to adults.

The expectations of parents who want their young children to give up their toys to share before they are able to understand and are ready to produce such behaviour suggest that the parents are unable emotionally to give their children what they need. Psychoanalyst Alice Miller, who has written about the emotional needs of children, says that children can experience their feelings only in the presence of a person who takes them seriously and understands, accepts, and supports them. If these elements are missing children will repress their emotions and become unable to experience them even secretly. The feelings of emotional abandonment experienced by the children will remain unexpressed but will be stored and resurface when set off by some later event.

Appeals for toddlers to share their toys imply that we do not believe children are social creatures by nature. We do not believe children are competent to determine their readiness to share belongings. Appeals that children wait their turn suggest we do not believe that children will become social beings who are considerate of each other if left to their unchecked inclinations. We believe they must be deterred from a tendency to hold and keep the objects they possess. We believe that children will be aggressive unless they are trained to be otherwise.

Watching toddlers at play, this idea seems reasonable enough. They grab at toys held by others, scream when someone takes the toys they are playing with, and slap at each other when perturbed. They try, repeatedly, to have their needs satisfied by whatever means they can. Their needs of the moment take priority over everything and everybody else. Occasionally children are afraid to be assertive, afraid to ask for what they want and need. Sometimes children withdraw and cry. However, most young children venturing into the world of peer interactions attempt to meet their own needs by acting in ways that adults label aggressive.

Kendal's parents are devoted to him and want only the best for him. They do not want him to grow up self-centred and alone. They want him to have friends and enjoy a meaningful life, to make emotional connections to other people. They believe, as do most parents, that teaching their child to share is a first step towards preparing him for a life of quality social interactions. The dialogue between Kendal and his mother is one that is repeated many times every day in millions of households and daycare centres. A tacit agreement exists that we need to civilize our children, but it is less clear that the methods we use to accomplish the goal are effective or whether Mother's attempts to separate Kendal from his dump truck are reinterpreted by Kendal and manifest in his aggression towards other children. It seems reasonable to expect that the proof of the effectiveness of parental methods should be evident in the product — adult behaviour.

That picture is not encouraging. Despite all attempts to enforce sharing and tolerance, adult behaviour suggests that parents are not meeting their goals. Some adults try to get as much as possible of things they desire, even at the expense of others. We are envious. We lose our tempers and loosen our tongues or find less direct ways to release our frustrations to the point of hurting — most often the people closest to us — when we feel impatient. We lie to each other. Some resort to fisticuffs when perturbed. In the privacy of our vehicles we rage at inconsiderate drivers even though we, at times, are guilty of the very same offences, which amount to refusing to share the road. We substitute sports for war and, eventually, we wage war.

The difference between adults and toddlers is that adults — you and me — take what we want in more sophisticated and often clandestine ways. We take what we want but spare ourselves from facing this reality in a number of ways: We pay as little as possible to people upon whose services we depend, telling ourselves at least they are getting to earn money. We minimize and trivialize the contributions made by people whose labour we need to ease our own load. We have created a society in which a tiny minority of people own an abundance of material goods and most others own very little. Even though some of us have much more than we need, we want to keep what we have and gain more. We have created a justice system to pursue the culprits who take our belongings, whether it be a thief or a former spouse, a system that best serves those who can afford to hire quality legal help to use it. We jump queues for everything from movies to medical services whenever we can find a way and convince ourselves our need is greater than other people's. We use connections with people to further our own interests, even at the expense of other people.

Considering the efforts of conscientious parents whose objectives belie all of these adult behaviours, we might ask what goes wrong. How do attempts to turn our children into sharing individuals get derailed? Perhaps, given the adult behaviours I mentioned, we simply are not very successful at civilizing our children. Perhaps there are genetic impulses for individual survival that are so strong they cannot ever be transformed to produce more co-operative behaviours.

The behaviours I have just described seem a long way from niceness, the bland form of interaction that is the focus of this book. In fact, the two types of behaviours are closely linked because niceness becomes the cover for our self-centred ways of interacting. We learn ways of interacting that allow us to appear civilized and benevolent while we continue to hold and protect our own possessions, hurt and deprive other people, and take, or try to take, what we think we want — in short, we learn to be nice. We learn to heed the multitude of directives to "be nice." Be nice, share your toys. Don't say that, it's not nice. Why can't you be more like Mary? She's such a nice little girl. But the ability to produce this behaviour does not mean we are sharing, kind people. All it means for certain is that we have learned to present an image that complies with cultural requirements. It does not mean we have learned to be genuine and to act from an ethic of authenticity rather than from the insecurity of an overriding wish for acceptance.

LAYERS OF LEARNING

Along with the expectation of sharing, toddlers are denied access to places where older children can go. For a toddler's safety caregivers must set limits. This can be done in many creative ways. Offering choices that are all within acceptable limits, helping a child safely experience the consequences of an undesirable action, helping him admire or carefully touch precious household objects to satisfy and nurture curiosity, and physically removing a child from danger are a few examples. In an ideal world, the caregiver acts in a creative and compassionate manner, exercising patience and working from a basic understanding that learning requires repetition. No child learns to resist temptation on the first trial, and often it takes many attempts to learn. In practice, caregivers who are fatigued and stressed from the multiple demands on their time, energy, and creative thinking resort to saying no when a child attempts to exceed whatever limit is being reinforced. Although "no" has a place in the training of children, especially when their imminent safety is at issue, the word is a too-frequent replacement for more original and effective options for limit-setting. When "no" is what a child hears, it will also become what the caregiver hears out of the mouth of the beginning speaker. If that were as far as it went, it might be a good thing, for he is learning to internalize limit-setting, which is a necessary part of socialization. But the story does not end here.

Kendal has been told not to touch things in the house or go into certain rooms. Listening to him is like opening a door with direct access to the environment in which he has lived. Kendal has begun to say no to any request put to him. He repeats "no" to himself as he stretches an inquiring hand toward a forbidden object and he says no to his playmates when they come too close and he fears they will take a toy he is holding. Frequently he tells his parents no, often with defiance, when they ask him to do something. He is echoing what has been said to him, time and time again. When his caregivers hear the constant echo, their first reaction of amusement soon gives way to annoyance and frustration.

DON'T SAY "NO"

For tired adults a toddler's "no" may set off feelings of helplessness. They recall with certainty, through the fog of long-term memory, their own precocious compliance with authority figures and expect the same of the child, giving no thought to the larger implications of such an expectation. The adult's mistaken perspective may lead, in frustration, to the next layer of silencing: telling the child not to say no. This directive may seem harmless enough as a desperate measure, but in all likelihood it is confusing for the child. How is it that Mommy or Daddy or the daycare worker can say no but he cannot? As adaptive creatures do, the child learns that saying no is not allowed, especially in the presence of authority figures. Enforcing silent, protest-free obedience is once again the training of choice, and the child has learned a powerful lesson in being nice.

CONFUSING MESSAGES

Growing up to become social creatures is difficult enough when the messages from parents are clear. When messages are confusing for children the task is made still more onerous. Even though parents may believe they are speaking clearly to their children, they may not understand the ways messages to children can be confused.

Confusion may derive from a difference between adults and children in the ways they understand the spoken word. Professors Sandra Trehub and Bruce Morton studied the responses of people between ages four and twenty-two to recordings containing happy and sad messages. The research subjects were asked to determine the speaker's feelings. The messages varied in the consistency of message and voice tone. Morton and Trehub found that younger children responded to words rather than intonations, taking words literally when the words and voice tone were inconsistent. Thus, if an adult comments on bad behaviour with sarcasm — "way to go" — children may respond as if the comment were positive and repeat the behaviour. Parents who rely more on tone than on the literal word in communications with their children may be sending messages they do not intend.

This research has implications for parents who rely on sarcastic humour as a way of relating. Many times I have heard clients who achieved high grades in school say that no matter how high their grades were their fathers always wanted more. If they brought home a 90+ grade but were second in the class the comment was "Why weren't you first?" If they brought home a 98 the comment was "Why not 100?" As an adult it is possible to see that some parents might think these were absurd statements and find humour in their own sarcasm. But all the children heard was "You should have done better; you're never good enough." If there was humorous intent, it was lost on them. The adults, remembering these experiences from childhood, felt only pain and a terrible sense of inadequacy. They grew up believing they were unable to please their parents and that they were never good enough for the important people in their lives. These are serious repercussions for the children of parents who relate this way, but there are also serious implications for the parents. Such relating suggests that they are uncomfortable expressing direct, loving words of appreciation to their children. The problem is the parents' but they pass it along to their children, who grow up doubting their abilities and feel they have fallen short of expectations. If they doubt their own abilities they may be more likely to comply to others' wishes and judgments in order to win approval, rather than trusting their own.

Parents may send messages they do not intend in other ways. Most would agree that it is important for their children to feel heard and accepted, and yet in practice the parents' own needs may get in the way. A client, Pamela, reported to me about some exchanges with her mother. She recalled telling her, as a young girl of six, that her teacher scared her. Her mother replied, "Oh, that can't be. Miss Jones loves children. I'm sure she wouldn't do anything to frighten you." Pamela said her mother's defence of Miss Jones made her angry and quiet. It was only one of many times her mother had made comments in contradiction to what she told her. With an accumulation of such experiences Pamela gave up confiding in her because she always came away feeling she did not believe her. She learned to tell her what she apparently wanted to hear — only pleasant things.

We could never be sure why Pamela's mother chose to respond as she did to her confidences. She may have felt that by denying her daughter's fear she could smooth things over for her, make them better for her. Pamela's mother may have felt scared herself at the thought of having to question her daughter's teacher. She may have thought that her fear was a one-time occurrence that Pamela would get over if she did not pay it too much heed. Although the mother did not accuse Pamela of lying, Pamela heard the implication in her mother's words. Mother might have been horrified if anyone had said she accused her daughter of lying, but Pamela felt she did not believe her. The impact was clear. Pamela felt that her mother did not want to hear her, did not want to hear about any concerns or unpleasantness or issues that might demand action from her. She felt invalidated by a person whose support she needed most. She learned that despite her mother's frequent invitations to talk to her, she did not want to hear what she had to say.

Parents may voice opinions about how people, including their children, should behave and promote responsible behaviour but be conflicted themselves when there is a call to action. In a classic illustration a client, Marian, related an incident that occurred when she was a teenager, still living with her parents. Together at home one day, they heard loud noises coming from the street. They ran to the front window in time to witness a robbery in progress. The thief struck and injured his victim, a woman, and escaped with purse in hand. Marian, who had the presence of mind to make careful observation of the robber's appearance, was outraged and started towards the telephone.

"What are you doing?" asked her father.

"Calling the police," she replied.

"Don't do that," her parents instructed in no-nonsense tones.

"But I have to. He got away with her purse and the woman is hurt," Marian protested.

"Don't do it," repeated her father.

"Why not? I don't get it: you've always told me to help other people," Marian shot back, confused by the discrepancy between her parents' ideals and actions.

"We don't want to get involved in that kind of thing. The police will be over here asking questions and then the robber might find out and hit on us," her father replied. "So get away from the phone."

Although she protested at first, Marian felt she had no choice but to comply. She had a history of being silenced, roughly, by her father, and felt uneasy. She heard her parents say no to her wish to telephone the police and she heard the "no" in her head in response to them. Years of conditioning told her she could not say no to her parents. But she never forgot that incident and the shame and guilt she felt for failing to report what she saw. The anger she felt towards her parents for forcing her to be silent emerged even many years later, with the retelling of the story.

Marian's parents were respectable people, like millions of other folks who consider themselves responsible citizens but who live in fear of retribution for speaking out. Their daughter had developed social consciousness at least in part by following their early instructions to her to be responsible. She was ready to act on it, but they were afraid to support her. Their response left her with feelings of confusion and a sense of alienation from her parents, along with a tendency to silence herself, punctuated by bursts of anger or tears when she could no longer contain her feelings, that accompanied her into middle age.

There are many ways in which families teach silence with confusing and conflicting messages. Often, appropriate behaviour is dictated but not modelled by parents. In varying degrees, parental arguments, parents' abuse of each other or their children, and drug and alcohol abuse may produce chaotic home scenes. Children must somehow reconcile these conditions with parents' admonishments that they keep silent about such goings-on and present a stoic face in public, that they produce exemplary behaviour in the face of their parents' misbehaviours. Children of such circumstances find themselves straight-jacketed into silence. They try to reconcile parental actions with parental words and conclude that the only way to be sure they are doing the right thing is to say as little as possible, especially to caregivers and other authority figures in their lives.

MISGUIDED TEACHING

Children in North America remain dependent for a long period during which parents are expected to provide financial support. Most children do not or cannot leave home until they are at least sixteen years of age, although many remain dependent even until their late twenties. Their dependency is a product of our culture. In North America we do not have legal ways for children or adolescents under the age of sixteen to survive without their parents' or guardians' financial support. University and college are expensive. The cost of living is expensive. Many adult children are unable to support themselves without financial assistance.

During this lengthy period parents are expected to teach children appropriate behaviour. There are no laws or official guidelines that tell parents what or how to teach. No one tells parents they must raise their children to comply with cultural standards, but implicitly they understand that it is their responsibility to ensure that their children "learn how to behave." Translated, this means teaching children to submit to authority, to be obedient, to silence their objections and dissension in the face of people who hold power over them — their caregivers, teachers, religious leaders, elders.

I was flying back to Toronto from a conference in New Mexico when I noticed a pale little boy of about seven attempting to return to his seat after using the lavatory. He was walking against traffic in the narrow aisle and was struggling in a sea of much taller people. His view was limited to the often-oversized midriffs of his fellow passengers who were all attempting to get to where he had just been. Suddenly, his mother caught up with him, pulled him aside into a row of seats, and told him to say "excuse me" to the passersby, who were all much larger than he was. A dutiful boy, he did as he was told while he held in his breath to make himself even smaller, whereupon his mother complimented him, saying, "That's a nice boy." She gave him the message that it was good he took no space for himself. Even worse, her comment suggested that being obedient is a character trait — a desirable one — rather than a behaviour. The boy was being told that making himself small and unobtrusive was being nice, a message that was expected, no doubt, to be generalized to other situations.

When the behaviour in question — obedience — is designated as a positive character trait without an accompanying critical analysis, the suggestion is planted that obedience is always a good thing. But sometimes disobedience is healthy and necessary, and sometimes obedience is dangerous. When the rules are unjust, disobedience or protest may be necessary, both for children and adults. When obedience compromises a child's safety or emotional security it is dangerous. Children need to be helped to discriminate between these possibilities, not taught to turn off their brains and comply blindly with any authority.

Many parents seek out information about raising children, in libraries and bookstores, from the family physician, and from friends and family members whose methods they respect. Despite this, at least some of the time most parents repeat the methods their parents used with them, even if they wish to train their children differently. Although they have the best of intentions, they do not recognize that they are repeating. Many people who have been criticized by their parents vow never to do the same to their children. In great effort to avoid that eventuality they go out of their way to praise their children and offer them emotional support or hands-on help. They are mystified, then, when the children sometimes reject their offers of help and accuse them instead of criticism. The parents fail to see an important aspect of their children's sensitivities. Children do need and want help from their parents, but when parents substitute their own ideas for the child's or contribute too much to the child's projects the unspoken message conveys the parent's lack of confidence in the child's capabilities.

The line between supportive help and criticism is crossed when the parent has a too-great personal investment in the child doing well, assuming some minor celebrity or ego stroking for the child's successes. Then the "help" might inadvertently discourage the child. The conversation might take the form of: "You played a good game tonight, son. When we get home I'll show you some moves that will help you score instead of just assisting." This kind of help can be experienced by the child as criticism and shut him down. Given that his father thinks he requires information about techniques, he assumes his work or play is not good enough to merit his father's unconditional approval. He needs to hear his father's support in that moment. In the wake of implied need for improvement he becomes shamed and quiet. He has no way of telling his parent that the help he did not request makes him feel criticized and the criticism makes him feel irritable or inadequate, that he feels he has been a disappointment. On the topic of his performance he remains silent, adding the criticism to his arsenal of bad feelings. He learns to be nice, to nod in agreement to the suggestions he experiences as criticism in the hope of pre-empting more of the same. He hesitates to bring up his own observations about his performance and requests for help with the skills he believes need improvement. Later, irritability might erupt in another context and neither his parents nor he will be able to explain it. Worse, the child learns to become critical of himself and others, an expression and projection of the anger and self-hatred he feels.

Parents must offer help to their children, but there are ways of offering help while remaining sensitive to the child's real needs that parents must learn. When parents' needs drive the perception of the kind of help required, the child's need for positive regard may be ignored. The tricky part is to remain sensitive to the child's real needs, which means that parents must listen to their children and get to know them on their own terms. It is not only criticism but also oblivion to the voices of children that reinforces the message of silence. When a parent monopolizes conversation or fails to pay attention to the child's conversation and respond in a meaningful way, the message is "Don't talk" or "Children should be seen and not heard." On the other hand, when parents and other adults in children's lives encourage them to speak and they listen respectfully and responsively, children gain confidence in themselves and learn to expect that they will be heard when they express themselves. When parents listen to their children and also set clear limits with them, acknowledging the importance of the children's words while pointing out that adults, too, like to get a word in, children learn both to speak and to engage in dialogue.

INFLUENCE   OF   SIBLINGS

Siblings teach the lessons of niceness by intimidation. Older brothers and sisters — and sometimes younger ones — can make life unbearable for their sibs. Their victims learn to protect themselves by withdrawing or fighting back in ways that don't expose them to additional threats, at least not in the moment.

Charles, a man in his late thirties and a lawyer in private practice, told me about the agony he experienced as a child at the hands of his older sister. She would taunt him when he talked about his favourite television programs, imitate his mild speech impediment when they were alone or in the company of other children, and tell him he was stupid. He hinted to their parents about the ongoing abuse, but they believed he was exaggerating because to them his sister presented a convincing picture of sisterly concern. She was clever enough to terrorize Charles out of sight of their parents and to threaten him into silence about actual details.

Charles's self-esteem suffered. He became shy and withdrawn in social situations, particularly with girls, and he stopped informing his parents, keeping the terror he felt, and his sister's behaviour, to himself. As a child he learned to hide out in his room where he might be forgotten. In adult-hood he was moderately successful in his profession, though he always felt he could do better if he were more comfortable taking calculated risks. Relationships with women were always difficult, deteriorating into struggles of power and control when the initial excitement calmed. After a few months he would become quiet and restrained in the presence of a new woman, keeping his thoughts and opinions to himself because he was always expecting that she would turn on him. Afraid of long-term commitment for this reason, Charles paired with women who were in some way unsuitable for him so there was never any question that the relationships must end.

Lucy was a woman who could not say no, and she was not at all mystified about the roots of her problem. She knew her relationship with her brother, who is three years older, was responsible for the tension she always felt with authority figures and her tendency to give in to their demands. In her family, her brother was an authority figure, having been given the job of watching Lucy after school while their parents worked. Her brother forced her to do his chores, left her alone while he went to hang out with his friends, and occasionally confined her to her room. On several occasions he sexually molested her. Lucy was confused by the molestation. She knew there was something wrong about what he did to her, and yet those were the only times her brother treated her gently. If she threatened to tell their parents he became obsequious and invoked guilt in her, and was successful in quieting her. How could she tell, she thought, if he was so sorry? As she grew older she protected herself against further attacks by authority figures, cushioning herself with extra weight and adding a crusty exterior to her compliant nature. She said no with her appearance and her manner but could not say it when anyone who gave the appearance of an authority figure asked her for something directly.

Silencing by siblings is not confined to boy-girl experiences. Boys pick on and are terrorized by their brothers, and sisters pick on and are terrorized by their sisters. Cousins who are frequent visitors or companions can also become quasi-sibling terrorists to younger children. To make matters worse, in the interests of treating children equitably and with the handicap of being out of sight at the onset of questionable events, parents sometimes inadvertently support the perpetrator rather than the victim.

I N F L U E N C E   O F   P E E R S

At school, children may be afraid to answer questions in class if they or someone else has been laughed at for giving an incorrect response to a teacher's question. Children are highly sensitive to the ridicule of their peers, so the power of children to censor each other is great. Rejection by the group is one of the cruellest relational incidents that can occur to children. No one wants to be isolated on the playground; no one wants to be left standing alone when teams are chosen or partners are paired for projects. As much as they are able, they want to avoid ridicule, and if that means keeping quiet rather than participating in a lesson, so be it.

I remember well the chant of my childhood, meant to ward off name-callers: "Sticks and stones may break my bones but names will never hurt me." Of course, it's not true. On the playground children may have to contend with bullies, students who terrorize their peers with verbal threats and sometimes with physical violence. In Manitoba, several children were forced to leave a school because authorities said there was nothing they could do about the children who were bullying them. In Surrey, British Columbia, a boy, fourteen, was not so fortunate. He committed the ultimate act of self-silencing, jumping to his death from the Patullo Bridge because he had been tormented with name-calling by his peers. Rena Virk of Victoria, British Columbia, was beaten to death by classmates because they took a dislike to her. What young person would not take the tormentors seriously when some taunts result in murder? The voices of peers saying, in effect, "shut up and disappear" are powerful.

Many teachers and administrators feel hamstrung in the face of bullying behaviour, but one educator, featured in a national television documentary, thinks differently. Cindi Seddon, principal of Seaview Community School in Port Moody, British Columbia, and co-founder of the Bully B'ware program, refused to tolerate bullying and developed a way of dealing with the children who were acting out in this way that was humane and firm. One child who had formerly bullied his peers said that as a result of Ms. Seddon's intervention he felt good inside, that he had needed help to curb his behaviour. The bullying, it seems, arose out of his own silence. He was unable to express what worried him, too, until Ms. Seddon helped him, setting limits and showing him respect.

A client recalls the pain of other children shunning him in elementary school because of his weight, appearance, and intelligence. The impact has been lifelong. In adulthood, he has overcompensated with food and played down his intelligence, in essence dumbing himself down. He carries the taunts of bullying classmates deep inside, keeping him in bed in the morning when he needs to get up for work, even as he approaches his thirtieth birthday.

In schools, children are categorized in formal and informal ways, by school staff and peers alike: according to achievement levels, by sex, age, sports skills, family wealth, political views. One young client said she became quiet in classes and casual situations at school to avoid categorization. Educated in alternative schools, at age twenty she was a critical thinker who gave original thought to complex topics in the fields of biology, adoption, and genetics, based on her own experience. Her thinking about these and other topics was different than her peers', and the few times she spoke up netted her ridicule. She soon learned that if she said nothing she could pass for one of the group and maintain some degree of connection. However, more often than not she was lonely and felt frustrated that she could not express her thoughts.

REINFORCING SILENCE AND OBEDIENCE

Irving Janis carried out research on group dynamics and, in 1971, identified a phenomenon he called "groupthink," which he defined as "a mode of thinking that people engage in when they are deeply involved in a cohesive in-group, when the members' strivings for unanimity override their motivation to realistically appraise alternative courses of action."

Janis's work was inspired by faulty decisions that produced significant consequences, such as the 1961 Bay of Pigs fiasco of the John F. Kennedy U.S. presidential administration, in which the U.S. attempted to forcibly overthrow the government of Fidel Castro. Efforts to validate Janis's theory have been limited, and he cautions that not all bad decisions are the result of groupthink and not all cases of groupthink fail. Nonetheless, Janis's model may be applied to describe characteristics of groups of nice people who may not be making life and death decisions together but who have attempted to maintain a cohesive unit. Symptoms he identified in the groups he studied included:

- the demonstration by group members of strong confidence in the group and belief in the rightness of their cause;
- a shared feeling of being special or invulnerable and an illusion of unanimity;
- rationalization of their decisions;
- stereotyping of people outside of the group and pressure on dissenters to conform;
- an inclination towards self-censorship; and
- censorship of others by group members and protection of the group leader from assault by contradictory ideas.

We live in groups, are educated in groups, work in groups, socialize in groups. In our daily lives we may interact with several groups on a regular or one-time basis. In varying degrees, they impact on us and we on them. We like to feel that we belong and therefore are vulnerable to the constraints and support of the groups we encounter. Several of the characteristics Janis named are particularly apt in describing nice people: they believe they are doing the right thing, rationalize their choice to silence themselves, stereotype people who are outspoken, and censor themselves and others. Applied to niceness, groupthink is obedient people reinforcing one another, buying into the notion of niceness, perpetuating what they have been taught. Its by-products are apathy and suppression of real thought, passion, and expressiveness.

Social psychology studies in which people's behaviour in individual versus group situations is explored confirm the impact of groups on the individual. Texts are laden with studies of the willingness to help strangers in distress when others are present (much less) and various other forms of bystander apathy. One study demonstrated that people are more reluctant to help even themselves when others are present.

THE TYRANNY OF NICENESS

The net of niceness is widely cast. When people who value this quality freeze out others who dare to speak up or live their lives in a manner consistent with their authentic beliefs, the impact is subtle but far-reaching.

The power of these people lies in the tyranny of niceness. They may not stop a determined person from speaking her mind, but their presence ensures that timid observers remain silent. Perhaps you have been in a crowd where someone challenged a speaker with a reasoned argument and yet the crowd remained silent, backing away from him even though in private some supported the challenger's view. The non-support that is suggested by such silence disempowers the speaker. In a culture of niceness, one lone voice informing the world of a preposterous but important truth is an outcast. To speak out is to risk isolation.

It is not surprising that after years of being trained to silence opinions, many people believe that even if they did speak out their thoughts and feelings would be negated by their audience. They are not mistaken. History has examples of just such instances, on grand scales, to reinforce this thinking. Cassandra warned the Trojans of their impending doom as the horse was to be rolled in, but they would not listen. Drunken and full of their own importance the Trojans brushed her off and restrained her when she tried to attack the horse with an axe. They silenced her for the moment, and they were the losers.

In today's world, anticipating non-support for our thoughts and feelings, we let apathy take over, and both positive and negative feelings are dulled. Comments are diluted to the extent that they lose any real significance. Eventually, people have difficulty forming opinions. Sometimes it is less troubling to remain uninformed.

The tyranny of niceness is a bit like a baseboard with chipped paint. From our usual position of distance the chips are invisible to the eye at a casual glance, but the baseboard is unable to withstand close scrutiny.

SOME ARE SILENCED MORE THAN OTHERS

Niceness is thrust upon us at a time, early in our lives, when we want only to be free spirits, when we want to express whatever feelings we have. With the assistance of the culture in which we are raised we learn to silence opinions, deny what we feel, censor and suppress thoughts we have learned to believe are inappropriate. Individual differences and experiences mean we do not all learn to suppress thoughts and feelings to the same degree. Gender, sexual orientation, and financial position all pave the way for us to be silenced in varying degrees. Racializing is another determinant of silencing, and it is woven through all of these.

In her novel *Cat's Eye*, Margaret Atwood describes girls at play, incidentally teaching each other how to be nice. The girls in question are creating scrapbooks, comparing their work as they put the books together:

> Grace and Carol look at each other's scrapbook pages and say, "Oh, yours is so good. Mine's no good. Mine's *awful.*" They say this every time we play the scrapbook game. Their voices are wheedling and false; I can tell they don't mean it, each one thinks her own lady on her own page is good. But it's the thing you have to say, so I begin to say it too.

In this illuminating novel about girls growing up Atwood goes on to distinguish between genders. Atwood notes that as a girl she does not have to worry about aiming well, running fast, or making loud noises. All she has to do is sit on the floor, cut out pictures from a catalogue, assemble them in a book, and say she's done it poorly. Denial is the core of Atwood's exposition of niceness: denial of competence, denial of authentic interaction, denial of competition. In their wish to be accepted girls silence the parts of themselves that they believe would jeopardize their membership in the group and remain obedient to the undefined but powerful standard of niceness that has been imposed on them.

Atwood warms to the topic in *Dropped Threads: What We Aren't Told*. She contributes a chapter, titled "If You Can't Say Anything Nice, Don't Say Anything At All," in which she describes the double bind that plagues women. To paraphrase: if women are nice they are weak but if they are not nice they are not proper women. Better to say nothing.

Hence, the silence of nice women.

One evening a friend and I were attending a movie at a local theatre. We arrived several minutes early and found seats with an unobstructed view of the screen. There were two free seats on both sides of us. We were waiting for the film to begin when a woman approached us and said, "Excuse me, ladies, I'm wondering if you would mind moving down one seat. I'm here with two friends and if you move down we could sit together in the three seats at this end of the row." We did not budge and my friend replied, "We sat here specifically so we would have an unobstructed view." The woman's obvious unhappiness with this answer was underscored with a curt "Well, fine then," as she continued her search, glancing briefly at the lone man in the row ahead. This exchange might not have been so notable if she had also asked the man to move. He was alone, and there was one empty seat on one side of him and two on the other side. But the woman did not ask him to move. It seems she was much more comfortable asking two women to move than one man.

The woman did not invent the notion that women are more amenable to being displaced than are men. Women and men are oriented to this idea at a very young age. Girls are encouraged to be compliant and contained, while boys are allowed — even expected — to be rambunctious, to push the margins of social conduct, and to have their space respected. Women are given messages throughout society that tell us we are inferior to men. Although some religious denominations now allow women to become priests and ministers, women still are not allowed to become Catholic priests. Women are a long way from occupying 50 percent of professorial jobs in universities or 50 percent of the principal positions in elementary and secondary education. Some women now fill seats in middle management, but rarely are we allowed into the real halls of power. Even though women make up 46 percent of the workforce in the media, they occupy only 5 percent of the top executive positions in communications corporations and only 9 percent of media company board seats. Women who make substantial contributions in their fields may be ignored, as was Rosalind Franklin, a scientist whose research was fundamental to the discovery of DNA. The men who received a Nobel Prize for the discovery, James Watson, Francis Crick, and Maurice Wilkins, not only used her work without acknowledging her contribution but also defamed her, saying that she was unwilling to share her research, that she was a complainer — and that her clothes were unattractive.

When a woman is asked to do something she is expected to do it, even if it is inconvenient for her or it robs her of her accomplishments. Conditioned to powerlessness, women can often be heard rationalizing their compliance with comments like, "It's easier for me to do it," or "It doesn't matter to me, I'm happy just knowing I can do it." Men, on the other hand, are less often encumbered with the kind of compliance that puts everyone else first, and many are therefore able to refuse requests with impunity.

Women who are not-nice — that is, who refuse to be silenced — are considered socially unacceptable, and women who are successful are deemed to have either slept their way to the top or to be deficient in some essential female quality. On the other hand, if women follow the invisible rules of niceness they also lose out, because for women being nice implies putting others first. Women are divested of niceness if they dare to contradict anyone, including other women. They are in a contest to put everybody else first in order to avoid the dreaded labels that relegate them to social isolation and disgrace, but when they win that race they become losers, particularly in the world of self-expression. The message is clear: don't speak. Even better: don't know. Women who "make it" in a competitive world walk a hair's-breadth line, adapting so well they are unaware of what they have lost.

Tennis champion Monica Seles was the first of the women grunters. Every time she hit the ball she emitted a karate-like yell, a yell that became her trademark. But male sports announcers ridiculed her, and during a tournament in 1993 a man stabbed her — to shut her up and make way for a non-grunting woman to be number one. Would this have happened to a male grunter? John McEnroe was known to hurl obscenities at opponents and judges. At worst, he was labelled "tennis's bad boy," more a term of endearment than disapproval.

Men are expected to be nice too, but they can push the limits further and still be considered nice. Men are admired for having opinions, but there are requirements: They must dress for their context, carry an air of authority, and appear rational. They must be well-packaged and stifle their words when a real authority enters the scene, in the form of a more powerful male. Still, a man who might qualify as nice might not be considered so because of some quirk of character or habit and may pay a high price for that unsolicited judgment. Guy Paul Morin was wrongly convicted of murdering a little girl, his next-door neighbour. He was quiet, shy, and inoffensive, but more important and damning, he was reclusive, preferring solitary activities to the company of neighbours, so he was judged by the people of his town to be an oddity. Not a nice man

in a way his town could understand, he was "different" by some undefined standard and therefore suspect. He endured two convictions and
years of legal wrangling before a DNA test proved his innocence. Chances
are if he had been considered nice — if his silence meant obedience to the
standards of the town in which he lived rather than a perceived rejection
of them — he would never have been subjected to his long ordeal. A case
in point is the nice guy accepted by all — maybe in your community —
who does so much for children in his community but turns out to be a
pedophile. His actions can go undetected for years.

The cliché "nice guys finish last" is often uttered by men who are
looking for a way to excuse their greed and competitive behaviour. It
allows them to pursue their goals while using the acknowledgment of a
deviation from niceness to hold on to the appearance of niceness. It also
underscores the differences in the expectation of niceness between the
sexes. No one would say "nice women finish last."

It is quite all right, even expected, that men finish first and use
whatever means they must to do so, unless they get caught —
although even that doesn't stop some. Finishing first turns a man into
a valuable social commodity, at which point his position affords him
the opportunity to again think of himself as a nice guy. Thus, women
and men are differently silenced into niceness.

SEXUAL ORIENTATION

A friend and her partner were enjoying some entertainment in a public park one evening. They were doing what most other couples at the
concert were doing, sitting with their arms around each other, sway-
ing to the music. My friend noticed a woman nearby, watching them
in the dim light with a smile on her face. But as the lights came up
when the concert ended my friend saw a look of horror sweep the
woman's face and heard her exclaim in shock to the man she was
with, "Ohmigod! They're lesbians!" Although the shocked woman did
not say, "That's not nice," my friend felt the judgment was implied by
her tone. Similarly, if a couple walking hand in hand turned out to be
two men, the observer's thoughts might be quite different, unless he

or she was also a gay male or a lesbian. In our society, we expect that to be "nice," women and men follow the socially designated sexual orientations: men couple with women, not other men, and women couple with men, not other women. Homosexuality is still considered to be "not nice" by many people.

People whose sexual orientation is different than the prescribed norm learn to be nice — to be silent about it in order to avoid the overt judgment of others. Even though gay pride days and, more recently, the issue of gay marriage have raised the consciousness of many people and forged greater acceptance, it would be naive to assume that these events have not also increased some people's negative judgments about homosexuality. Therefore, many — perhaps most — gays and lesbians prefer to keep silent about their orientation in all but the safest of environments. This may seem like a small concession to make until we examine the ease with which heterosexuals express their orientation. Images of women and men together abound and some physical contact and expressions of affection are accepted in public, whereas a gay couple walking hand in hand place themselves at risk for harassment.

The Funky Butt, a bar in New Orleans, turned niceness on its ear. Outside the entrance management posted a sign that stated, "If you can't be nice, go away." In a clever twist they were telling people who were unable to silence their objections to homosexuality that they were not welcome. The ones who have so often been accused — in one way or another — of being not nice would decide who qualified for niceness, silencing the silencers.

HAVES AND HAVE-NOTS

Paul Krugman often writes in the *New York Times* about the inequity of wealth in the United States. The gap is widening, he contends, between the small numbers of people who hold the greatest wealth and the middle class, which is being sucked dry. While there are many concerns for people who do not have even the financial resources of the middle class, the gap Krugman describes is a serious one. In a culture that promotes the idea of unlimited growth of wealth, fewer people hold more of the spoils than ever before. Yet people whose own financial well-being is threatened by policies that allow such disparities to be created support those very policies.

This phenomenon of the middle class described by Krugman signals that they have learned to obey, to honour the right to privilege invested in the very wealthy, by silencing what they see — even supporting it — and buying into the rhetoric that they too can have it all. These people are afraid. They want to keep what they have and believe they can have more, much more. They fear that if they protest the policies their own right to wealth will be threatened. In the process, they wind up on the losing end because they do not recognize that they can never benefit from policies designed to protect the very rich. David Brooks, also writing in the *New York Times*, points out that as long as the very rich stay "real" — that is, downplay the importance of their wealth and play up their down-home ordinariness — they are not resented by the American public. He claims that most Americans think their community is the nicest, and they feel pity for the poor folks who have lots of money but no true neighbours or free time. They effectively block their own protests to unfair income distribution.

At the other end of the have/have-not continuum lies the most silenced and obedient of all, people who are dependent on public assistance to stay alive. Many years ago I worked as a welfare caseworker in Toronto calling on recipients of public assistance. The people I met lived in some of the direst circumstances, drug-infested buildings owned by slum landlords or public housing that had become ghettoized. A few lived in rooms in relatively clean buildings. These people receiving social assistance were the most silenced of us all. None wanted to attract attention because raising a voice could mean losing their lifeline. Their very survival was dependent on their obedience. Sharing their position for most silenced are the inmates in prisons throughout the world, many of whom have a foot in each environment.

In the U.S. presidential election of 2000, the greatest threat to the people's voices occurred when people were denied the vote. Most of these people were African-Americans who went to the polls only to discover that their names had been omitted from the voters' lists without their knowledge. This act suggests disrespect for the right to speak that belies the Constitution itself. Disenfranchising some of the already weakest voices in America is a blatant silencing of the worst kind.

The yells of infancy are silenced into adult compliance and compliant adults shape the next generation. People co-operate in this process to create a culture of shared knowledge and values, but in this culture of silence and obedience it is the loudest voices that carry the greatest weight. Does the culture we have formed express the values of the people, or do the loudest voices merely make it seem that way? The next chapter is an examination of the institutions that shape us.

CHAPTER 4

CAREGIVERS ARE THE first to teach that niceness is achieved through silence, but they are far from being the only ones to do so. They are supported and guided in the curriculum of niceness by cultural influences. As children grow up and head into the larger world parental silencing often takes a back seat to influences outside the home. In adolescence, the pace of outside influence quickens, with varying impact, as children attempt to differentiate themselves from their parents. Teachers, religious educators, employers, government agencies, and the justice system become the standard bearers for niceness, reinforcing the message that parents have begun to teach and peers have reinforced. All are products of the same school of social deportment that turns demanding infants into silenced, obedient — frustrated — adults, generation after generation.

These individuals and groups operate as apparent free agents, but they are part of a much larger phenomenon, the society in which we all live. This framework is made up of articulated and unarticulated agreements that are instituted and reworked from generation to generation. The social agreements are both developed and reinforced by the agencies that have been formed around both visible and tacit agendas — agencies of education, religion, government, medical science, justice, and commerce. These agencies are operated by people, all of whom have grown up influenced by the very agencies they now run or work in. Each new generation of operators creates an impact on the agencies, so small changes are made, some to reinforce the silencing, some to free people.

A few brave individuals will attempt to correct some destructive situations: A politician may oppose rampant building, labelled development, because it is destroying ecosystems. A minister may attempt to convince a conservative congregation that loving their fellow humans includes accepting homosexuals and both genders as ministers. A scientist may report drug findings that might be in conflict with the interests of pharmaceutical promotion. These voices do gather support and mitigate inadequate or harmful policies and actions, but they are often drowned out by a cacophony of self-interest, greed, and hatred that is passively reinforced by the apathy of the silent. Facing that noise with small, protesting voices can be discouraging, and sometimes those who would make change do not survive. Instead, they become part of the system that silenced their voices, perpetuating it by complying. Many sidestep this entire process by simply following without protest, believing this to be the best way for them.

INFLUENCE OF FORMAL EDUCATION

When I was training to become an elementary school teacher, in the mid-1960s, a teacher advised us: "Never smile in September and you'll have a wonderful June." His message was clear. He was telling his class of budding teachers to restrict the human portion of interaction with young students early in the school year in order to effect compliance. Control in a classroom is important. No one can learn if chaos distracts her. On the other hand, control is counterproductive if children's self-expression is squelched. There must be limit-setting and encouragement, both.

Some teachers encourage students to express their own opinions, to explore ideas and push the envelope of learning. They are open in their encouragement and validate children's attempts to explore and stretch their own wisdom. They encourage children to take pleasure in the sound of their own voices as they speak out in class. Any children who experience even one such teacher in their school careers are indeed fortunate, because it can be difficult for students of any age to speak out, formally, in institutes of learning. To do so risks exposure. The speaker risks exposing ignorance of the topic at hand, and for many of us that is a position of extreme vulnerability, one that we often choose to avoid. Therefore, any parents who discover teachers in their children's schools

CONSPIRACY OR COINCIDENCE?

who create safe environments in which children can practise voicing their opinions, asking questions, or opening up a different way of thinking about a topic would do well to support them and to lobby for more of the same.

With sadness, I believe teachers who make children's expression of their own opinions a priority are rare. It is more common, in classes from daycare through secondary school, for teachers to expect students to enter the room, sit down, and listen. The adage "speak when you are spoken to" is alive and well in education. Messages of encouragement often get lost in efforts to control. Although there are exceptions, in general, the teacher imparts information and students are expected to absorb it. From daycare through graduate school learning is prescribed; opinions expressed are valued if they fit with those of the curriculum. Of course, teachers ask questions and want students to respond, but they ask questions to elicit a particular answer rather than to stimulate exploration. The guiding principle is that the "correct" information should be taught. The program is content driven, testing knowledge of facts. There are no tests for ability to ask questions that might stump the teacher. Rarely are there marks for different or critical thinking. Teachers demand respect in the form of quiet compliance, and students win rewards, in the form of grades, for giving what is expected. Too many students asking questions or expressing opinions would interfere with time needed to absorb the required material, subject matter that the teacher is required to teach. Diminishing education budgets mean there are fewer teachers and larger classes, allowing little time for anything but the most expeditious transfer of information. Therefore, even in those instances when teachers want to hear students' opinions there is little time to spend in this exercise. Students who endure long rides to their schools may have to fight fatigue, which interferes with their alertness. Sometimes a student will form opinions and succeed in making them heard, but this takes a determined or charismatic student.

In the United States the Bush administration passed the No Child Left Behind Act of 2001. The legislation that has been put forward as an initiative to raise the standards of education will, more likely, silence children. Although the program has not yet been funded, it is scheduled to become fully operational in 2005 with a mandate that demands that each state administer standardized tests to third- and eighth-graders in language arts and mathematics. Science knowledge will be tested beginning in 2007. The legislation has been criticized by many, including psychologists, journalists, educators, and legislators. Molly Ivins and Lou Dubose articulate many shortcomings of the plan in their book *Bushwacked: Life in George W. Bush's America*. A fundamental concern is that school funding, and principals' and teachers' salaries and jobs, will depend on students' performance on the exams. What this means to students is that their education is in danger of becoming even more focused on exam performance, not on learning how to think. Teachers anxious to hold on to their jobs will find that they are better off to concentrate their efforts on students who show ability to excel on exams, for that is where their own fate lies. Many students will fall between the cracks, some will be (some already have been) forced out of school because they keep the standards too low, and all will be deprived of opportunities to be inspired by their educational experience, to think.

Margaret Malone, a friend and an inspirational teacher at Ryerson University in Toronto, has found that students are stymied when they first come to her classes. A professor of nursing with degrees in nursing and sociology, Dr. Malone's primary concern is that her students learn how to think critically. She has found that this is a near-unknown concept to her students who, with a few exceptions, have been trained by elementary and secondary educational systems to suppress critical thinking. It takes exceptional effort for the students to let go of their quest for the "right" answers and think for themselves. To do this they must embrace the notion that they will be rewarded for learning a process that has previously been closed to them, the process of exercising their capacity to observe and make comments based upon their own experiences.

Dr. Malone's approach is unusual. More often than not, silencing of the students by grooming them to think in particular ways is the hidden by-product of formal education. Critical thinking is not encouraged. Children are taught to learn by rote methods to memorize and regurgitate facts and to avoid drawing conclusions intuitively. While these methods are necessary and helpful for some learning, such as multiplication tables, the basics of grammar, or fundamental factual information in any discipline, they are not appropriate for all learning.

History, for example, is often presented as a kind of gospel according to battles, treaties, heroes, and villains. The stories of women, men, and children who struggled through the ages to survive and thrive through wars, weather, and plagues are rarely visible. The stories of people meeting the challenges of everyday life are omitted in such renderings of history, and yet those individuals were and are responsible for the perpetuation of the species. Cultural influences such as art, crafts, and dance are taught, but as marginalized adjuncts to the real history — as optional courses — despite the fact that these expressions of creative thought are the roots of cultures that shape us now. Yet, the history of governments and battles is taught as if it were written in a completely objective way encompassing all we really need to know. It is taught as truth rather than subjective accounts of events in the past, accounts that are influenced by the period in which they are written and the authors' own limited views.

Technology has secured its own place in the influence of education on silencing en masse. In 2003, the state of Maine initiated a project in which fifteen thousand seventh grade students were provided with lap-top computers and a high-speed Internet connection for their work in the classroom. The expectation is that children will be given advantages in a computer-driven world and the teacher-student experience will be changed for the better. And yet, a program such as this limits students' ability to voice opinions or enter into critical discussion. It is difficult to enter into intense dialogue while riveted to individual computers, except perhaps to discuss what is on screen. Programmed to accept right answers, computers command obedience from their users. Approval, in the form of its feedback, from the inanimate computer is a powerful reinforcer for doing things in the expected way and focusing on finding right answers.

Computer use in the classroom fails to encourage discourse, and according to several research studies it also fails to provide educational benefit. One Israeli study carried out by MIT economist Joshua Angrist and Victor Lavy of the Hebrew University of Jerusalem showed that the mathematics scores of students in Grade 4 actually went down after the classroom acquired computers, while in eighth-grade maths and language there was no effect either way. A study carried out by the New

Jersey–based Educational Testing Service also showed a decline in fourth-grade math scores while some eighth-grade scores rose and some declined. The *San Jose Mercury News* in California funded a study that could find no significant link between the presence of computer technology and higher achievement.

The emphasis in education is on achievement of goals. Children learn in order to pass or, better yet, to excel on exams, to win points for the class or school, to get into the best universities, and ultimately to secure plum jobs. The attachment is to the outcome, not to the process of learning to think. Compliance with the methods and curriculum of the institution or educational system is expected. Analysis based on gender, race, or age may be dismissed as lacking significance or relevance if it is addressed at all. Critique by students of an institution's operations or teachers' methods is discouraged if not forbidden.

A few students learn to satisfy the system while expressing and acting on their own opinions. A few can overcome the strenuous systemic silencing played out in most institutions. More often the story is different. Students learn to keep their opinions to themselves, be very careful to whom they suggest them, and learn to craft their responses and work in ways that will be acceptable to authorities — who happen to be their teachers. Good grades are top priority. Learning how to think independently is not a requirement and not encouraged. A fortunate few may encounter teachers or professors — or have parents — who believe critical thinking is the educational goal of real value.

In universities there is greater tolerance for critical thinking, but even then it is not always welcomed. A friend, Carol, told me about a professor she had in undergraduate political science who encouraged critical thinking and discussion. Carol was so stimulated by his class that she took two more courses with him. Some time later she applied to graduate school at the same university. Her grades were more than adequate, and yet she was not accepted. Mystified and upset, she visited the professor to bend a sympathetic ear. To her surprise he told her that she probably was not admitted because she had used his name as a reference. Not everyone in the school approved of his methods. Although any number of political conditions may have been operating in the department and affecting acceptance of a student, one can only wonder, as did Carol, could it be that other professors felt threatened by students who learned to trust themselves and to question authority? Carol applied to and was accepted at another university where she completed her master's degree.

Whether or not professors value and encourage critical thinking, by the time students arrive at university they have already been indoctrinated into the ways of the education system. A telling sign is the question inevitably asked at the beginning of each course: how are we graded? Students ask detailed questions for specifics about how to achieve the highest possible grade, and then they tailor their thinking and work to meet the requirements.

Make no mistake — teachers do not act in a vacuum to silence students. Governing bodies determine what curriculum will be taught. Teachers are legislated to follow it. Decisions about what to teach are often driven less by thoughtful consideration of that which stimulates and expands young minds than by economics, time constraints, and political agendas. The arts and physical education are cut back in public schools because they are viewed as unnecessary extras in a system struggling under inadequate financing and focused on preparing children to earn money. In the interest of economics, education has become job-oriented, while the valuing of a solid education in the liberal arts has become lost in many public systems. Rather than broadening the purview of students, employment-focused schooling narrows the range of understanding. It creates worker bees, not creative, critical thinkers.

Thinking is also dulled when books used as part of curricula have been laundered for political reasons. In her book *The Language Police*, Diane Ravitch rails against the taboos that have been placed on textbooks. Faulting both political correctness and fundamentalist moralism she notes that views of the world are whitewashed. Rather than presenting facts as they are with thoughtful and critical discussion — which is possible at even the earliest levels if we simply access children's observations of their world — children are "protected" from everything. Dinosaurs are excluded because they suggest the controversial subject of evolution. Stories and pictures showing a mother cooking dinner for her children are cut because they are thought to suggest gender bias. A black family living in a city is deemed suggestive of racial bias, and Mickey

Mouse is out because mice and other creatures are considered to be upsetting to children. Rather than becoming more inclusive, with increasing frequency textbooks exclude anything that is deemed upsetting to interest groups with the result that children are being taught from texts that fail to represent reality.

Books that censor material because it might be upsetting are no better than the history texts I grew up with that failed to tell stories of women and children — or ordinary men, for that matter — births, deaths, or marriages. Life outside governments, geographical discoveries, and battlefields was non-existent in the history I was taught in my early education. The question of how to write texts to be inclusive is a difficult one that is subject to a variety of opinions, but it is one that must continue to be addressed, for it is inclusion, not exclusion, that assists greater understanding.

The current educational agenda makes sense if we are interested only in maintaining a world in which people focus their energy on going to work in order to earn money to spend on a multitude of products and services. If we are interested in developing a world of people who are unafraid to think for themselves, to question and discuss, it does not make sense. Neil Postman says, with tongue in cheek, that educating children to be critical thinkers is risky. He says it has the potential to damage home and nation because if children learn to think critically they will become skeptical and question the system in which we live. Of course, if we are to move ourselves out of blind acceptance or rejection we must first ask questions, we must suspend our belief, or disbelief, and challenge our assumptions. The likely product of this process is the emergence of skepticism, and with it, enlightenment. But this is risky if we want to maintain life as it is, because chances are the status quo will be found wanting. Postman suggests that parents do not want their children to think freely because the result could be the children's alienation from them. The alternative, however, is to keep children fettered and immature. So, following Postman's logic, if we want to protect the goals and smooth functioning of the nation it makes sense to prevent individual enlightenment by discouraging critical thinking. On the other hand, if we believe that it is healthy and desirable for children to mature and act on the basis of doing their best for themselves and others, to develop an informed skepticism about the institutions that govern and shape them, and to comply — when they do — not out of fear but from an informed position of understanding, it makes sense to educate them to be critical thinkers.

The psychological price, for individuals, of continuing to live in an unenlightened state can be great. The big picture, which includes human relationships and caring for something outside ourselves, gets lost. People lose sight of — or never understand — the value of teaching children to think and question. Parents concerned about secure financial futures for their children buy into popular thinking and encourage children to focus on achieving high grades or winning games. High grades mean the most prestigious schools become available. Entry into the best schools offers the illusion — and sometimes the reality — of a secure financial future. Yet by focusing all energy on these goals, parents may silence a vital energy that could land their children in a world of experiences that appears to be riskier materially while more in tune with their children's authenticity and ultimately more psychologically and intellectually enriching.

Everyone you encounter has been influenced by the education they have received. When you go to your dentist, physician, psychologist, or lawyer, when you request the services of a plumber, contractor, or financial planner, or when you send your child into a teacher's classroom, you want to know that these people are knowledgeable. You want to know that they have been educated thoroughly, have a broad and deep understanding of their work, and are skilled in applying their knowledge. For this reason, the straightforward transmission of information is important. There are times, however, when problems you present to these people are not straightforward, that you also want to be assured that they are able to think creatively, outside the box of accepted knowledge. You may need them to be sleuths, linking the information they have absorbed in new ways, in order to resolve your problem. Whether you need a plumber to find the source of a water leak or a physician to find the source of symptoms that defy the usual protocols of testing, you will need to rely on the creative and critical thinking abilities of these helping professionals. When you send your child to school you will need to rely on the ability of the teachers to provide a welcoming and stimulating environment for learning. For this reason, a complete education must include basics that are taught by the most efficient methods, and it must include instruction in and the encouragement of critical thinking. It must not silence, but liberate.

INFLUENCE OF RELIGION

Many people feel the need to enter into a community of like-minded religious observers, and many are introduced to such communities by parents who wish to expose their children to a spiritual or religious experience. These connections can benefit society in general because religious leaders teach guiding principles and attempt to encourage followers to a better life. At its best, religion is responsive to the needs of people while guiding them to become exemplary beings. Unfortunately, it is often practised as monolithic dogma that its followers are expected to swallow whole, without question or debate. Nuances are emphasized that divide groups. In monotheistic religions, people learn to attribute events to their god's will. They learn to ignore the contradictions of a god who is described as loving and all-powerful, but who allows small children to be molested and killed, wars to destroy lives — in the name of their god — and a few people to exploit and ravage the physical world that we all need to sustain life.

Organized religions use methods of teaching similar to those of education. Rote learning begins at a very early age, creeds are recited in weekly services, stories are repeated that are crafted to teach lessons according to scriptures. Singing, which is a vital component of many religious experiences, reinforces the message emotionally. Jewish children are taught to read and chant from the Torah in preparation for their bar or bat mitzvahs, when they attain the age of religious responsibility and duty. In the Roman Catholic Church children are taught to memorize the correct answers to formal, church-formulated questions in preparation for their first communion. One client, Carmela, was a questioning child who, in her first communion class at the age of seven, questioned the validity of the sin of pride. To her, it made no sense, and she raised her objections. The teaching nun's response was to send her outside the room to stand in the hall. Convinced the nun was wrong, Carmela had no change of mind, standing there alone. She had always been encouraged by her mother to question and learn. Still, her experience with the school was not forgotten, and the nun's failure to take up her question and the banishment to the hall left their mark on Carmela. It is not a stretch to imagine that the rest of the class, who witnessed their classmate being punished for asking a question, understood the message that was being delivered: do not question the teacher. As people are inclined to do, many of the children doubtless generalized the message to mean they must not question authority.

Almost anyone can participate in an educational institution of some sort up to post-secondary school, when the costs may make it prohibitive. Religious institutions have a different protocol. People are welcome to attend services at churches, synagogues, or temples, but the words "Everyone Welcome" that so often appear on notice boards outside the buildings may exist on the margins of honesty. Two principles govern membership in a religious organization: payment of dues and compliance with the belief system. Many synagogues are straightforward about payment: seats for services during the high holidays must be purchased. Other religious groups attach envelopes to their service programs for donations, and members solicit funds on behalf of the institution in the form of annual pledges. The plate is passed at weekly services and donations are expected. If people are unable to contribute they may still attend services, but tension develops if attendees do not eventually contribute money — the more the better — into church coffers.

The belief system of the Roman Catholic Church applies to many aspects of life. It includes weekly attendance at Sunday or late Saturday services, frequent participation in the Eucharist, early baptisms, last rites ceremonies, abstention as the method of birth control, and marital instruction before marriage from an unmarried priest who has taken vows of celibacy. If people fail to comply, the sacrament of confession and the old stories of penitents who flagellated themselves to atone for their disobedience reinforce the belief that it is wrong to disobey the church's teachings. Many people attend masses without obedience to these requirements, but if they revealed their practices or did not contribute financially, they would not be considered members in good standing.

Attendance without obedience to the requirements means that people must perform mental gymnastics to justify their position, something that might include referencing the experiences or justifications of others.

In every religion followers are expected to learn and accept the basic statement of beliefs, to contribute financial support, and to follow the instructions for daily living that the faiths prescribe. People sometimes self-identify with a religious denomination but fail to practise or make financial contributions. Requirements for membership involve setting aside other beliefs and accepting those of the religion in question. Such is the nature of membership.

The outcome of these practices in religion is the silencing of dissension. The price for not observing the rules is forfeiture of membership — a serious threat because many people want to belong to something that promises to give their lives meaning or relieves them of the fear that this life is all we have. The need to belong and believe in something is important, so people do not want to be deprived of their religious connections. Christianity teaches love, but in a practical sense, fear of being locked out of heaven takes precedence over the love message in keeping people in the fold. Religions that promote the idea of a life after death contain the most elegant of silencing mechanisms. Some people may accept inequitable work or living circumstances or succumb to physical abuses if they believe life is mere preparation for heaven. People may be convinced to sacrifice their lives to enjoy a divine hereafter. In the here and now, people sit through uninspiring sermons that are out of touch with their lives if they believe such endurance is the key to belonging to a community.

We are a species that thrives on connection and belonging. Religion is one way to achieve connection with other people. If you have ever sung a hymn with a large group of people you understand the life-affirming power of voices united in song. Yet the liturgy often detracts from that positive experience when it is rigid, demanding, and unchanging. A Roman Catholic might argue that changes in the church keep it abreast of the needs of the people. Latin was dropped from the mass following Vatican Council II in 1964, and around the same time the prohibition against eating meat on Fridays was removed.

Yet the most significant message is the one implicit throughout the ages, the thread that never changes — that children of the deity must be obedient. Fear of the consequences of being disobedient permeates the lives of the faithful as well as people who purport not to be religious. I remember an old woman acquaintance, a staunch follower of the Roman Catholic faith since childhood, who was unable to accept the declaration that eating meat on Friday was no longer sinful. For her it remained a sin and she fulfilled her perceived duty by avoiding meat every Friday for life. For her, obedience had its roots in the church she had always known, and she was not going to change.

When it occurs, change is long in the making and follows prescribed, lengthy processes. Traditional religions are understood as constant. They are not responsive to the needs of followers except as those needs are defined by the institutions. How different might peoples' experience be if they learned as children that religion is an important agent of social organization that provides a home to explore one's spirituality. How validating and encouraging for people to follow their spiritual quests with the help of theologians interested not in promoting a particular point of view but in supporting the journey. How different might people respond if they were taught that the great religious books such as the Koran, Torah, and Bible were accounts of some people's experiences at particular times in the history of the world. How different might it be if they were taught about the similarities in these points of view as well as the differences. Some ministers in some denominations are attempting to develop new theology that is relevant to the lives of their members, but these are still in the minority.

Religion changes with glacial speed, with the exception of splinter groups that initiate change to express differing philosophies. An entity that could be affirming and unifying is divisive and alienating because its focus has been on eliciting blind obedience to dogma. Followers are treated, all too often, like children who are not encouraged to mature and develop their own relationship with a spiritual entity, a relationship open to questions and doubts. When an opportunity for healthy change comes along, many followers are caught in lessons learned too well, remaining obedient to outdated dogma and failing to see the benefit of evolving and of reconciling traditional ideas with new understanding.

CONFLUENCE OF EDUCATION AND RELIGION

It has become policy in many jurisdictions to do away with morning prayers in public schools. Although this is an affront to people who wish to protect the tradition they grew up with and who want their children to be trained in religious practices, it can only be a relief for children who would otherwise be expected to participate in rites that are meaningless to them. A friend, Daniel, who is Jewish, attended public schools in a primarily Jewish neighbourhood in Montreal. According to the ruling of the Board of Education, Christian hymns were sung and the Lord's Prayer was recited every morning. Daniel and the other Jewish students were not excused from these exercises. When the high Jewish holidays, Rosh Hashanah and Yom Kippur, came around the Jewish children missed classes. There were so few non-Jewish students remaining that it was pointless to keep classes running as usual, so those who attended gathered in a single classroom on those days.

All through the year, Daniel and the other Jewish students in his school were expected to participate in Christian prayers and songs. They did so obediently, silencing the objections they felt even though they were the majority of students in the school. They kept their feelings about the situation to themselves, discussing the matter only with children and adults of their own culture. On a small scale Daniel's school illustrates what happens repeatedly: the dominant culture or religion perpetuates its supremacy. Even though they outnumber the dominants, subordinates silence themselves in public and bond in adversity as did Daniel and his Jewish family and friends. Nothing is accomplished except a deepening chasm between cultures and religions.

Many North American Natives were taken from their families in the combined interests of education and religion. Children were sent off to residential schools at the ruling of the dominant culture, where they were taught to read and write and pray to a Christian god. In addition to the physical and sexual abuses that many experienced at the hands of their keepers, the children were removed from their own culture and families. Some adopted the ways of the culture that took them over and have struggled with or become alienated from their own families as a result. Many have suffered trauma and pain that has cast them into lifelong emotional struggles; families are fragmented and social problems abound because compliance was forced. The impact cuts into generation after generation.

GOVERNMENTS, JUSTICE, AND THE CORPORATE WORLD

In North America we are fortunate to live in democracies where we have a right to vote for people who we believe will best represent our interests. We can raise our voices through this instrument of freedom, the secret ballot. Moreover, in theory, any of us can choose to run for public office and realize a dream of working to create a better country, a better world. Yet people feel frustrated with government — or at least with politicians and bureaucracy. The structures that oversee our lives and interests are unwieldy and insensitive to the needs of the people. Politicians sometimes respond to interest groups or individuals who promise to support the incumbent government, serving their own interest in maintaining power rather than the well-being of people they govern. Sometimes this is accomplished with campaigns that are designed to convince us that our interests lie in places that better serve those who wish to hold on to power.

After the attacks on the World Trade Center and the Pentagon on September 11, 2001, the president of the United States, George W. Bush, declared, "Either you are with us or you are with the terrorists." He was responding to challenges to his policy. This unsubtle silencing of the American people flies in the face of a constitution that reveres freedom of speech. It makes sense, however, in the context of a comment made by George Orwell, who maintained that political institutions capitalize on our silence and social control depends on it.

Not often is silencing so blatant as President Bush's post–September 11 dictum, but it exists nonetheless, and it has generated the uneasy feeling that our governing bodies are not friends of the people they govern. Before and during the war on Iraq millions of protestors gathered in countries all over the world to protest the United States' threat and then decision to launch a "pre-emptive" attack, to no avail. People feel powerless in their dealings with government. Yes, we can write letters or telephone our representatives, but our concerns disappear into a cauldron that churns out form letters and impersonal responses. Protests fall on state-of-the-art deaf ears. When people attempt to make their voices heard by those in power, as they did when economic summits were held in Seattle, Cancun, and Quebec, barriers are erected, extra police are called in, and people are beaten into submission, carted off to jail, or slain. During the Vietnam War tens of thousands of war objectors left the United States because their protests were ignored by a government that was intent on waging war for its own purposes.

Politicians run roughshod over the concerns of people who, feeling unheard, insignificant, and helpless, become apathetic. The proof is in the voting — or lack of it. Believing their votes mean nothing, many people can no longer be bothered to exercise this right. Even when they do, they may feel their votes do not count. In 2000, George W. Bush managed to take the presidency of the United States with a one-vote majority in the electoral college, mandated by the Supreme Court of the United States, even though he failed to win the popular vote by over half a million ballots.

The justice systems created by governing bodies are also oppressive. Under a laborious system the wheels turn slowly for people who are sometimes wrongly accused of everything from traffic misdemeanours to major crimes. Whether it is a police officer who bullies a disadvantaged person to admit to crimes she has not committed or courtrooms run by ill-informed judges, the people who depend on the system to be chaste are often disappointed and silenced in their attempts to secure justice.

I received a parking ticket for "failing to display receipt" in the windshield of my car. The ticket was issued in error. I had paid the fee and properly displayed the receipt on the windshield of my car. To challenge the error I would have to go to the city administration offices during a working day, wait in line to be told I would have to arrange for a court date sometime in the distant future, and then spend another day pleading my case. Instead, I sent a letter explaining the situation and the difficulty entailed in protesting something that should not have happened in the first place, along with a photocopy of the receipt on which the time covered was displayed. Some time later I received a letter stating that "no apparent error" was found in the issuing of the receipt. I was hamstrung. At that point, all pertinent dates for protesting having passed, I had no choice but to pay up. If I did not, I would not be able to renew my vehicle licence for the following year. And of course the fine had inflated from the original $20 to $56.

A picayune matter? Perhaps. But not long after this incident occurred, a local newspaper ran a full-page story on a similar situation. The reporter took her protest to court and was still ordered to pay $10 of the original fine. It was impossible to plead not guilty and be excused when a car owner's word was in conflict with that of the issuing officer. The ticket frustration is a small matter in terms of implications for my life but enormous if it is but a sample of how justice systems stampede over the citizens they purport to serve. The picayune becomes serious and questions arise: are parking enforcement officers required to fill a quota? Well, no, says Doug Reynolds, superintendent of the parking-enforcement unit in Toronto. But they are required to meet "performance standards," and the officer who issues the greatest number of tickets gets a cash bonus. And issue them they do, to the tune of 2.8 million a year — worth $75 million — in Toronto. In Los Angeles $86 million in tickets are issued every year, comprising 2 percent of the city's revenue. In Chicago 3.5 million tickets are issued for a total of $100 million, and in New York City 9 million tickets are issued with revenue of $375 million. No small matter.

How many people as a ratio to tickets wrongly given actually protest? One Toronto resident who parked his vehicle on a downtown street on the strength of a parking permit was issued twenty-one tickets in eighteen months despite the fact that he had parked legally, under the conditions of his permit. Was he going to take time off work to protest each time? He moved instead, to a place with a garage. Many people don't have the flexibility to choose moving as an option in the battle against parking tickets, and my guess is that most people do not bother to protest an occasional ticket issued "in error," believing the dollar amount is not large enough to warrant their time spent. They pay up and shut up.

This example from everyday living illustrates that methods of silencing are in full, frightening evidence when we peer below the surface and understand that they do not always involve face-to-face confrontation and demands. An effective method for silencing masses of people can be to induce frustration and feelings of powerlessness. Small lessons learned with parking tickets may generalize to more important issues for which a great deal more effort would be required to protest. Although higher stakes may incite people to action, it is important not to underestimate the conditioning to feelings of powerlessness produced by mundane events such as the issuing of parking tickets for offences that did not occur.

The methods of silencing are legion. I witnessed an unnerving scene while working in a prison for women. An inmate was with me in my office when she was called upon to meet with a police officer. She requested that I attend the meeting with her. The officer did not object to my presence, nor did he make much effort to cover up the fact that he was badgering the woman into admitting to a crime that she said she did not commit. It became clear that the officer wanted the crime off the books. The inmate was indoctrinated in the ways of the justice system and familiar with many police officers, giving them lip when she felt like it. Still, she was cowed by the man and agreed to admit to the crime on a vague suggestion of a light sentence. After the meeting she reiterated her innocence to me. Of course, police work is difficult, sometimes dangerous, and often thankless, and there are many instances in which people say they did not commit crimes when they have. But many people have also been wrongly accused and convicted. This woman had no power and no hope of having any. Whatever angry protests she could still summon were ignored or laughed at. She died in her mid-thirties of a drug overdose, a victim of a life of poverty and abuse that led her into a justice system where her victimization was repeated, not, perhaps, because there were no people willing to help her, but because they, too, were rendered powerless. She fell between the cracks and died.

In a democratic society oppression takes the form of onerous and excess paperwork, contradictory policies, laboriously slow procedures, and meaningless responses to the concerns of the people. Sometimes it takes extreme forms, such as the shooting of students protesting the Vietnam War at Kent State University. In our frustration we often give up trying and say we could not have made a difference anyway, and then the silencers have been effective.

Those who continue to protest are rare. David Milgaard was convicted of murdering a young woman in Winnipeg, Manitoba. The evidence was flimsy and another suspect was ignored in the investigation. Still, Milgaard was powerless to secure his freedom. His mother, however, proved to be a formidable and vocal opponent of the law enforcers who convicted him. Accepting no less than absolute freedom for the son in whom she believed, she managed to turn the case around, and he was eventually exonerated by DNA tests. Nonetheless, Milgaard languished in jail for over twenty years before her tireless work paid off. If his mother ever learned the lessons of silence and niceness she threw them out in her fight for her son, exhibiting a courage and diligence that is rare indeed.

The layers of silencing incorporate, as well, people engaged to enforce laws, those who interpret the law, and those who break the law. Many jurisdictions now have screening tests for candidates for their police forces, and they aim to recruit high-calibre people who are able to interact well with the citizens they meet during their working day. They may arrive at their jobs intending to serve the populace with compassion, but the requirements of budget-strained administrations and the hostility of jaded citizens can be enough to move police officers off the high road. It may be safer for them economically and socially to quiet themselves when they see practices with which they do not agree rather than speak out in the interest of integrity.

At the other end of the justice scale, inmates have their own methods of silencing those who do not meet the standards of the heavies or who dare to "rat" on a co-inmate. At the level of administration inmates are subject to rules and standards that have been developed on the assumption of their guilt, within a system founded on the assumption of innocence. Thus, their behaviour in prison is interpreted accordingly, despite protestations of innocence or nuances of culpability. At another level, in almost all jurisdictions in the United States, inmates and parolees are not allowed to vote. Their right to participate as citizens is stripped from them when they are convicted, even though policies and judgments still affect their lives.

Lawyers must interpret, prosecute, and defend within a system that forces complex issues into adversarial positions and often frustrates all the players, especially those at the lower end of the socio-economic scale who await judgments, encumbered by near-endless delays and technical exceptions. Judges, too, make their decisions within the context and confines of this system that is dependent for its functioning on the observance of process, which is, ironically, blind to certain complex issues.

In British Columbia a seventy-five-year-old woman, Betty Krawczyk, was jailed for contempt of court after refusing to sign a court document agreeing not to return to the sites of her protests, logging road blockades. A strong defender of the environment and protester against the logging policies of British Columbia, Ms. Krawczyk had been convicted of contempt twice before, for refusing to obey court orders to stop blockading logging roads. The judge said that although she saw herself as a political prisoner the court saw her as a lawbreaker. Unfortunately for Ms. Krawczyk, and perhaps for the environment of British Columbia, the court was not authorized to act on principles of scientific investigation and thus became the handmaiden of corporate logging interests. How many people have the determination of Ms. Krawczyk, to go to jail for their beliefs, to fight for the quality of life of generations of people yet to be born? Rather than fight corporations and then be silenced by the courts, most people silence themselves, taking the pragmatic view that someone else will fight the fight or rationalizing that the situation is not as desperate as this radical protester claims. Henry Thoreau was jailed when he refused to pay his taxes in protest over the United States' invasion of Mexico in 1864. Ralph Waldo Emerson asked him, "What are you doing in jail?" Thoreau replied, "Why are you not in jail?" He was rare, like Betty Krawczyk. Most of us are not so principled that we would risk such confinement in defence of our beliefs. We silence ourselves instead.

The structure of the corporate world is also effective at silencing. Employees who want to keep their jobs and move up the ladder of success learn the argot early on, what to say and — at least as important — what not to say. Before you can "put your best foot forward" in the job interview you must subject yourself to a process of grooming that will make you acceptable in the world of business. There is little tolerance for opinions that question company policy, for "positive thinking" is *de rigueur*. There is little room for personal expression in dress or grooming. Books have been written underscoring the need to dress for success, a euphemism for obedience and silencing of personal expression. Employees are expected to respect the hierarchy of status and remuneration. It is accepted that chief executives earn many times the amount of money those lower down the ladder make and that the gap is increasing even when the same companies are faltering.

Their silence does the employees no real good, for they will be let go despite their obedience if officials in the company decide this is necessary. Now researchers are beginning to recognize that their silence does the companies no good, either. Harvard University professors Leslie Perlow and Stephanie Williams say their research has shown that employees' silence generates anger and resentment that contaminates every interaction, shutting down creativity and decreasing productivity. In a dubious beneficial stroke, companies may encourage expression when they realize employees' silences are cutting into their profits.

In the name of profits, creativity has been stifled; entrepreneurs purchase franchise operations rather than setting up individualized versions of restaurants and food, clothing, hardware, and office supplies stores. The quest for fast money has led people to set up businesses based on applied formulae that promise high profits rather than trust that one's individual expression in business will find a market. In the wake of mass acceptance of this rationale, the world has begun to look homogeneous. Our choices are diminishing, and many of us go along with it, convincing ourselves that predictable mediocrity is better than the unknown, which may provide a range of experiences from exciting to disappointing. Predictable mediocrity seems to offer stability and choice, but the reality is that we end up with a significantly reduced range of options. There may be restaurants on every corner, but if they consist of Burger King, McDonald's, Pizza Hut, and Tim Hortons we have very few real choices from which to pick.

MEDICINE

In its own ways the medical profession silences people. David Healy, a Welsh psychiatrist, teaches that power relations between physician and patient are such that patients are afraid to disobey their doctors and, I add, many are afraid even to question them. A physician has the power to terminate service to a patient. Patients, facing a choice between non-compliance with doctors' orders and a fear of being without a physician in a time of crisis, will do as told, even if they feel the proffered help is not what they need.

A client, Terry, reinforced for me the power of physicians' words. She had been taking antidepressant medication for a long time but felt ambivalent about it. She was also in psychotherapy, had made good progress with the depression she had been experiencing, and had been working on issues that had troubled her for years. Even though she was feeling much better, the physician who prescribed the pills advised her to continue with them through the winter and then return to him for advice about weaning off them, a process he said must be slow. Three days before Christmas Terry ran out of the pills and did not renew the prescription. By Christmas Eve she was experiencing symptoms — heart palpitations and anxiety — and on Christmas Day she sought out a pharmacy hoping to get even one pill to carry her through to the next day when her usual pharmacy was open. The pharmacist she found co-operated and gave her a supply of the pills. Terry left the store, got into her car, and swallowed a pill using saliva to wash it down. The pill was only halfway down her throat when her symptoms disappeared.

As she related the story to me Terry expressed amazement. She realized that it was impossible for the pill to have such an immediate effect and was stunned at the impact of taking it. As we explored the possible reasons for her remarkable recovery she said it was her doctor's words — his cautions about staying on the antidepressants over the winter and weaning off them very gradually — that had the greatest impact on her. She believed she should not have disobeyed the doctor, and her recovery was a direct result of re-compliance with his instructions, not of taking the pill. A short time later Terry decided to stop taking her pills and did so, in a more gradual manner. The insight she gained seemed to strengthen her. Within a few short months she was dealing in greater depth with the real issues in her life, finally disclosing problems to her husband that she had never talked about because she had doubted her own perceptions vis-à-vis her husband's insistence that he was right. She had also been mired in guilt because she was not contributing financially to the family and she felt paralyzed. When she risked talking about what she really felt she was able to begin moving forward in her life.

Terry's experience underscores what any good psychotherapist knows, that the words of an authority figure carry a lot of weight for the people they touch. Because of their special position in our culture physicians must speak with care and never underestimate the impact of their words on patients. Anyone working with a vulnerable client or patient needs to be realistic about the power their position holds in the minds of the people of our society, positional power that is deeply embedded in our social structure. In full awareness of this aspect of the professional-client relationship, they must practise with caution and compassion.

In years past, enforcement of social conformity has been practised by the medical profession in a number of ways. One of the most notorious and repulsive that rose to prominence in the 1940s was the ice-pick lobotomy, designed to turn patients into compliant, mediocre personalities. The procedure was performed by attaching electrodes on the temples of the victims and shocking them into a faint. The doctor would then lift the left eyelid and plunge an ice pick into the head. The operation was performed on about twenty thousand people worldwide, some veterans of the world wars and sufferers of trauma. Twice as many women as men were lobotomized. Frances Farmer, a beautiful and successful Hollywood actress in the 1930s and 1940s, was one of them. Ms. Farmer had a tragic flaw: all her life she had rebelled against every form of authority and in addition to her movie stardom had been a radical political activist. At the age of thirty-four, she was incarcerated in a state hospital in Washington. There, she was cured of her communist sympathies and her aggression against authority by Dr. Walter Freeman. Dr. Freeman, then president of the American Board of Psychiatry and Neurology and one of the pioneers of the procedure, ensured that she would never again be a "threat" to society. Farmer drifted off into oblivion, ending her days as a hotel clerk.

A particularly alarming feature of the lobotomy-era tragedy is the lack of resistance from others in the medical profession. Although individual psychiatrists and psychoanalysts objected to the procedure in private, they evidently silenced themselves in the interests of conforming to current thought and practice, for it took more than a decade for medical professionals as a group to put a stop to the unconscionable act of ice-pick lobotomy.

Medical professionals expect compliance, and often it is wise for patients to comply. In the case of antidepressant pills, for example, the safest way to stop using them is to wean oneself off because physical dependencies can develop, and therefore stopping their use produces withdrawal effects. Weaning minimizes these effects. In other instances it is important to co-operate with a trusted physician to best help ourselves.

Many times I have been helped by physicians, and it is not an over-statement to say that I would not be alive to write this were it not for the skill and knowledge of some excellent medical doctors, whom I could never thank enough. At the same time, I know it is important not to comply blindly with advice from experts. Whether we are purchasing items or services we must take responsibility for informing ourselves as thoroughly as possible. A fear for many people is that they will be labelled, and then not helped, if they object to or question the authority of physicians and other experts. The fear is not without a basis in reality. Medical professionals sometimes do label individuals who do not con-form to particular ways of behaving and thinking and who appear to be problem patients. Nowhere is this more likely to happen than in the practice of psychiatry.

In the absence of a definition of normalcy, the bible of psychiatry, the *Diagnostic and Statistical Manual-IV* (*DSM-IV*), is used to label as mental disorders behaviours of certain types. This manual has generated a great deal of controversy, in part because of the labelling of problems that have no proven organic origin. Whether perceived as useful or not, psychiatric labelling has gotten out of hand, in part because mental health care is often paid for by insurers on the basis of *DSM* diagnoses. That the patient experiences difficulties in living, in relationships, or at work is not enough of an explanation to justify reimbursement for services. Each problem must be identified as a disorder, syndrome, or condition to be eligible for funding. As a result, listings include anything for which a person might seek out counselling, including parent–child relationship problems, problems with mathematics, suicidal depression, and personality problems.

The listings, though wide-ranging, are selective. For example, eating disorders such as anorexia nervosa and bulimia nervosa are included, as is binge eating. Yet, even though chronic overeating that results in obesity is a common problem in North America, it is not listed in the *DSM-IV*. Many people eat so much food on a regular basis that they accumulate extreme amounts of fat, putting them at risk for such life-threatening diseases as diabetes, hypertension, and heart disease and creating a high degree of physical, psychological, and social discomfort. Despite this, their behaviour, laden as it is with self-destructive effects, is not considered a psychological problem worthy of inclusion. Similarly, there is no listing for people who fail to provide their bodies with physical exercise needed to sustain good mental health. Why these problems should be omitted when others are included is unclear.

Early in my clinical training I noticed a circularity of reasoning that was sometimes incorporated into diagnoses that contributes to the silencing of certain people seeking help. Patients who had been diagnosed with borderline personality disorder were marginalized because they were known to be difficult to treat. Mental health professionals were reluctant to work with them because they felt their efforts would be futile. The patients were difficult, yes, but it was unclear to me whether the reluctance to work with them was a result of the patients' problems, the diagnosis made by the treatment industry, or some interaction between these factors. When a patient is given this particular label, treatment is likely to be limited because many therapists believe the person cannot be treated. However, one of the features of the diagnosis is an inability to sustain relationships. If the patient, disheartened by therapy that is not helpful, decides to seek out help from someone else — and must do this several times — her actions could be used as one element in the confirmation of the diagnosis.

Attention Deficit Hyperactivity Disorder (ADHD) is a diagnosis given to rambunctious children who cannot sit still and concentrate on tasks. Referring to the criteria for ADHD in the *DSM-IV*, Dr. Peter Breggin, who is a leading critic of the diagnosis, argues, "There is no disease; it's a list of behaviors that annoy adults." If that is true the diagnosis is particularly troubling when it is coupled — as it so often is — with treatment such as the drug Ritalin. The drug, which is a stimulant, has a paradoxical effect with children and subdues the child and makes him or her (though it's usually boys) nice and acceptable. Parents all want their children to comply with their expectations of behaviour, in part because they believe it will make the children socially acceptable, but sometimes — maybe even often, in this age of overloaded schedules — the expectations are simply beyond a child's developmental level. The child is subdued with medication and receives a powerful message about silencing and obedience. The diagnosis allows parents to deny that their, and society's, expectations may be too high, that the lifestyle to which they believe their children must conform is too demanding, or that events in the child's life are overwhelming. It supports the idea that the problem rests in children's brain chemistry. If the problem is chemical, a drug can fix what might in reality be problems in children's lives — confinement to city lots, demanding school programs, parental discord, abuse and other trauma, peer pressure, and tight schedules that leave no time for children simply to be children. The drug makes life easier for the families of children who are not ready to become inhibited. The drug subdues children to enable them to better conform to a socially constructed notion of age-appropriate behaviour. Sometimes it subdues children so they are more able to speak and work in a focused manner. It does not address the deeper problems facing the child. The diagnosis lets an excessively demanding culture in which parents are trying to raise their children off the hook.

There are many problems in making diagnoses of mental health problems, which Paula Caplan addresses in her book *They Say You're Crazy: How the World's Most Powerful Psychiatrists Decide Who's Normal*. One argument Dr. Caplan makes is that the normal reactions of women to an oppressive culture are pathologized in the manual. In an effort that underscored the gender bias in the manual's listed diagnoses, she introduced a potential new category to the committee writing the *DSM-IV*, one that describes the dominating behaviour of men in our culture. Although the issues in her proposed diagnostic category have been studied and documented by competent researchers, the committee produced nothing but roadblocks to the inclusion of this category in the manual. Thus, in its very development, the manual silences individuals, and it labels groups differentially. Nonetheless, although the *DSM-IV* has been found lacking by many scientists, and despite its biases, it is considered to be the defining instrument of diagnosis in mental health.

Some critics have raised the possibility of a link between the development of drugs by pharmaceutical companies and the development of new disorders for commercial purposes. Forest Laboratories is promoting its antidepressant Celexa for compulsive shopping, exposing the extraordinary lengths to which drug companies will go to sell their products. In this case, individuals' shopping problems are redefined as a psychiatric disorder, and it is being considered for inclusion in the next revision of the *DSM*. The rationale for inclusion is that shopping is acceptable unless it interferes with other functioning, whereupon it becomes a disorder. This myopic approach separates the problem from the culture in which it arises — a culture that promotes excessive consumerism and the accumulation of material goods as a fundamental measure of success and happiness.

There is a large and growing tendency to treat depression and anxiety with medication. Patients who confide in their family physicians about mood problems are likely to be offered antidepressant medication even if the person's preference is to talk through problems with a trained professional. The explanation given is that a chemical imbalance in the person's brain is responsible. But how did the alleged imbalance suddenly occur, and how will medication resolve the problems that the patient experiences? The answers are not clear. Still, pills are the solution of choice for physicians, even though evidence for their usefulness is flimsy. Even children are being prescribed antidepressants, despite the dearth of knowledge of the long-term impact of these drugs on developing children. So predominant has this trend become that when the British regulatory body banned the prescribing of antidepressants to children under eighteen because of adverse side effects, some American psychiatrists were flummoxed, evidently concerned, but not knowing what to do with children who presented as depressed other than prescribe drugs. Understandably, many parents were alarmed, having trusted their doctors' advice only to have it called into question by the actions of another country.

In his book *Blaming the Brain: The Truth about Drugs and Mental Health*, Elliot Valenstein exposes the influence of pharmaceutical giants in perpetuating the notion of chemical imbalance as the root of mental illness. They are interested in profit and they have been highly successful in marketing the claims that justify prescribing and taking the pills they manufacture. It is not in their financial interests to encourage patients to talk instead of medicating. The complement to this is patients who want an easy or quick fix to long-standing and difficult problems and who have been taught that medicine is the solution to psychological problems.

For some people medication seems to help severe depression, and doctors and researchers provide examples of successes treating such patients. But often the treatment far outlasts and outweighs usefulness, and some researchers have argued that a placebo effect is at work. The patient believes the pill will help and so it does, for a while. In another study it was found that improvement using the highest doses of medication was not different from improvement at the lowest doses. Moreover, there was only a slight increase in improvement using drugs rather than placebo, an improvement that the study's authors suggested might be invalidated with further studies exploring placebos in greater depth.

Physicians are the usual first professional helpers sought out by people who are feeling depressed. Some physicians refer patients to professionals trained in talking therapies but often only as an adjunct to drug treatment. Sometimes physicians attempt to counsel patients themselves, but many do not have adequate training in talking therapies, so their counselling may take the form of advice-giving rather than empathic listening with appropriate and timely interventions. If they have not been through psychotherapy themselves they may unwittingly bring their own emotional issues and limitations to the counselling relationship. People who have difficulty talking about their feelings are acutely tuned to subtle messages from others that either encourage them or discourage them from talking. Even though people speak to mental health professionals for the express purpose of helping themselves through difficulties, they may feel inhibited to use language that they believe may be offensive or relate thoughts that they believe might cast them into disfavour or make them seem psychologically unstable. They may silence the very parts of themselves that most need to be expressed because they have learned not to offend. Some are skilled at giving the impression of disclosures while effectively keeping hidden their deepest shameful secrets. They have learned to silence themselves in the belief that they are protecting themselves. Although they want to feel better they struggle to speak about the things that would help them. To release these people from their bonds requires a great deal of skill, acquired with intense and lengthy training and experience.

When people are seeking help to deal with their emotional problems they often become confused about whom to consult with or look to for treatment. Many people do not know the difference between psychologists, psychiatrists, and psychotherapists. All of these people might practise psychotherapy, but some psychologists do not and some psychiatrists do not. The most reliable statements about the differences are that psychologists have earned Doctor of Philosophy (Ph.D.), Doctor of Psychology (Psy.D.), or in some cases Doctor of Education (Ed.D.) degrees; psychiatrists have earned Doctor of Medicine degrees (M.D.); and psychotherapists may hold any degree or none at all. Psychologists, to use the title, must be registered with or licensed by the body in their geographical area that is responsible for licensing and quality of service, usually a College of Psychologists. Like medical doctors, they are licensed to make diagnoses based on the *DSM-IV*. Psychiatrists are registered with a College of Physicians and Surgeons. Psychotherapists may have affiliations with bodies that oversee them, especially in the case of registered social workers, but some may be unregulated. Of these groups, only psychiatrists can prescribe medication, although there have been some experiments in which psychologists have been trained to prescribe medication.

Counsellors and psychotherapists working from a variety of perspectives place differing emphases on the importance of helping a client open up and speak about deeply personal issues. Some approaches are focused on changing behaviour without delving into understanding the causes of the behaviour, while other ways of working to help people with their problems involve exploration of childhood, relationships, the social world, and any traumas the person may have experienced. Perhaps the most important variable of the work is the person who, regardless of theoretical persuasion, will help clients speak freely and work through their problems to the extent that their own capabilities allow them — to listen, hear accurately, interpret, and be authentic as persons — thus helping clients understand themselves and make changes in their lives.

When it is working well, psychotherapy can free people to speak out and give up niceness. Like other helpers, psychotherapists grow up and are trained within a social world that values and encourages niceness. They must become aware of the ways they might silence clients. You, the consumer, must decide whether they have learned to help people open up.

We live in the age of experts. People are taught to heed experts' advice rather than think for themselves, and even if they do attempt to chart their own paths their efforts may be thwarted. This phenomenon, powerfully in evidence in medical practice, was reinforced for me several years ago. Through the investigation of some minor symptoms, I learned that I had a cyst on one of my ovaries, which grew slightly during a three-month monitoring period. This was a difficult time in my life. My marriage was ending and I was completing a master's degree while raising my teenage son. My gynecologist, Dr. Steal, a woman whom I had begun to see the previous year and who was highly recommended to me, said she wanted to investigate the cyst surgically as a precautionary measure. Although she did not expect to find cancer, she wanted to open my abdomen to see what was happening because I am a cancer survivor. I was alarmed and felt pressured to go ahead with the procedure sooner rather than later because the doctor was going away on holidays and because of my medical history. The cancer I had survived many years before had been a fast-growing one, but the vigilance and quick actions on the part of the attending doctors saved my life. In this new situation my gynecologist was reassuring: she did not believe it was cancer, only a cyst, and the peek inside was intended to confirm this supposition.

The night before the surgery a medical clerk brought a consent form for my signature. I refused to sign the form as it was written because it gave unlimited licence to the doctor and I was well aware of the controversy surrounding the alarming number of hysterectomies that were being performed every year. With the help of the resident oncologist I wrote in a stipulation that there was to be no hysterectomy or oophorectomy if there was no cancer. This addition to the consent form left me feeling reasonably protected. I would not lose my reproductive organs unless it was necessary to save my life.

When Dr. Steal spoke with me after surgery she informed me that there was good news — she found no cancer. But she had performed a radical hysterectomy because I had had endometriosis spreading through my pelvic region. Endometriosis is a condition in which the lining of the uterus separates from the uterine wall and implants itself on the ovaries or in other parts of the pelvic region. It can be painful and in some cases debilitating. It is not life-threatening.

I was shocked and in hindsight realize that I was traumatized by the experience. Prior to surgery, the doctor had never mentioned the possibility of endometriosis to me, although I now know that the cyst was an indicator of its presence. I knew that my symptoms did not warrant such drastic action. There are other ways of dealing with the problem that are far less drastic. If she had apprised me of the possibility of endometriosis, one she should have considered judging from my symptoms, she would have learned of my preference for less drastic measures, a cleaning away of as much of the endometrium as possible followed by treatment with medicine. Surgical castration is the last resort, and yet it was the doctor's first approach to my problem as I lay unconscious on the operating table. Dr. Steal erred twice, by failing to advise me of a condition that was a clear possibility and by taking the most drastic action without consultation. When I heard the news I felt powerless and bereft. Within a few days I developed a powerful urge to see the parts she had removed, the parts that had determined my womanhood, but the physician told me it was too late. The organs had been disposed.

Feeling robbed of my power to protect myself by the physician's actions I was left speechless. The fact she was a woman worsened the sense of betrayal and rendered me more helpless than if the doctor had been male. I saw her on occasion for a check-up but could not express my anger to her. Such are the silencing effects of trauma and the powerful authority of the physician in our society. I continued with graduate school, purposely avoiding thoughts of what had happened to my body, believing I needed to get on with my life. Two years later I began to cry while listening to someone else's story of hysterectomy. It was only then I realized the extent of my own trauma, and it was still much later until I was able — with great trepidation — to confront Dr. Steal. Her response? Silence, then defence: "I still think I did the right thing." And with that the subject was closed. With that she committed another grave error — no apology.

I never pursued legal action but did once discuss the issue with a lawyer. He suggested that the outcome of such an action would be determined by the judge, who would assess whether the doctor had acted in my best interest. One layer of silencing reinforced by another: the justice system potentially negating my ability to act in my own best interest. I chose not to have my day in court, rationalizing that I did not want my life bound up in the matter — the same decision I had made years earlier in the post-operative period. But the emotional wound has left a scar. An apology might have helped but that was not forthcoming. Now I retain my biochemical womanhood with hormone replacement medication and live with its incumbent, unasked-for complications and concerns, including an increased risk of breast cancer. Each time I read a study about the health hazards of estrogen replacement therapy my anger resurfaces. All this because a person took her authority too far and failed to respect my vulnerability. All this because she made a decision she had no right to make and in doing so negated my attempt to determine my own course of healing.

How does a surgeon determine what is the right thing to do? Confronted with unexpected findings in a patient lying vulnerable on an operating room table, decisions must be swift and correct. A margin for error is always a reality, but how much error is acceptable? How much is too much? At the same time, a patient needs to accept that risks are a part of surgery and that surgeons are humans often pushed to the limits of their capacities. But how much risk and to what extent does the patient accept the error based on these variables?

There are times when we need to trust a doctor's integrity and knowledge. We need to believe that he or she is appropriately educated, skillful, and has our best interests at heart. We need to feel reassured that the doctor will make recommendations and decisions based on the benefits for our health, not on what is easiest, most profitable or economical, or raises prestige. I believe the vast majority of physicians have integrity and want to do their best for their patients. I believe they are horribly constrained by financial resources and cumbersome administrative systems. However, in order to know who best can serve us we must inform ourselves and satisfy ourselves that the physicians we choose will respect us and tell us everything we need and want to know about the state of our bodies and the options they can offer to help us. They must relay this information in a way that we understand so we need not act out of fear and ignorance. We, in turn, must be active investigators, considering that a surgeon's decisions may be influenced by his or her care for you and also by economics or matters of efficacy. We must be vocal participants in our own health care, and for that we must resist all attempts, intentional or not, to silence us.

For me, the lesson in niceness gleaned from my experience is about breaking the silence imposed by the presence of authority. We must ask questions until we are completely satisfied when we are entrusting ourselves to others. We must make our wishes known and then be sure they are. We must check to be sure that the other person is doing what we think they are. We must be vocal, questioning consumers of medical services. Good doctors will respect you for it.

AGENCIES OF NICENESS AND CLICHÉS WE LIVE BY

The structures that support our existence also have potential to silence us. Education, religious training, governments, the medical establishment, the justice system, and organized workplaces assist us through our lives. They are useful entities, essential to a civilized society, but at the same time, by design or by accident, they become the instruments of silencing and enforced obedience. We are encouraged by every means possible to think of these lessons in compliance in other terms — how to be successful, how to get better, how to be saved, how to be educated. The culture we live in promotes the idea of freedom but delivers oppression in doses that are hardly noticeable because we have been taught the basic lessons — don't think, don't ask, don't speak.

Part of our training includes learning to monitor ourselves while we collude in the idea that it is for our own good. We learn to do it without thinking and over time lose the capacity to decide what really is in our best interests. Our language assists us in this learning. Laden with clichés — "Don't speak unless you're spoken to," "Children should be seen and not heard," "If you can't say something nice, don't say anything at all," and the all-purpose "Be nice" — language reinforces the lessons that start from the moment we emerge from the womb.

We become passive in many ways because the qualities of niceness lend themselves only to action based on satisfying the real or perceived wishes of others. Ironically, there is a great deal of work in the act of silencing because it is not our natural inclination. We must work at silencing our feelings and words. We actively pursue passivity as we learn to be nice.

We have lots of help in our learning to be nice, and agents of silencing into niceness come in surprising forms. Often it is nice, rational people who toss skillfully disguised slurs to a roomful of listeners in order to silence one of them. Without seeming like antagonists they succeed at rendering the unidentified target impotent to respond. If these people were forthright and invited their targets into a discussion — as if all opinions mattered — the target would not be silenced. The message from silencers is clear: don't speak, don't say what you think and know. Remain silent and, if necessary, feign ignorance or you will be marginalized or disowned. Implicitly the message is "I am more powerful than you. You must fall into line."

CHAPTER 5
NICENESS AS PROTECTION: NICENESS AS MASK

AT SOME POINT in our early lives, if we learn our lessons well, we come to believe niceness is our own idea. No longer do we resist it. We internalize the concept and behaviour, taking it in with our emotions and intellects to such a degree that it becomes part of us. We do this because we believe we are helping ourselves. Some of us believe we need niceness to protect ourselves from rejection and ridicule. Some discover that niceness can mask our true intentions and use it in this way to further our own agendas.

In his insightful book *Nocturnes: On Listening to Dreams*, Paul Lippman suggests it is sometimes necessary for the human mind to disguise itself. He says the "modern world has the ability, the equipment, the need, and the will to gain entrance to our most private experience." He adds that disguise is necessary for humans' survival, just as it is for plants whose harmless berries resemble poisonous ones, fish that resemble the rocks they hide under, and insects that resemble the plants on which they climb.

For humans, one effective disguise is being nice, a way of relating that lets us move around in situations we believe will otherwise endanger us or deny us what we want. It seems essential for our emotional survival because its importance as a social tool has been emphasized in our training since babyhood. The teaching has been effective. We have learned no other way of being so we believe we need the disguise of niceness. For those who are most susceptible to the training it becomes a way of life.

There are two uses of niceness — as protection and as mask. Although the outward presentations are similar, these two variations of niceness are produced by different motivating factors.

NICENESS AS PROTECTION

Niceness is a shield for people who feel overwhelmed or frightened. Some take it on as protection from threats they feel from the world around them, especially the threats of non-acceptance and being seen as inadequate. Others use it to protect themselves from internal threats of a psychological nature such as guilt. Neither of these groups is able to see that the silence and obedience imposed on them in exchange for protection is anything but beneficial, although a niggling discomfort, a sense of something amiss, may occur over time.

If niceness protected without incurring any side effects, its use might be justified, but the personal impact of niceness — denial or dismissal of our deepest feelings, thoughts, and understanding — can lead to illness, addictions, injury, and even death. By being nice we can fall into self-sabotage and stress our immune systems into paralysis, which I describe later, in some detail. At the very least it leads to relationships based on false premises and a gnawing sense of dissatisfaction with life. Behind the agreeable, silenced exterior lies loneliness and alienation.

Even though the benefits are fallacious and the threats to our security that seem to necessitate the use of niceness have been exaggerated, we continue to take up the lessons of silencing and obedience, acting as if they do not affect us in a negative way. We believe that if we do as we are told and as we believe is expected of us, we will get what we want — acceptance, approval, a good life, and a clear conscience.

We protect ourselves with niceness in two ways: We use it to prevent rifts with other people that might mean we are not accepted by them — this is protection from threats originating outside ourselves, whether real or perceived. We use it to ease our guilt when our thoughts and feelings are unfriendly or aggressive — this is protection from threats originating inside ourselves. By separating these two types of threats I am creating an artificial split for illustrative purposes. Threats from inside and threats from outside are woven together in many instances. For example, when I am treating a client in psychotherapy I sometimes hear the words "I don't want to be judged" — expressing a fear of external threats. This fear leads clients to withhold words and thoughts that they believe will make me judge them harshly, even though the premise of psychotherapy is to speak one's mind. At the same time these clients are judging me, assessing whether or not I will think they are bad people if they say what they are really thinking or if they speak the way they would with someone whose judgment does not concern them. At the core of this lies their own feeling that their thoughts and words are wrong. Unless they have had experiences in psychotherapy that were disrespectful or harmful in some way, there would be no reason to fear my judgment, and so the fear of external threats is generated by the internal threats. They withhold until their own internal judges have relaxed enough to allow them to speak authentically with me. Their willingness to do so is based much less on any direct reassurance I might give them — for example, in a preliminary discussion of the way psychotherapy works — than on their own feeling of safety in the psychotherapy situation. Some people have learned so well the lessons of suppression, silencing, and obedience that it takes many months for them to grant themselves permission to speak freely about their deepest secrets and feelings of shame, even in psychotherapy.

PROTECTION FROM THREATS OUTSIDE

We use niceness as protection because we are afraid. Our training has limited our experience of interacting with other people. Rather than learning to be direct and honest with respect, we have learned to stifle ourselves, and in the absence of practice in self-expression we have become afraid. We are afraid that the sound of our own voices telling people our honest opinions will offend, afraid that honouring our own needs will seem selfish, afraid that pointing out our discomfort with another's behaviour will create difficulties. We have no practice testing our inner wisdom by acting upon it and, like Max, who failed to heed its warning on his wedding day, we have learned to squelch it. Our silence is rooted in fear of taking a risk, no matter how small the risk may be. We are afraid that if we speak, our words will somehow generate problems.

Fear of non-acceptance and abandonment

More than anything, we want to belong. Being held and touched is as important to the survival of infants as the food they eat, and our need for contact with other people continues throughout our lives. Whether we acquire our sense of belonging from spouses, extended family, friends, colleagues at work, or community groups, we feel better when we are affiliated with other people. We fear shunning and act from a belief that even mild confrontation will chase friends away.

Fear of non-acceptance distorts and replaces many of our other emotions and at the same time determines many of our actions. So powerful is our fear of being left out of the group that shunning has been used since ancient times to discipline group members. Today, some Native American bands and Mennonite sects use it as the ultimate form of punishment for breaking their rules. The Roman Catholic Church uses excommunication for the same purpose. All of these groups know the impact of non-acceptance into the group. In schools, misbehavers are set apart. Parents use "time out" as a form of discipline. Our fear of non-acceptance is great, and in our desperation to calm it we shroud ourselves in the cocoon of niceness, which has earned the following of an entire silenced culture as the prophylactic for non-acceptance.

Why should a fear of non-acceptance be so powerful that we sell ourselves out for approval and acceptance? There is a moment in Jean-Paul Sartre's play *No Exit* that sheds some light on this question. His characters Inez, Estelle, and Vincent are beginning to analyze the reasons that they have been locked together, for eternity, in a room in hell. Vincent makes a desperate attempt to leave and suddenly the locked door springs open, and remains open. Stunned, Vincent is faced with a decision at this apparent gift of freedom. But he cannot move himself through the open door. Inez observes, with a sadist's satisfaction, that he is too attached to leave. Vincent moves, but not through the door, and rationalizes staying on. The door swings shut.

Vincent's attachment to his colleagues in hell is one thing, but there is more than an offer of freedom in the open door. Were he to take that path and leave what has become familiar to him, he would venture out into an encounter with his past. Vincent was acutely attuned to the approval of his colleagues in life, and in death he tuned in on those same colleagues, from time to time, to try to hear what they were saying about him. He was desperate to have their approval but did not know if he had it. When he was confronted with the open door he chose instead to succumb to the wiles of Estelle and involve himself in a repetition of his life's drama with his wife as the abusive, exploitive male. Although he could never win the approval of Inez in hell, the open door represented the unknown. It is the unknown, fraught with the possibility of isolation, that we fear when we are looking for approval, acceptance, and the apparent favourable judgment of others.

No one knows the fear of this judgment more implicitly than families. Family members who seek to speak the truth as they see it or who wish to make changes in themselves that threaten to rock the family boat may be judged as outcasts and excluded from the circle or pressured to stay true to their assigned role. Although family members may overtly encourage change and believe they mean it, their resistance to the changed person suggests their roles are threatened and they feel safer interacting in familiar ways.

Rosa, a client, always avoided confrontation, at great costs to herself. She feared the judgment of those close to her would leave her friendless, so she would never complain when friends postponed get-togethers. She was the "understanding" one who endured cancellations and resched-uling, time and time again. Often the reasons seemed flimsy, even hard to believe, but she always gave her friends the benefit of the doubt. As a single person living alone she counted on her friends for companionship. She was their confidante and she believed the wish for friendship was mutual. When they needed to speak with her about some crisis or important event in their lives she made herself available even when she had other things to do. For years this was her practice until she tired of hearing, over and over, the same reasons for rearranging evenings out or lunches when her friends were not in crisis. Her resentment mounted to such a degree that she brought the problem to therapy, where it emerged that her reasons for tolerating her friends' inconsiderate behaviour was her fear of losing them, of being alone. She believed she had no options if she wanted to keep her friends, and yet she felt the relationships were insincere and she was simply tired of listening and responding without being heard in return. She felt her needs had not been dealt into the equation of her friendships.

As Rosa grew stronger in therapy by working through her concerns and learning how to relate to people in a direct way, she began to speak out when her friends cancelled plans and to talk more about herself with them rather than always playing the role of listener. Like other clients who have made the choice to give up niceness, her fears were both confirmed and dashed. Some friends dropped out of sight and others became more considerate of her. Despite her losses, Rosa's resentment and insecurity lessened over time and she found she enjoyed, much more, the friendships that remained. As new people entered her life she made sure the relationships were more balanced or she did not pursue them.

People will often cover up the abuses and addictions of their spouses in order to avoid the scrutiny, judgment, and shunning of others. Kathryn was one of those. Always pleasant with people, rather quiet and somewhat self-effacing, Kathryn thought she had met her ideal match in Peter. He was a typical "nice guy" who was friendly and helpful. Her family took to him quickly and accepted him into their circle. In short order, she had taken up his offer and moved into his apartment. She set about cleaning the place because Peter never had enough time, and it seemed logical for her to wash his laundry with hers rather than waste time and money duplicating effort. It was only after a few months in the relationship that Kathryn let a queasiness she had sensed in her body since they met seep into her consciousness. She could not identify what it was, though it created emotional discomfort. She tried to understand it, and when she could not she tried to dismiss it, reassuring herself that everything would work out.

One day Peter returned from a golf outing with some business colleagues. He was drunk. Alarmed, Kathryn upbraided him for driving when he was inebriated. Peter did not handle her concern well, became very angry, and the two were soon embroiled in their first serious argument. The next morning Peter was silent and stayed that way the whole day, breaking his silence only long enough to warn her never to speak "that way" to him again. Kathryn was devastated. She did not recognize the man who issued the warning. The queasiness finally made sense to her: it was her body saying what her head could not admit, that Peter had problems he had not disclosed when they met.

The situation settled down after that because Kathryn heeded the warning. She decided, though feeling some reservation, that the incident was an isolated event precipitated by the stress Peter was experiencing at work. She reasoned that under the circumstances his behaviour was somewhat understandable and, not wanting to judge him harshly, she let the issue go. No sooner had it been assigned to the nether regions of her memory than Peter again came home drunk. Kathryn was alarmed and this time also felt anxious because she was afraid to speak to Peter about his drinking. His anger that first time had been fearsome, and she did not want to see it again. She remained quiet, hoping it would blow over, thankful he had gotten home without killing someone with his car. Her silence did not please Peter, however, and he became antagonistic, asking her why she was so quiet, what she was thinking, and, it seemed to Kathryn, baiting her to take up the gauntlet for an all-out battle. When she told Peter she was afraid to speak he became enraged, yelling and punching the walls. Kathryn's fear heightened, and she meekly implored him to stop. He told her if she didn't like it she could get out. Kathryn moved to the sofa that night after Peter fell asleep and lay awake hoping he would not wake up anytime soon.

Less time elapsed before the next incident, and it followed the same pattern as the others, except that this time Peter bloodied Kathryn's nose. When she awoke the next morning her eyes were blackened and her face was swollen. There was no mistaking she had been hit. She called in sick to work, not wanting to fabricate an explanation to curious co-workers. She had not mentioned Peter's drinking and previous outbursts to anyone, hoping they would just become part of a bad dream, and she did not want to jeopardize his relationships with her friends and family. This time she kept quiet because she felt ashamed and humiliated.

In a classic tale of escalating violence, Peter and Kathryn were soon embroiled in the cycles that are typical of violence against women. To the world, Kathryn continued to be a nice, quiet, though increasingly self-effacing woman. Everyone continued to think Peter was a nice guy. The fear Kathryn felt was real, and while it is easier to see and understand than someone's fear of having no friends, it produces a very similar response: the silencing of opinions and subordination of needs to those of the other person. At root is the wish to protect oneself from aloneness and judgment. Abusers, like Peter, understand this fear and use it to control their victims.

Fear of being seen as inadequate

The need for protection is sometimes motivated by fear of being seen as inadequate. Perhaps this is most in evidence in the workplace and in school. Frank, mentioned earlier, was a super-employee. A bright man and hard worker, he knew that he was doing a good job, but his emotions would not concur. He doubted his abilities and as a result believed he had to work harder than anyone had a right to expect of him in order to maintain the positive regard of his boss and colleagues. He took on far more work than anyone else in his office, but he did it because he felt inadequate and feared being judged deficient. He never said no to a request from either boss or colleague, even when he was struggling under a crushing workload. If he did not know an answer or how to complete a task he would drop what he was doing and research to get the answer for whoever had requested it. The phrases "I don't know" and "I can't take that on" were not part of his vocabulary.

The fear of being seen as inadequate in social situations paralyzes some people into silence. Rather than take a chance by contributing to a conversation, they smile, nod, and make agreeable and supportive noises. Charles, the lawyer who was browbeaten by his sister, was one who voiced opinions in social settings only on the rarest of occasions. Although he felt somewhat more able to contribute to a conversation with one other person, rather than in a group, he preferred the scripted exchanges of the courtroom to social interactions and hid behind his work. The only relief he had was when he played squash. He was a formidable competitor, smashing the ball with all the energy that he withheld in his social niceness.

Women have learned that in mixed social groups their role is to listen to the men, to stop talking and defer when men interrupt them. They protect themselves from judgments of being inadequate women by monitoring their voice tone and keeping their contributions to a minimum, paradoxically masking their intelligence and opinions. One woman I met who was institutionalized in a prison had learned the role of the nice woman so well that clinical staff at first failed to realize that she had less than average intelligence. Until her capabilities were clearly understood it meant much more was expected of her than she was able to deliver. But she could pass for a woman of greater intelligence because we are accustomed to seeing women mute and smile themselves into social acceptability, obscuring their capabilities. That is what is expected of them. Niceness, for women, all too often means denying a fundamental strength — their intelligence. In turn, the silencing discourages women from exploring and developing their potential with the result that they often do fail to stretch themselves intellectually. With time, they may doubt their intelligence, and the doubt reinforces the silence, for they do not wish to be perceived as inadequate.

Many people are afraid of being perceived as weak. When they feel an affront from an offensive person they remain silent rather than protest or complain to someone who might help. They live out the notion that it is best to suppress emotions. Our language is riddled with expressions that reinforce this idea. One such phrase, "stiff upper lip," originated in eighteenth-century Britain. The British noticed that when people are upset their lips tremble. During that period in Britain most men wore moustaches, so a trembling upper lip was very obvious. Hence the call for the stiff upper lip — to hide the trembling that spelled emotions. "Keep your chin up" is another common expression, playing on the idea that when we are happy we hold our heads and thus our chins high, but when we are sad we hang our heads and our chins. Holding one's head up is thus a way of hiding undesirable emotions such as sadness. These injunctions are still used, along with names such as "crybaby" and "wimp" that suggest that expressing any hint of emotion is weak, infantile. Even today, children being harassed in the schoolyard are discouraged from seeking out solace from yard supervisors. Boys learn that big boys and men don't cry or talk about their fears, and some children learn that if they are reprimanded at school they will be reprimanded at home.

People in relationships sometimes fall victim to the fear of being perceived as abnormal by their intimate partners. Faced with partners who are close enough to know their greatest vulnerabilities, some hide their real feelings behind a protective layer of niceness, which takes the form of conforming to socially designated roles. Men feign independence when they don't feel it and don't want it. Although they may harbour a wish to be taken care of by their partners, they cannot risk seeming dependent. Women feign dependence even though it robs them of stimulation and self-respect. Although they may be ambitious and achievement-oriented, they may feel they cannot ask for the support they need to realize their dreams, support that women routinely give to men. Each sex fears being found out by the other. People fear being seen as lacking the qualities expected of them by the society they occupy and so they hide, forfeiting the possibility of attaining an emotional balance that would reflect the complexity of their very human needs. When couples maintain these deceptions they become estranged from each other, but they also become angry and act out this anger with each other.

Another kind of Mr. Nice Guy, the helper, is a study in contradictions. His protection is an artificial optimism visible in his perpetually happy face. He pitches in to the task at hand without hesitation. While his behaviour may be appealing to the people in his life, his failure to consider his own needs suggests eroded self-esteem. Although not conscious of it, this man is cynical at the core. His behaviour suggests that he never expects anyone to do things for him or show him kindness, and he has adopted the belief that to give as much as he can and then give some more is his only path to acceptance.

Fear of giving offence

Diane was lunching with a friend. It was a delicious lunch of well-prepared trout, but midway through the meal she felt an uncomfortable sensation in her throat. Worried that she had swallowed a fishbone she began to panic, thinking that if it moved down her throat it could do damage. She happened to be in a restaurant near a physician's office where her aunt worked as the receptionist. She telephoned her aunt, who agreed to ask the doctor to see her even though Diane was not a patient of his. Within the hour, the doctor had peered down Diane's throat.

"Nothing there," he declared, to Diane's surprise. The sensation persisted. "Nothing?" she asked. "No. I don't think there's anything in there," he replied.

Reluctantly and in silence, Diane left the physician's office. The discomfort persisted into evening. Unable to endure it, she went to the emergency room at the hospital. By the time she was seen by a physician she was in distress. He looked into her throat, said "There it is," reached in with tweezers, and carefully extracted a long, sturdy fishbone. "No surprise you were uncomfortable." Diane felt immediate relief and a great deal of gratitude.

The next day, Diane's aunt telephoned because she had neglected to ask Diane for her health insurance number. Diane reported none of the events of the previous evening to her aunt, nor did she request to see or speak to the physician again so she could inform him of his error. She did not want to seem ungrateful for her aunt's and the doctor's efforts to squeeze her in to his busy schedule. Besides, she rationalized, the incident was over and it could not be undone, so what was the use of dredging it up again?

Diane's reasons for saying nothing to her aunt or the physician who could not see the fishbone were the same ones that many people give when they wish to avoid confrontation. Fearing the possibility that others will be offended they choose to silence themselves, even though the impact of the other person's actions on them have left them feeling angry or resentful. And yet, if the physician had been told of his error he might have been more observant and less dismissive the next time a patient brought him such a problem.

Often, reassurances are given to other people, even when they are not invited, in order not to give offence. Perhaps you have had someone in your presence express a need for some help but who does not say so directly. In fact, the message is sent in a negative way: "I'm sure you don't have the time to spend doing this for me, so don't worry about it." It's true, you don't have the time, and you would rather be walking the dog or spending time with your family, but you do feel some pressure to offer your help. It is clear to you in that negative statement that the person does want your help, and you believe it would be rude not to offer it, even though not offering would mean agreeing with the words of the person seeking help. You reply, "Oh, no matter; I can do that for you," reassuring the person that you do not mind helping out. In doing so, you betray your own preferences and you reinforce the passive manner in which the person made the request. Agreeing with the person would have affirmed what you wanted and alerted the person needing help that the respectful way to ask is to be direct.

Fear of retribution

People sometimes co-operate with others in ways that compromise their own preferences and beliefs because they do not want to risk a payback. They fear that an honest opinion will encourage others to criticize them in return. They fear a physician might end service to them, so they heed doctors' instructions and prescriptions despite their own misgivings. A student may fear that criticizing a professor will result in a poor grade. Sometimes the fear of retribution takes people to unexpected irony, when they agree with a person who badmouths a third party or fail to voice a different opinion — being nice to the perpetrator — hoping to avoid similar treatment themselves.

The stakes may seem very high. In Henrik Ibsen's play *The Pillars of the Community*, protagonist Karsten Bernick spent fifteen years building a reputation as benevolent patriarch, held in high esteem by the towns-people, who believed the image of community service and selflessness that he portrayed. As the play unfolds we learn that his reputation is built on lies that besmirched the reputation of Johan, his wife's brother, who had idolized Bernick, colluded with him, and fled the community years before. But Johan did not realize that Bernick had taken the lie further than agreed upon, and when Johan returned Bernick was devastated and tried to hush Johan. He feared that if the community knew the truth he would be cast out in disgrace and that he would lose his reputation and his wealth. After events forced him into a confrontation with himself, Bernick finally disclosed the truth to the community. He was not cast out, and the story ends on a positive note with a foreshadowing of much-improved relations with his family.

Of course, life is not a play, and giving up the protection of niceness does not guarantee that you will be accepted by other people. But your chances of solid relationships with other people are improved when you interact with them with honesty and openness.

PROTECTION FROM THREATS INSIDE

Niceness can be a defence system implemented to cope with a hostile and conflicted internal world in which guilt and self-hatred prevail. People using it in this way remain nice by denying their own anger and aggression, which they unconsciously fear will destroy others and leave them alone. As long as they deny these qualities that they have learned to consider undesirable they can keep their world intact. They fear exposing the parts of themselves that feel unacceptable in some way, the parts of which they are ashamed.

Guilt

People like Frank, who feared the judgment of colleagues at work, are also struggling with internal attacks. Abrasive prods from their own psyches badger them into holding onto the notion that they are not good enough. The internal and external dovetail to keep them in a state of niceness that verges on emotional paralysis. For Kathryn, who had spent a lifetime struggling with low self-esteem, niceness was an effective cover. By the time Peter came into her life and revealed himself as an abusive alcoholic, she had learned to say only those things that she thought would project the safest image. She was unable to speak out or get help, fearing that his problems would somehow be construed as her fault. Of course, Peter assisted in strengthening this belief. With his help, the emotional pit she was in became deeper and deeper.

Self-sabotage and underachievement are typical of those who suffer from internal threats. Luke, a man in his fifties, told me in a session, "I haven't gotten what I want, but at least I haven't hurt anybody." He rationalized his inability to act on his own behalf in his marriage by believing that getting what he wants means hurting someone. Ruthlessly taking what we want does hurt others, but there are ways of fulfilling our needs without hurting other people. It is true that if a relationship has been built on dishonesty people do get hurt when one decides to change. However, when the choice is continuing to relate in a mutually destructive manner or taking a step outside of that dynamic, it is most often for the better of both to step outside, despite initial pain. Holding and acting upon the duality — one's own needs and wishes along with an acted-upon understanding of the needs and wishes of others — is possible. For Luke, however, pursuing what he wanted was a concept saturated with guilt.

Rosa, who was afraid to lose her friends, was reluctant to speak out in part because she felt guilty about being critical of them. She did not like everything they said and did and sometimes she felt angry with them. At the same time, she was afraid of losing any of her friends and she was sure that if she expressed the anger she felt she would hurt them deeply. She was trapped by guilt that pre-empted finding creative ways to resolve her anger. Rather than exploring ways of telling her friends, with kindness, about behaviours that offended her and opening up a discussion, she silenced herself, hoping the attacking thoughts would subside. Her intention was to preserve her friendships, but instead the relationships suffered because the objections she had towards their behaviour, the unexpressed criticism she felt, wracked her with guilt, and she could not be fully available to and expressive with her friends.

Margaret came to therapy plagued with self-esteem problems and a great deal of unexpressed anger. She was successful in her work in a retail business, and part of her success was no doubt due to her unassuming manner. She always maintained a low profile and went to great lengths to please her customers. Her trademark was her smile, but she confided that the smile was her way of eliciting acceptance from other people and seldom reflected what she was feeling. She had learned years before that a smile can control others' reactions to her, so if she thought someone was angry with her, as she often did, she smiled to disarm them. People responded with a return smile and Margaret thought her strategy worked. For years she failed to realize the anger was her own, projected onto other people.

There are far worse ways than a smile to get what we want in the world, but the smile was a problem for Margaret because it was protection from her inner, unhappy world. It was not an authentic expression of her feelings. More often it was part of an act designed to elicit acceptance and subdue anticipated danger or disapproval. As inviting as it was for some people, her smile was not backed by genuine feelings of warmth and friendship or even collegiality. It was akin to printing money without the backing of real assets, a counterfeit smile at best.

For many people, niceness is an acceptable alternative to speaking the unspeakable — those things they are afraid to say. They have convinced themselves that their opinions or real feelings will devastate their friends or family. Like Max, who married for all the wrong reasons, they live in fear of hurting others' feelings and anticipate living with guilt if they were to do so. The daughters of Louise, who was dying of liver cancer, were unable to tell her that she looked ill, even when she asked them, because they were unable to face the truth about her — that she was dying — and they needed to pretend it was not happening. Louise wanted validation. Her daughters backed off, defending themselves, denying the extent of the illness because they did not want to lose her, afraid of being honest in a world that is given over to the white lie and feeling guilty because her illness had become a burden to them. Like most of us they had never been taught to be unafraid of truth. Confused by her request and fearful of doing the wrong thing they acted from their training, attempting to placate their mother, attempting to make her feel better when in fact she only felt lied to.

Even death fails to stop the masquerade. People tell grieving relatives how natural the corpse looks. We focus only on good qualities, ignoring pain the deceased may have inflicted in life. We avoid talking about the inconveniences or the benefits of someone's death. In the wake of death we see our own mortality but skirt the issue. Rather than face the kind of legacy we might leave and change our ways, we talk about the person who died as if he or she had lived a two-dimensional life, as if this act will one day protect us from unfavourable judgment. The most we seem able to do when someone's life and death has been difficult, by character or by illness, is to say that death relieves the deceased of suffering or declare that the person is "now at peace." The more authentic grieving, attempting to come to terms with the entirety of the person's impact on family and friends in a respectful way, escapes our imagination. We feel superstitious about speaking of the dead with candour, so we absolve them of their humanity to avoid being struck down or maligned ourselves.

In life, couples go to great lengths to suppress feelings for fear of damaging the relationship. They do not want to face the possibility of abandonment, so they hide their darkest thoughts. This does not mean silence in the literal sense. These couples may spend a good deal of time arguing, but the deepest fears, the darkest critiques of their partners, or the fantasies or thoughts that they fear will damn them remain undisclosed. Arguments between these couples all begin and end in the same manner, repeat the same patterns, and feel to the partners like wheels in a familiar groove from which they are unable to move.

At the same time, people in relationships fear hearing things from their partners that may eat at their doubts and force them to make choices about the relationship or to make changes in themselves. A great deal of security in a relationship is required before we can hear and embrace the insights and darkest thoughts or feelings of those closest to us. We want the silence of our partners because we fear our own reactions to their words, but the silence erodes our sense of security. Acting as if an issue doesn't exist if it is not said or heard, we refuse to hear what our loved ones say. Those couples who retain this kind of non-communication often develop a pattern of expectant idling riddled with injections of bickering, impulsive behaviour, physical or verbal abuse, addictions, or depression.

One of the most difficult tasks of a relationship is to engage fully in it. We all seek to retain a strong sense of self, and although we also want strong intimate relationships we do not know how to be in them without losing ourselves emotionally. The fear of losing oneself in a relationship lies at the core of many relationship problems and leads to withholding thoughts and feelings. Paradoxically, the withholding — the specific behaviour that keeps us from engaging fully in the relationship — means we are not expressing ourselves, and we lose ourselves in non-expression even as we struggle to hold on to our sense of self.

When a relationship does not work for one person, the unspeakable may be the words "I do not want to continue in a relationship with you."

To avoid saying those words, Judy suggested to her lover, Dan, that they change their relationship, that they stop dating and become "friends." Dan was not happy with this because he felt in love with Judy, but he agreed because he had no choice, and he believed that if he waited for her she would, sooner or later, love him as a partner again. He was shocked and hurt a short time later when she refused to answer his calls and treated him with cool reserve when they met by chance on the street. He was in tears, trying to understand.

"How could she act that way and call me a friend? Friends treat each other with respect. They don't ignore each other's calls or simply disappear from their lives." Dan, like so many who have heard the same words from former lovers, felt cheated and betrayed. It would have been much better for him had Judy told him, face to face, the words she did not have the courage to say but which were evident in her actions. He would have been more able to let go of the hope that held him to her.

There are times when niceness is useful and healthy as a protective measure. If real danger is present and the only escape is to appear compliant, it makes sense to call upon niceness. The dilemma is knowing when danger is real or a product of one's own fears.

A particular problem with using niceness for emotional survival is that the disguise is often invisible to its wearer. The potential for misuse increases with its owner's inability to perceive it in himself. We need to see how we disguise ourselves and understand the ways others use it so we know how far to take it and how much of it to accept in others.

Judy may have felt a great deal of guilt at ending the relationship. Not wanting to hurt the other person is the usual reason given for suggesting an intimate relationship be changed to friendship. However, it may be that Judy was also masking her unconscious wish to be considered a nice person. She could not bear to have Dan think of her as someone who was anything but good because if he did it would affirm her guilt about hurting him. Although he still would have been hurt at the loss of her, Dan likely would have retained his respect for Judy and he may have recovered more quickly if she had been honest with him.

Dan had his own reasons for not saying what he knew to be true. In his heart he felt Judy had ended the relationship, but he wanted so much to be with her that he failed to act on the unspoken signals he picked up from her. His choice would have been to tell Judy they could not be friends, that it was not the way he imagined them in relationship, or he might have addressed the issue of how they felt about each other. However, he did not want to expose his shameful weakness, his needing her, so he went along with her request, saying nothing about the feelings that were sounding a warning signal.

Self-hatred

In an age when the concept of self-love verges on a new religion, self-hatred is the ironic outcome of propaganda that floods us every day. When we read a magazine, take a trip to the supermarket, enter a bookstore, or watch television or movies, we are bombarded with images and articles that tell us how we should look, what products we should own, how we should act — in short, how to become the cultural ideal. If we cannot do so we blame ourselves because that, too, is part of the cultural script. We feel shamed and inadequate. We learn to hate ourselves and then to hide our self-hate behind a protective layer of niceness. One of the difficulties in writing a book such as this is that readers, left alone with their thoughts, may see only the worst in themselves. It is my hope that should this happen, that self-view will be short-lived. I know from personal experience that the road to self-love is riddled with moments of self-loathing as we learn about our weaknesses. But our trip along that bumpy road inevitably encompasses these moments as surely as it encompasses an increasing amount of joy as we also recognize our attributes.

Although no individual or group has exclusive claim on self-hatred, some groups and individuals are especially susceptible. The cultural ideal is a masculine one. Men of a certain ilk are most valued, but, with some exceptions, all men are valued more than women. Men are considered more interesting to listen to and their ideas are attributed more worth. Women are valued for their usefulness to men or, more correctly, to the masculine culture. For this reason, women in their natural state are shunned. In North America a woman with hair on her legs, under her arms, or on her face is seen as a non-woman, devoid of sexuality. Large women are threatening. Old women are superfluous. All women are potential objects of ridicule.

Like men, women have learned to value men and denigrate women and all things designated to be woman-like. They have internalized the hatred that forces them to emulate the images of constructed femininity that accost them in every supermarket and pharmacy, on billboards, television, and in magazines. They perceive men as better and they become the rivals of other women. They put themselves and other women second to men, always subordinating themselves and rarely championing their own contributions and abilities.

Homosexuals also suffer prejudice. Despite gay pride days and greater acceptance of same-sex spouses, homosexuality is still outside the accepted norms of our culture. For many gays and lesbians this cultural rejection becomes internalized and they, like women, devalue their own qualities in favour of those of the dominant culture.

NICENESS AS MASK

Social etiquette columnists Kim Izzo and Ceri Marsh writing in the *Globe and Mail* advised readers to forget using *nice* as an adjective and instead to begin using it as a verb. "Nicing," they said, "is the verbal deployment of sweetness in order to get your own way." They went on to describe how to manipulate people — "nice" them as much as necessary to get what you want. They were describing something already entrenched in our culture, the use of niceness to mask an agenda that might not be well received if it were exposed.

A recent spate of elections took place across the continent. Watching the candidates, on television, working the crowds, presenting themselves in ways they and their handlers believed would win votes, was an education in image-making, or impression management, as it has come to be known. They presented themselves in prescribed ways that were formulated by people who earn their living creating personae. Any intersection between what we saw of them on the news and their non-affected behaviour was, in all likelihood, coincidental. The affected behaviour was niceness masking a professional agenda. When niceness achieves its goal in this context, it overrides other publicity that may not be flattering. This may include newspaper, television, and radio reports of the comings, goings, and shenanigans of candidates, critical analyses of candidates' speeches and activities, their promises made and broken, their undisclosed agendas and inconsistencies, and reports about activities and events in their pasts that they might wish to forget. Some of this information is presented strategically by their opponents, who may also exaggerate it. When the image-making machinery is effective, the public believes the image more than the criticism and almost never knows the worst of what lies behind the mask. Nonetheless, from time to time the cover is removed and the public gets to see.

When you first heard of Bill Clinton you may have thought of him as a nice man. For a while, the media loved the saxophone-playing president and provided lots of evidence to back up this impression. There were photos of him walking arm in arm with his loyal wife and daughter across the White House lawn. On occasion he was photographed in the company of their chocolate Labrador retriever. One picture showed him and Hillary emerging from church, Bill clutching a bible. Anyone who owns a Lab and goes to church on Sunday carrying a bible must be nice. But who among us can look at Bill now without remembering what he was doing while he was talking on the telephone to some head of state?

Baby-kissing politicians cultivate sincerity as their most valuable commodity, encouraging the public to overlook and rationalize war-mongering, grand-scale manipulations, questionable ethics, and double-speak. The cover-ups can be blatant. When Colin Powell addressed the UN Security Council promoting a campaign of war against Iraq, organizers covered up a painting at the entrance to the chamber with a large cloth. The painting was *Guernica* — Picasso's mural-sized depiction of the ravages of war. The cloth masked any visual connection between Powell's words and the famous artistic rendering of war's blood and destruction. A few days later, the *New York Times* ran a photograph of George Bush standing in front of a painting of Jesus Christ. Cover-up and suggestion are all part of impression management.

Terms like *collateral damage* have been popularized to separate images of the act of killing and reality of death from the people responsible for it. Four Canadian soldiers were bombarded in Afghanistan by a U.S. war plane, a killing that was labelled "friendly fire." Six British soldiers were killed by U.S. friendly fire in Iraq, and U.S. soldiers were similarly downed in Iraq. Whole countries have been called "evil," raising xenophobia and religious fundamentalism to frightening levels. In Walkerton, Ontario, seven people died from E. coli poisoning because the provincial government, in its "Common Sense Revolution," privatized water testing services and failed to ensure that adequate controls and well-trained, responsible people were in place to protect the public. Less serious but affecting more people are sleights of phrase that politicians use when they want the public to accept fewer services in the face of higher taxes. At election time, politicians offer partial truths or outright insults to denigrate their opponents and to cover up their mistakes and focus on their successes if they are the incumbents.

Impression management and doublespeak that covers up everything from the atrocities of war to day-to-day mismanagement results in confusion and fear. People see and hear the image and are left to make sense of it when it proves to be untrue, when politicians reveal themselves to be less than honest, less than scrupulous, less than capable of acting with integrity or competence, preferring to protect their power. Some people become cynical and trust none, while others find ways to rationalize the politicians' actions and keep believing the image because, psychologically, they must make sense of the discrepancies.

There seems to be a certain illogic that politicians' actions should generate confusion and fear in the very people they purport to serve. Surely, they should be doing everything in their power to reduce these destabilizing factors. Indeed, much of the rhetoric around the diluting of people's civil rights since September 11, 2001, has focused on protection and security. Ironically, the emphasis on protection from terrorism has helped keep fear alive. Keeping fear alive, whether it is the fear of terrorism or loss of life, loved ones, home, or property, ensures that people are malleable and more obedient to authority. Especially, perhaps, authority figures who speak the language of protection.

Politicians aside, in everyday life there is a continuum in the use of niceness to mask harmfulness, from the relatively innocuous to the life-threatening. The mask is used for reasons ranging from the mundane to the dangerous, from image protection in families to cover-ups for pedophiles. Sales people use it to earn a living and provide a service. People with serious pathologies use it to maintain a steady source of suppliers to satisfy their own out-of-control needs.

At one end of the scale we find Bernadette, an efficient woman and wife who likes to maintain friendly connections with her husband's family. She is concerned that they think well of her and her husband, so, long ago she took responsibility for sending greeting cards to his family members on their birthdays and special holidays, signing the cards from both of them. She is the one who makes the telephone calls to them. She relays messages from her husband to them. Although she finds it irksome that her husband refuses to do any of this work, she does not stop doing it herself. Her husband says he doesn't care whether cards are sent; in fact, if left to him he would not send any. He also says he would make telephone calls but she always does it first. Bernadette says that if she waited for him to do it, the cards would never get sent, the calls never made. She believes his family's feelings would be hurt if they received no cards, but she is also concerned about the image of their son — and her, by extension — that would be created. Based on these concerns, and ignoring her husband's position, she continues promoting the image of the good son. This is not lost on her in-laws, who, when in need of a favour from their son, ask Bernadette to intervene on their behalf rather than ask him directly.

Families often put on the act of niceness to try to convince others that theirs is a happy family. Although members may be unhappy about the facade they collude anyway, believing that if they did anything other than pretend that family relations were perfect they would be "airing the family laundry in public," which is felt to be not nice.

Individuals will be nice and lead unsuspecting others into believing that favours will be done. A client, Anne, had the experience of being told by someone she had just met, the relative of a friend, that there may be a possibility of a job with his company. Anne clung to the hope that the man would contact her until she finally realized it would never happen, that the man's musing was empty.

Judy, who suggested she and Dan be friends instead of lovers, wanted to be seen as a nice person. It was Dan's perception that she privately relished the thought that Dan was in love with her, even though she did not want him in her life. The thought of him carrying a torch for her appealed to her wish to be the centre of someone's universe without having to give of herself. By suggesting they remain friends she did not have to continue loving Dan, nor did she have to face the antagonism and hurt he would have expressed had she told him she wanted to end the relationship completely. The suggestion that they remain friends exposed her to less antagonism in the moment, and she went away feeling desired rather than the object of Dan's anger. As it happened, although she did not stab him with words, her actions caused Dan a great deal of emotional pain. In the end, he also thought much less of her than he would have if she had told him the truth. There is little doubt that Dan's perception of Judy's motivation was affected by his pain. However, it would have been less open to his questioning if she had been straight-forward, if she had asked him about his preference, given that she did not want to be involved in an intimate relationship with him.

Raising the bar on harmfulness takes us to Peter, the abusive husband of Kathryn, who hurt her physically and emotionally on an ongoing basis as he continued to wear the mask of niceness in public. He under-stood Kathryn's fear of abandonment and the judgments of other people and used it to his advantage to control her. Peter was like the father of my client Natalie, who was also a tyrant at home. Natalie's father made every shared mealtime a terrifying event for her, her mother, and her siblings. It was his time to rant and vent his anger on his captive family audience, often picking on the children. No misdemeanour at the table was too small to escape his attention, and the rules were exacting indeed. His voice was booming and his facial expressions frightening. The punishments he meted out for loud and visible chewing, speaking without first being spoken to, and scraping knives on plates were harsh. Mealtime was also the time Natalie's father chose to reprimand the children for any failure they may have made in perpetuating the image of happy family to the community. He, himself, did a superb job of presenting an image of loving father, dedicated family man, and united family to the com-munity. For Natalie, the discrepancy between her father's behaviour at home and in the world outside the front door was crazy-making. It is hardly surprising that she emerged from her childhood with an eating disorder, anxiety, and low-grade chronic depression.

The mask of niceness has tragic results for the one masked as well as those who come into contact with the mask. Jason was the quintessential Mr. Nice Guy. Like most of us, he was trained for this role throughout his childhood. Along the way he realized that he could use it to his own advantage. He modelled a persona of niceness with his agreeable manner, passivity, and implicit support of whoever was speaking at the moment. He never complained unless he was agreeing with someone, and he never confronted anyone when he disagreed. Rather, he kept quiet or expressed a throwaway sentiment to deflect the discussion. No one suspected that such a nice guy could be so dishonest. And yet, the persona was built on lies, including lies of omission. It was built on evasiveness and blurring of the truth. He lied to all he knew, including his wife and his employer. He carried on affairs with several women over the years of his marriage and became an expert at cover-up.

By the age of forty, he had built a monument to dishonesty, and it was becoming uncomfortable. He could see that he had constructed a monster that was out of his control and began to feel guilty. He agonized over the pain he would cause his wife by revealing his lies to her and realized she might never trust him again and might end the marriage. He worried about losing his job if his shortcuts were exposed. He imagined his life would crumble if he took a step into honesty. Faced with the choice of continuing the masquerade and living the rest of his life as a lie, he was a man trapped. He was in complete discord with the man he preferred to show to the world. Jason would hurt many people and risk disrupting his wife's life if he unmasked. He was hurt whether or not the mask was removed. Yet, underneath it all, I saw a man who wanted to access his own fundamental honesty, the feature that brought him into therapy and kept him confronting the awful truths about himself.

Ernest, too, suffered behind his mask. He was a successful businessman. He had risen from humble origins to take the business his father had started in a machine shop in his garage to international acclaim. He had attained financial success and appeared to be enjoying the trappings it afforded them. He wore flashy jewellery and drove an expensive car, but his most noticeable accessory was the smile that was etched onto his face, and anyone might have guessed that his was a story of the American dream come true. Until, that is, he went missing and was later found dead of a self-inflicted gunshot wound, apparently unable to come to terms with the life he had created for himself.

On the extreme end of the continuum of harmfulness lies the mask that hides pedophiles and the Ted Bundys of the world. It may be difficult to think of these people as nice once the mask has been removed. Yet one of the reasons people are vulnerable to them is because they masquerade as nice people. In her book *Dancing Devil: My Twenty Years with Albert Walker*, Barbara Walker describes her life with the husband whose mask was pulled off when he fled Canada with their daughter and a million dollars of clients' investment money. He was later found living in England, posing as the husband of his daughter, who by then had two young children. The extent of this masked man's atrocities were revealed when a body that was caught in a fish net off the coast of England was identified as Ron Platt, the name Walker had taken. Walker was convicted of murder in England but was recently returned to Canada where he is incarcerated.

Barbara Walker notes in her book that anyone who met Albert in the 1970s and 1980s was impressed with his fun-loving and outgoing nature. He wore his mask well and for years was able to fool a great many people, many who entrusted their money to him. Although his wife suffered during even the first years of their marriage, the fun times and his acting left her slightly off-balance, usually leading her to question herself and give him the benefit of doubt.

A common feature among the pedophiles I have met and counselled is their ability to be charming, nice men. They have been courteous and often exhibited boyish qualities that could be endearing to some who are vulnerable and enjoy the non-threatening demeanour. I have heard, first-hand, tales from the offenders — pedophiles — themselves. Some befriend single mothers and embark on a campaign of winning over the mother and child in order to molest the child. Some become involved with sports or cultural programs to provide themselves with opportunities for sexual contact with children. Some ingratiate themselves to their community so they can pursue their innocent prey undetected. Many are well thought of by their families. Other pedophiles hide behind institutions that provide the mask for them.

Perhaps the most startling disclosure of sexual abuse of children has come from the Roman Catholic Church. Women who have been seduced by their parish priests have received less attention in the media, but the public has finally been made aware of the harm that has come to children. We can only guess at the number of children, mostly boys, who have been molested by priests in North America. Jason Berry, author of *Lead Us Not Into Temptation: Catholic Priests and the Sexual Abuse of Children*, estimates that at least eighteen hundred priests have been named in civil and criminal cases in the United States. Among the many stories that have been disclosed in the course of the investigation there are accounts of priests with a history of molesting boys, one who supplied cocaine to teenagers in exchange for sex, and one who recruited girls as nuns and then abused them. Yet the church helped priests hide by dispatching them to new posts when transgressions were discovered. The mask of niceness was worn by men at the highest levels of the church.

Paul Dintner, who spent more than two decades as a priest, knows from personal experience how silence and deference to authority are enforced in the clergy. As head of his seminary's student body he attended a dinner where he found himself seated next to the cardinal. Eager to relay the results of a student council study of issues affecting seminary life, he broached the topic only to be silenced by the cardinal, who advised him to approach him through appropriate channels so the chain of authority would not be broken.

Dintner described a culture of deference and silence that encourages ignorance and denial of important issues. Such a culture, he believes, fosters the idea that priests can be predators with impunity. Accountability, in such a climate, is for lesser mortals.

All of these masked predators have in common their refusal to take responsibility for what they have done. Although some may say the words, that they should not have molested their victims, they add that the children did not refuse their advances, did not resist them. From this apparent lack of resistance the molesters infer that the children enjoyed and wanted the attention. The molester speaks of the child victims more as equals than as children in relation to their adult role. It becomes obvious that these men will do anything, including saying what they believe the listener wants to hear, to exonerate themselves. At the same time they cannot miss an opportunity to drop hints to the listener that they are desirable to the children and the molestation was, underneath all the social restrictions, one of mutual pleasure.

On January 20, 1942, at Interpol Headquarters in the Berlin suburb of Wannsee, a meeting was held. Reichsmarshall Hermann Goering requested his subordinate, SS-Obergruppenfuhrer Reinhard Heydrich, to call a meeting of the relevant German government and Nazi party ministries. The purpose of the meeting was to "carry out all necessary preparations in regard to organizational, practical and material matters for a total solution of the Jewish question." This one-hour meeting codified what became known as "the final solution," and not once during the meeting did anyone ask for or question the wholesale murder of the Jewish people. In the official minutes of the meeting, prepared by Adolf Eichmann, terms such as "evacuation," "elimination," and "treated accordingly" appear with great frequency.

When captured by the Israelis in 1961, Eichmann was asked, "Was it difficult for you to send these tens of thousands of people to their death?" Eichmann replied, "To tell you the truth, it was easy. Our language made it easy." Asked to explain, Eichmann said, "My fellow officers and I coined our own name for our language. We called it *amtssprache* — 'office talk.'" In office talk, "you deny responsibility for your actions. So if any-body asks, 'Why did you do it?' you say, 'I had to.' 'Why did you have to?' 'Superiors' orders. Company policy. It's the law.'"

Eichmann and his co-conspirators agreed to carry out the mass slaughter of Jews. They found ways to disconnect any emotional sensi-bility they might have felt from prohibitive thoughts in order to con-tinue their grisly work. They did it by developing a language that helped them to deny the reality of what they were doing and transfer the responsibility for their actions onto a faceless entity: company policy. In this extreme disconnection of thought and feeling innocent people died and the perpetrators continued, immunizing themselves with their words and rationalizations. They blinded themselves to what they and their colleagues were doing in order to satisfy the orders of a monstrous leader, perhaps to save their own lives, the lives of their families, or their jobs. We would not think of Eichmann and his associates as nice people, and perhaps they wouldn't have filled that description even before they committed their unspeakable deeds. However, his explanation suggests

THE TYRANNY OF NICENESS

they were able to blind themselves to what they were doing, and the result was harm to others on a massive scale. On a lesser scale, people are complicit in harm done to themselves and others every day when they hide behind their own brand of office talk, the niceness of protection or mask, and fail to speak the truth of what they see and know.

The use of niceness for either protection or to mask agendas is widespread. Fearful people believe niceness will give them a measure of safety. People who want something, whether it be some innocuous favour or an invasive act, have learned their lessons and discovered that using the mask of niceness is an effective way to satisfy their own needs and desires. When the disguise of the seriously masked, the pedophiles and con artists of the world, is removed, these users of niceness are punished by the justice system, an institution that helps perpetuate the notion of niceness as it is expressed in silence and obedience. The impact on the remaining users of niceness is not always so obvious. This is discussed in the following chapter.

CHAPTER 6
THE HIGH COST OF BEING NICE

IN HIS DISCUSSIONS of anxiety, Kierkegaard wrote that the most common form of despair occurs when one does not choose to be oneself, when a person is "another than himself." By the definitions I have given, being nice means to be silenced, to deny one's authentic thoughts and feelings. A silenced person hides or compromises essential parts of himself or herself. What is being expressed in word and deed is not genuine. This lack of genuine expression of thoughts, feelings, and deeds — implicitly, the failure to be oneself — can lead to despair.

At the core of using niceness as protection lies the belief that if you are nice, your world will be safe and conflict-free, that nothing bad will happen to you. You will not lose your lover, your friends, or your job; you will be secure and everyone will like you. Your fears will be calmed, your guilt mollified. In many ways, using niceness is meant to ward off despair, and perhaps this is possible in the moment. By silencing yourself and being obedient and agreeable you may be able to ward off those eventualities that dash hope — the loss or judgment of a partner, friend, or employer — and you may be able to avoid confrontation for a while. But in the long run, niceness as protection is a flimsy covering at best, endangering and destructive at worst, and contributes to the despair we seek to avoid.

We crave ease, and niceness offers a spurious ease. It allows us to indulge in laziness with our language and our behaviour. We no longer have to think of accurate descriptive words, nor do we have to commit to our approval or disapproval. We can simply say "that's nice" or "it's not nice" in the careless way that suggests an absence of any real sentiment or thought. Niceness lets us act as if it is not work to be in a relationship or to live life, as if living is not fraught with risks. We want to sail through life and relationships with little effort, and everything in our training to be nice people suggests that this is possible if we just keep quiet and be agreeable.

Adding weight to this wishful thinking is the reality that the price of being labelled not-nice can be high. Many assume the price is too high. Social isolation and shunning are among the highest potential costs of being not-nice. Even within families this can happen when one member chooses to speak out about problems rather than collude in silence. Alcoholism, for example, often splits families when some members join the alcoholic in denial and others refuse to buy into that hallmark of the addiction. Failure to meet others' expectations for compliance in the workplace might cost people their jobs, however unreasonable the expectations may be. Guilt, the internalized product of other peoples' instant judgments over years, is a portable cost, moving with its hosts from relationship to relationship and situation to situation. The price of being not-nice is the exacerbation of our fear and guilt and it seems too high. We want to protect ourselves from moments of confrontation or conscience and we have learned to do that by being nice, believing that it is to our benefit and convincing ourselves it is better for the people with whom we are in contact. But we are letting ourselves be hoodwinked.

The relief that we might experience by being nice is short-lived, and the price we pay for it is much higher than the cost of speaking out, of being authentic. The social losses that we fear will occur and the guilt we may feel if we act and speak according to our own beliefs, needs, and desires pale in comparison to the alienation from oneself and from others that accompanies niceness. If people use niceness as protection they put themselves at risk of letting problems in their relationships fester, endangering themselves psychologically and physically, and compromising their health. They lose touch with that essence of being that we refer to as our "self." If people are complicit in others' niceness they are saying, "I don't want to know who you are." If they insist that their children be nice they are robbing them of the ability to develop and act on their inner wisdom. If people are not forthcoming with their life partners or business partners and accept niceness from them in lieu of honesty and directness, they are encouraging inauthentic relating and contributing to the dilution of communication.

Jimmy Reid, a British trade unionist, put it this way:

> A rat race is for rats. We're not rats. We're human beings. Reject the insidious pressure in society that would blunt your critical faculties to all that is happening around you, that would caution silence in the face of injustice lest you jeopardize your chance of promotion and self-advancement. This is how it starts and, before you know where you are, you're a fully paid-up member of the rat pack. The price is too high.

There is an essential dishonesty in being nice. We cut and paste ourselves into a facsimile of the cultural requirement without thinking that we are lying, denying our authenticity, and sacrificing our integrity. We believe our empty promises. We are appalled at a suggestion that we might lie. If, on occasion, we awaken to the reality of what we are doing, we rationalize: We tell ourselves our honest opinion would be hurtful, that people would not like us if they knew what we were thinking, that we would disappoint the people closest to us. We convince ourselves that we must do things because others expect them of us even though it is counterintuitive to comply. We minimize the impact of our inauthenticity on others.

The cost of our dishonesty is high. It extracts a bounty from us and from the people who are recipients of it. Although the implicit hope of niceness is that it will stop our fear and guilt, it does not do so. On the contrary, it keeps fear and guilt alive, and it stands in the way of fulfilling relationships.

IMPACT ON ONESELF

In Paulo Coelho's novel *Veronika Decides to Die*, a psychiatrist, Dr. Igor, identifies a disease of the soul that he calls Vitriol. The disease is progressive, a gradual release of bitterness —Vitriol — that poisons the soul and leads to death. Its main target is the will. Its victims lose all desire to either live or die. They go about their business without passion.

Like the fictional Vitriol, niceness weakens the will and leaves its victims passionless. Few of us are able to express ourselves without reservation and act on our own desires if we have constantly been told, in a variety of ways, to suppress our thoughts and feelings and behave in ways that deny our own needs and wishes. One early weakening of the fibre of authenticity takes place in toddlerhood, when children become casualties in the battle for control of some small area of their lives. They struggle to hold on to their toys as their parents exhort them to share. They attempt to explore their surroundings only to be told not to touch anything. When they protest they are confined to playpens and cribs and isolated in rooms. The conflict they endure weakens their spirits. With this kind of training in our early years, we are inclined to cave in, to submit to the higher cultural and parental authorities that, by the time we reach adulthood, have come to reside inside us. We forfeit our will to act and express ourselves in authentic, involved, passion-filled ways because we have been convinced that obedience is expected of us in exchange for approval, acceptance, and love. The plucky and determined among us may find our voices and begin to act in accordance with our own hearts' desires later in life, but many do not. Many have been lost along the way, victims of their unwavering obedience to their training and its fallout.

When we give up expression we also lose any real sense of what we feel and think. Andrew, a client in his mid-fifties, understood, after two years' work in psychotherapy, that he had been attuned to watching the reactions of other people all his life. When he saw what they thought or felt about something he would accommodate them. He wanted them to remain as friends because having friends meant status to him. He believed that to keep them around he had to comply with their likes and dislikes. Even in his therapy sessions he would describe his behaviours as if they were an accurate indicator of his preferences. Then one day, watching a play with his wife, he caught himself looking at her for her reactions and realized he did not know his own thoughts and feelings about the play. That moment was the beginning of his understanding of the extent to which he had lost touch with himself. It was a frightening moment, but it also gave him hope because he could begin to mine the depths of himself, to learn to know himself as he never had before.

Andrew used niceness as protection and was alienated from his own thoughts and feelings as a result. Rather than develop and articulate his own, he echoed others' thoughts, and in so doing he lost touch with his own responses and reactions. When people use niceness as a mask they are no less alienated from their thoughts and feelings than people who use niceness as protection. When they make the choice to use this mask they are deliberately suppressing their real thoughts and feelings. For example, it could be that Bernadette, who acted as the go-between for her husband and his family, was afraid of being thought inadequate or was afraid to alienate his family because she craved their companionship and approval. It could be that Judy, who said she wanted to keep Dan as her friend when she had finished with him as a lover, was afraid of commitment. Peter, who abused Kathryn, may have been afraid that she would leave him and attempted to keep her submissive so she would not. Jason was afraid of being seen as inadequate and in his depressive state created a grander persona for himself. Ernest, who smiled to his death, may have been a man who had suppressed anger or depression all his life, then finally released it on himself. The authentic feelings of these people were buried under mounds of self-deception.

Pedophiles such as the priests who have molested countless boys and psychopaths such as Ted Bundy, Paul Bernardo, and Albert Walker exhibit a degree of alienation from themselves that requires separate analysis. Although these people use the mask of niceness to further their agendas with devastating impact on their victims, they are in a different sphere of self-alienation than people who are seeking the approval of others. These people believe they are exempt from the rules that govern ordinary people, which makes them very dangerous.

There are a number of ways that being nice affects nice people themselves. Ironically, although being nice is meant to make life easier, nice people suffer. When it forces us to satisfy external demands, both real and perceived, rather than internal needs and desires, we cast into confusion the very essence of our selves. At a fundamental level, the level at which our innermost sense of self meets the world, we lose control of our interactions with other people and our development takes a path of self-denial rather than self-nurturing.

We are all unique. We have different genes, experiences, and ability to make sense of ourselves and the world. The tyranny of niceness is a demand not for uniqueness but for sameness. Our need to feel and believe in our uniqueness is frustrated by niceness, and out of that frustration emerges our discontent, which spells trouble for our bodies, our relationships, and our level of contentment.

LOSS OF CONTROL

Control has become a bad word in relationship jargon. Many times I have heard one member of a couple complain that the other is attempting to control him or her, behaviour that threatens the health of the relationship. I have also heard many individuals describe themselves as "too controlling," meaning they attempt to exert control over the activities of others. Too often, people make blanket assumptions from such observations and conclude that control of any kind is undesirable.

There is a vast difference between controlling others and being in control of ourselves. We all want and need a measure of control over our lives. On the other hand, attempts to control other people are ill-advised in personal relationships and are often a result of having little control over ourselves. We all need to control or inhibit behaviours that endanger ourselves or others, weaken us, or expose us to needless stress. We need to feel we have some control over the extent to which our environment impacts on us. People who are nice are confused about being in control. They have too much control over the expression of their thoughts and feelings, which means that in practice they relinquish control of their speech and behaviour in order to be nice. They let someone else decide what they should say and do, and when. They are encouraged, even convinced, to do this from the time they begin to explore their environment as children and discover that few things in it are subject to their wishes. For some people the imbalance in control develops to self-defeating proportions by adulthood. They fail to recognize that they are over-controlled in some spheres and feel frustrated and unable to see how they can take control of their own lives and get out from under the limitations imposed by the outside world. On rare occasions people are so frustrated and angry that they lash out in violence, sometimes doing harm to other people, often those closest to them, or harming themselves. This is one of the most extreme outcomes, when niceness covers severe suppression of feelings that may then take the form of attempted or successful suicide and suicidal thoughts, homicide, bullying, road rage, or other forms of aggression. At the other end of the continuum it leads, more often, to a quiet alienation from oneself.

Rosa submitted to people's needs in order to keep them on as friends. She became all things to all people except herself. Her troubled youth had led to one suicide attempt, after which she pulled herself together enough to finish school and go to work, but over the years she had become so alienated from her own needs and wishes that she lost her enthusiasm for life. In the throes of major depressive episodes she would be plagued by thoughts of suicide. At those times, not living at all seemed preferable to living an empty shell of a life.

Barry, in his late teens, was like Rosa in that he submitted to others' requests in order to keep them on as friends. In his case, however, the requests involved the things he owned. Material things came to him easily, being one of only two children in an upper-middle-class family. If a friend wanted to use his bicycle or borrow videos he always complied, lending the items with no questioning about the return date. He never requested to have the items returned; he simply waited. More often than not they never were returned. When his parents complained he would make excuses for his friends and promise he would ask for the items back, but he never did. Although generosity can be a wonderful thing, when it is generated out of fear of non-acceptance it is not real. Rather, it is another manifestation of someone who feels disentitled and who feels unable to take control of his own life for fear of losing his friends.

Some teens who feel powerless to make themselves heard by their parents express frustration in ways such as this: they remain nice, promising whatever the parents ask, but forget or do not bother to follow through. Unexpressed anger lies at the bottom of this kind of interaction. Parents feel the intensity of that anger as it transmits to them through their inability to make the passive child comply. This type of transmission of anger is not unique to parent-child interactions. Whenever it does occur, the individuals involved become locked in the tyranny of niceness that erupts when the tension becomes too much to bear.

Roland, a widower living alone, gave up control of the home he had shared with his wife and family for decades. He and his late wife had raised a family of three, and each had large families. Visits from his children and grandchildren were frequent and he always enjoyed seeing them. What he did not enjoy was their emphasis on material goods. It seemed the family felt compelled to bring him gifts whenever they came to visit. At holiday times and Father's Day they pulled out all the stops. Roland was a man who disliked clutter, but he was also someone who was unable to speak up about his preferences. His wife had decorated the house and she was a lover of bric-a-brac. He never protested the ornamentation that occupied every horizontal and vertical space in the house, reasoning that his wife spent a lot more time in it than he did.

When his wife died he wanted to remove her decorations but worried that his children might be offended, so he kept most things. His children, lacking any direction from him, assumed that he liked the objects in the house and that he liked to receive gifts, so they continued to give to him in the manner they had done when their mother was alive. The themes changed from cute statuettes and nostalgic prints to elaborate flies for fishing, assorted pipes, and miniature replicas of old trains — but the gifting continued.

Roland felt like he was being buried alive under a mound of paraphernalia that had little meaning for him. He felt the gifts were a burden. Many were not to his taste or represented long-forgotten interests and pursuits, and they simply meant he possessed more objects that sat around gathering dust. Nonetheless he continued to live with the growing clutter because he was too nice to tell his children to stop bringing gifts, that their visits were all he desired of them. He felt he had no control over his environment, but at the same time believed that the givers would be offended if their gifts were not displayed. Because he was so nice, Roland's children, well meaning though they were, inadvertently had more control over his environment than he did. He felt suffocated in his home and powerless to make changes to his living circumstances.

Despite his feelings, Roland did not speak up and take control of his life and living space. He was like many people who feel the life squeezed out of them by denying themselves the most basic of needs: control of their personal space.

A D D I C T I O N S

In their despair, people who feel no sense of control over their lives may succumb to drugs, alcohol, and ill health.

Marshall, like Max, knew his marriage was a mistake before he entered into it. He married because he felt guilty: he had impregnated his wife, Teresa, very soon after they met when they were teenagers. She was from a strict, religious family, and the embarrassment the family would have felt if she had had a baby without the benefit of marriage would have been hard to manage. Abortion was not an option because of her family's religious beliefs. Marshall decided to do the "right" thing in spite of having misgivings about marrying a woman he barely knew and at such a young age. They married anyway, and even though he soon realized how little he and his wife had in common, he kept up the charade of a marriage.

Marshall provided well for his family, never missing a day at work. He attended church services each week with his family and, on occasion, socialized with his wife and a few other couples. At the same time, he was sarcastic with his wife at home and made her the brunt of his jokes in public, "kidding" her about her housekeeping skills and her lack of sexual interest. He resented the child who was born five months after the wedding, as well as the one who followed ten months later, and he avoided spending any significant amounts of time with them by working late or busying himself with projects in the house. With increasing frequency, he hid behind television, computer games and pornography, alcohol, and his public face of niceness. He maintained that he did the right thing by marrying, but the habits he developed to hide from his conflict over the decision manifested in his body and face. His eyes had the glazed and yellowed appearance of overindulgence and he experienced recurring bouts of gout. His resentment cast a black pall over his home and his relationships with his wife and children.

Marshall would never admit that he was an alcoholic. He would say that a glass or two of wine with dinner was good for his health and a few drinks with friends never hurt anyone. The problem was that his words did not describe his drinking habits. He kept a flask of vodka at work to help him through the day — though he never sipped at it until noon.

Occasionally he took clients to lunch, which included two or three beers. A martini or two preceded dinner, and a bottle of wine or a glass or two of beer accompanied the meal more often than not.

Marshall is like many people who hide behind alcohol, drugs — either the street variety or prescribed medications — or other addictions when they become unable to face the life they have shaped through their failure to live according to their genuine needs and desires. They rely on their addictions to pull them through the day. Some smoke marijuana every day, some consume medication, over-the-counter or prescription or both, to ease the emotional pain that sometimes manifests as physical pain. Some draw from all these sources in misguided and unhealthy attempts to heal themselves of pain whose source they barely remember because they have spent a lifetime denying it. Some numb themselves in front of screens, television or computer.

Denial is powerful. For Marshall, the key to survival in his unhappy life was his belief in a false image of his own creation. His wife, in her way, bought into it. She had become dependent on the image he had created for her standing in the community as well as on the money he earned. Any wishes she might have had for a more satisfying relationship were drowned in these features of their life together.

For Josie and Rex, another couple haunted by denial, the circumstances were somewhat different. They met when they were in their early twenties. Both liked to "party," which meant they consumed substantial amounts of street drugs together along with their like-minded friends. Their relationship became serious and they married and began to take on some of the trappings of a suburban lifestyle. It was then that their use of drugs tapered to marijuana only. Within two years Josie became pregnant and made the decision to stop smoking. She asked Rex to stop with her but he refused.

Years later, when their two children were in elementary school, Josie and Rex found their way to my office. Josie was the image of the successful working — and overworked — mother. They sought out marital counselling because Rex had become nothing more than an incidental partner in the relationship. He worked at his trade during the day and spent his evenings smoking marijuana in front of the television. His smoking had become a central arguing point in the marriage and yet, Josie admitted, she had mixed feelings. Although she did not like the amount Rex smoked and she did not like his emotional distance, she was relieved that one of the effects of the marijuana was to decrease his sex drive. It meant she had one less thing to do.

In both these relationships the men were dependent, either physically or psychologically, on their substances. They had become entrenched in the way of life that went with their use of the substances and neither knew how nor wanted to change that, even though their families were being harmed. It could have been the women, although women are somewhat less likely to become addicted in circumstances such as these. All four people were, however, imbued in denial about the extent to which their relationships suffered for decisions they made earlier — to marry when all indicators suggested such a marriage would be a disaster, or to marry in the haze of substance-induced myopia.

The tendency to give oneself over to addictions often starts early in life. The culture we live in, peer groups, and the examples of older family members encourage alcohol and drug use as a way of coping, promoted under the guise of a "good time" or, in the case of prescribed mood-enhancing drugs, "medicine." If the alienation from oneself and others has taken hold these props may present a quasi-opportunity for the disaffected to connect with other people. Teenagers whose social skills have suffered because they know only how to obey rather than express themselves are lured into the anorexic language and behaviour of the drug culture. Older people's tongues are loosened under the influence of alcohol or drugs, freeing them to repeat the repertoires of stories that would lose all significance in the direct light of sobriety. None are relating in ways that might deepen relationships or offer the possibility of quality emotional connection, for these props create distance, not closeness.

Use of addictive substances underscores emptiness. On a large scale it reflects the emptiness of society. Approximately 18 million Americans have alcohol problems, and 5 to 6 million Americans have drug problems. Considering these numbers, and combined with people who simply consider themselves social users of alcohol and drugs, our world encompasses a huge void under its agreeable crust. Many who are addicted are caught in the jaws of niceness, numbing themselves in order to comply with images and roles they do not find comfortable or satisfying. Many

who would not consider themselves to be addicted use numbing substances regularly for the same reasons. We have learned to keep ourselves
nice by employing these illusory forms of pleasure. At the same time,
alcohol acts as a disinhibitor, and for some people this means a release of
anger when they have been drinking. They are then able to blame the
alcohol for their emotional display and maintain the passivity of niceness
and denial of their troubled feelings when sober.

HEALTH

With research money granted primarily for the pursuit of viral and
genetic causes of disease few scientists are motivated to look at the
nebulous world of emotions and their link to physical disease.

Still, some scientists are conducting groundbreaking research in this
area, and there is evidence that emotions are linked with the immune
system. Dr. Esther Sternberg published an article in the *New England
Journal of Medicine* in 1980 showing a connection between a brain chemical and a severe autoimmune disease. She has since produced a body of
respected research linking health and emotions and in 2000 published
The Balance Within: The Science Connecting Health and Emotions. Dr.
Antonio Damasio, author of *The Feeling of What Happens: Body and
Emotion in the Making of Consciousness*, has linked body and emotion in
his work with brain-damaged patients. Dr. Michael Gershon, Professor
Keith Sharkey, and Dr. Nicholas Diamant have discovered that nerve
fibres link the brain to the digestive tract, where most of our immune
cells are located. However, it takes no research other than personal experience to know that a healthy body produces a sense of well-being and
that sudden relief of stress can cure small aches and pains as if by magic.
A feeling of well-being can be thwarted by stresses including everything
from nightmares to a friend's disapproval, and when we feel stressed we
tend to locate the discomfort in our stomach and abdominal area.

Gabor Mate wrote about the mind-body link in his book *When the
Body Says No: The Cost of Hidden Stress*, based on his work with patients.
He discovered that many people with rheumatoid illness are extremely
stoical and show a strong resistance to getting help. According to his

research, these people have become hyperindependent to compensate for feelings of emotional loneliness. They tend to be perfectionistic, fear their own angry impulses, and feel inadequate. He found that the backgrounds of people with autoimmune illness often include the actual or emotional abandonment of a parent.

In his work examining the link between stress and disease, especially heart disease, diabetes, and depression, researcher Dr. Michael Meaney has found that personality traits are a differentiating factor between who gets sick and who does not. He has found that individuals at risk are competitive, ambitious, impatient people who are frustrated and hostile. Dr. Meaney also says that shy people have higher levels of stress hormones, and they are more likely to suffer from chronic illness. Shy people, like nice people, suppress their thoughts and feelings. A crucial factor emerges in Dr. Meaney's analysis: the role of the perception of control in the production of disease. He has found that if we believe we have no control in a difficult situation our stress increases. This means the hormones that respond in stressful situations, ones essential to arousing us to action, are activated. When these hormone levels are chronically activated the result is illness. So, although we need the hormones to help us out of stressful situations, chronic stress means we get too much of a helpful thing and the hormones cause trouble.

Does this mean we should vent our anger whenever it arises? Does it mean we simply give in to road rage and yelling our discontent at the supermarket cashier? Does it mean that we must weep whenever we are touched by something? Not at all. There is a sea of difference between the extremes of non-expression and the impulse to be vociferously cathartic, although neither is an aid to health. The real problem lies in the denial of feeling and the inability to link raw emotional impulse with understanding of that impulse and appropriate expression.

I have known people who talked as if they were in touch with their feelings. They stated the right words at the appropriate time. And yet it was their gift of observation that was at work, not the connection between their intellect and emotion. They knew that if a family member or friend died the appropriate emotion was sadness and they could say they were sad. They knew that if their spouse was upset the appropriate response was concern. But they had learned ways of coping that isolated the raw emotional impulse from their brain's processing of it because at some point they had learned not to express feelings. The impulse still occurred, but it was stopped before it could be expressed as a feeling and a thought. They had learned the subtle and powerful skill of emotional disconnection by obeying messages from important people in their lives. The messages for suppression of feelings were ubiquitous: "Keep a stiff upper lip," "Don't cry," "It's not that bad," and — that all-time favourite — "Be strong." Feelings were invalidated with these comments. The messages ensured that they had never learned to say directly to one another "I'm angry," deal with the feelings, and articulate the reasons for the anger. More often, they zapped through feelings of sadness or hurt, through anger and on to denial without being aware of their reactions. Although it can be helpful to deal with problems with humour or think about positive aspects of life and recognize our strengths in order to move ourselves out of despair, if these ways of coping are engaged before the emotional impulse is validated, the result is suppression of feeling.

On the other hand, impulsive raging, for example at other drivers, is also no expression of what is really going on. The anger and frustration are products of many circumstances. You might be running late, traffic is heavy, you had a bad day at work, or you're worried about your children. The catalyst for your rage may be an inconsiderate driver, but it is really the sense of having no control that underlies your rant. When people encounter situations that are packed with emotion, they feel and act out of control if they have not learned how to identify and articulate their feelings. They fail to see what control they might have in the situation and their stress hormones remain at high levels, exacerbated by the raging.

Dr. Alistair Cunningham, a Toronto psychologist, has worked with cancer patients for two decades. A survivor of cancer, he began, many years ago, to help himself by meditating. In his program at Princess Margaret Hospital he teaches others to meditate and helps them achieve some sense of control over the course of their disease and health. Meditation is a method of returning to the sense of oneness in ourselves that we lose when we give ourselves over to the demands of our environment.

In clinics across the United States, patients with various kinds of chronic disease are taught mindfulness meditation to help them deal with their symptoms. Dr. Richard Davidson, director of the Laboratory for Affective Neuroscience at the University of Wisconsin, has found that mindfulness, or learning how to monitor one's own moods and thoughts, seems to improve the robustness of the patients' immune systems.

There is a great deal more to be learned about the mind-body-emotion connection in health. What is clear is that there is an unmistakable link, that through our mental processes we can help our bodies stay well, and that unresolved emotional issues can lead to illness. As we suppress ourselves into niceness we fight ourselves emotionally and physically and sometimes pay the price for this conflict with our health.

PROTECTION BECOMES MASK

Being nice as protection sometimes transmutes into niceness as mask. Rosa, in her silent resentment of her friends' lies to her, was also lying. She heard their problems and stories with apparent interest and empathy. Sometimes she did feel that way but often she was angry and preoccupied with wanting to be heard by them. When she realized what she was doing, the insight was liberating for her. In time and with practice speaking up she was able to alter some of her relationships so that her role in conversations became more give-and-take, rather than only listening and responding.

In the same way, people who have been abused adopt the mask of niceness when they, in turn, hurt other people. They become the persons they never wanted to be while they carry on a display of niceness for the outside world. The point at which the victim's protective niceness becomes the abuser's mask of niceness is hard to discern and the shift is rarely absolute. Often people move with a great deal of fluidity between the two modes of niceness, so that one or the other will be the motivating force depending on circumstances of the moment.

Frank prided himself on the quality and quantity of work he accomplished. His willingness to do whatever he was asked was legendary at the office. But there was a downside that was spoken about less often. From time to time, Frank exploded. Out of the blue and usually at home, in a reaction disproportionate to the situation, his face would become red, his volume would increase, he would swear, and then he would deflate as if someone had popped him like a balloon and become the agreeable helper he always was.

It was no surprise to discover that Frank's explosions were related to other events in his life. Most recently, the catalyst was that he had been passed over for promotion. He was the one who worked overtime and was called on by others for help on a near-daily basis. He had as much seniority as his colleagues. Yet he was passed over for a colleague who was vocal in his own self-promotion, something Frank was unable to do. His superiors rationalized their decision to him — Frank was so efficient that his department was unable to spare him — but he had to face the fact that he had silenced his trumpet far too long and that his reticence to draw attention to himself was his contribution to his failure to advance.

It became clear with his reaction to the promotion that Frank's protective niceness had stepped aside to make room for the coexistence of a mask of niceness long before. The niceness that had been generated out of fear, put into place to protect him from rejection, had stretched to accommodate a much different undercarriage. Outwardly he looked the same. He still did everything he was asked and walked the extra mile to please people. The mask he now sported looked the same as the protective gear, but underneath lay resentment and anger alongside fear. In truth, Frank wanted to be recognized, wanted a promotion and salary increase, and had ambitious feelings about it, but, still holding on to fear, he revealed only his willingness to accept more work, without asking to be considered for the benefits of his labours. Without making effort on his own behalf, he wanted others to see for themselves what his needs and expectations were, but they did not. When the insult he felt became too much to bear, he exploded.

Frank thought of himself as a nice man, and other people shared that judgment. The smouldering and volcanic erupting nature of his personality was topped by layer upon layer of lessons in social expectations overlaid by a blandness that lent itself to the most innocuous of interpretations. His colleagues were the beneficiaries of this character construction because they availed themselves of his help. He achieved nothing more than lost hours of free time and threats of rising fatigue and blood pressure. In the end he felt deprived even of pleasure in a job well done.

The process of turning protection into a mask is slow and undetectable by most people because it coexists with protective niceness. Often people who have made such a change function for most of their adult lives in this mode without realizing what has happened to them. They fail to sense anger developing where fear had been the driving force before. When others, generally their partners, point out the anger that exists just under the surface they deny it, not because they want to oppose the partner for the sake of opposing but because they believe the image they project. If their partners tell them they are far too critical of their children they rationalize the need for strong discipline or deny the charge. They cannot see who they have become. When, at last, they are convinced that anger is a problem, they are shocked. People who have spent a lifetime protecting themselves from the cold, critical eyes of their own parents cannot conceive of themselves as angry critics of their own children or as abrasive partners, and yet the transformation has taken place in spite of their wishes to avoid just that. Niceness remains the cloak in which interactions are wrapped, but anger, not fear, determines the message. All the anger they could not express to their critics as children and later as adults emerges in ways that they vowed would never happen.

Sometimes niceness masks an undercurrent of manipulation. Max knew on his wedding day that he did not want to marry but he went ahead anyway. His feelings did not change over the course of his ten-year marriage. Far from it, he felt uncomfortable in his marriage and was determined to get out of it, although he may not have been aware of the extent or impact of his unhappiness. As he described his feelings and the interactions he had with his wife it became obvious that he had been angling for years to get her to ask for a divorce. He would not have to compromise his perception of himself if she was the one doing the asking. His wife's insistence on trying to make the marriage work left him frustrated and led him to seek help, but he could not give up his mask. He out-waited her, and in the end she initiated divorce proceedings. Max's perception of himself remained intact.

Many compromises must be made with oneself in order to use niceness as both protection and mask. Sometimes people become complicit with mean-spirited people, remaining silent while someone maligns a person who is absent from a conversation for fear of getting the same treatment themselves. People become different at home than in public, showing one side to the world and another side to their families. Often, entire families adopt this way of relating. Communication becomes distorted: we do not practise speaking our thoughts, so when we need to point out some inconsistency to another person, when things have gone too far, our approach is either apologetic or, on the other hand, attacking. As a result, the other person has a hard time knowing what is going on. Sometimes people who have lived extremes of protection and mask explode into violence. Most often, the difficulty that occurs is a blurring of the lines between people who are good and kind and nice, and people who are manipulative and dishonest and nice.

AT THE MERCY OF THE MASK

I went to high school with Barbara Walker. Back then, she was Barbara McDonald from a rural community. She was a quiet teenager with a shy, ready laugh, someone who might have been voted "nicest girl of the year" had there been such a contest. She describes her upbringing in her book, saying, "We were given a good grounding in the teachings of the Bible and the laws of man." She also learned to be her twin brother's keeper, at the urging of her mother. She developed a strong sense of responsibility for him and guilt when he failed to live up to his potential, characteristics she believes she brought to her relationship with her former husband. The training she received in her family home, which produced a law-abiding citizen in Barbara, did not prepare her for the likes of Albert Walker. Nor did the culture in which she grew up, the ubiquitous culture that perpetuates the notion of male supremacy and till-death-parts-us marriage. Led by example, most women in such cultures understand that they must make the best of the situation in which they find themselves. Barbara was no different.

Throughout her narrative she discusses her concerns about Walker, wondering about his inability to grieve his mother's death and his failure to express any real emotion. In retrospect there was almost nothing about the man that she liked. Yet, despite all her evidence, even early in the relationship, that she did not need him and that he was a detriment and danger to her, she did not leave him. She realizes now that she should have left when he had his first major outburst over a trivial matter in his parents' home, but even then Barbara had doubts about her intuitive sense of him and the situation she was in. The lessons she learned in her community and through her upbringing did not enable her escape from him and probably worked against it. Nice people do not act on doubt about the sincerity of others, even when any evidence of sincerity is in short supply or even when they sense danger. It took Barbara many years before she could attempt to free herself of her abuser.

Barbara's husband turned out to be much more dangerous than most wife-batterers, and perhaps nothing could have prepared her to deal with him. Still, in many ways, Barbara's situation was typical. Pared down to basics her case reads like that of many women who would never consider themselves abuse victims or survivors, women who are living the life expected of them in this society. Like other victims of abuse that has been perpetrated over a long period of time, she was first charmed, then led to believe in her abuser's superiority even while protesting it. She was filled with doubt about her own talents and brought to a point of doubting even her perception of reality. In hindsight it all seems obvious, but in the process of living life it is not, especially in the absence of a well-developed trust in one's own feelings and observations and thoughts.

Barbara Walker's story highlights the importance of learning to trust what we see and feel. Looking back, it was obvious to her that she had ignored what she sensed about her husband based on her observations and feelings. The cliché "Hindsight is twenty-twenty" is confirmed by the events of her life, but when the story was moving forward, instead of reflecting upon her own wisdom and acting on it, she doubted it. She could not trust it enough to end the relationship until the danger signals could no longer be ignored, until they were blatant, right in her face. Like most of us, Barbara had been trained away from her intuitive wisdom. Life might have been very different for her if that wisdom had been nurtured in her formative years rather than suppressed in the service of being nice.

People whose need to avoid confrontation is strong unwittingly collude with those who use niceness to mask exploitation and atrocities.

At a relatively innocuous level, people are taken in by assertive — even aggressive — sales types, well-dressed and personable, flattering their compliant prey. Joe, who feasted on expensive menu items while his companion dined frugally, then suggested they split the bill, used the mask of niceness to take advantage of his friend, but the friend went along with him because he wanted to avoid confrontation. At a dangerous level, the Ted Bundys and Albert Walkers of the world trade on charm while they carry out their hideous acts, sometimes helped by eyes that have learned to look away and lips that have been trained to remain closed rather than express doubt or concern.

CHILDREN WHO ARE TAUGHT TO BE NICE

Lisa, a professor, was forty years old when she first came for counselling. Her parents had separated when she was four years old and her mother married another man soon afterwards. This man, George, was the one she knew as her father, because her biological father was not active in her life. Her mother and stepfather had a difficult marriage beset by several separations. During one of these periods, when she was about twelve years old, her stepfather negotiated with her mother to have Lisa stay with him for a weekend at his cabin in the north. Lisa did not hesitate because she had spent some good times with him. Preparing for bed the first night of the weekend she noticed that George had made up only the bed in the main bedroom.

"Where am I going to sleep?" she asked him.

"Right here," he replied. He patted the bed.

Lisa was startled. She was bothered by the thought that she would be sleeping in the same bed with him. Yet George was the only father she had known and she trusted him. He had taught her to ride her bicycle, stayed with her when her mother was working, cooked for her, helped her with her homework, and sometimes cuddled with her. All the same, she felt uncomfortable with the sleeping arrangement.

As an adult, Lisa was no stranger to public speaking. She was articulate and challenging, able to question and express her thoughts and feelings. But she was inhibited sometimes and, in particular, found directness on a personal level difficult. She made jokes to cover her anxiety and was quick to tears.

As an adolescent of twelve, Lisa was obedient to the authorities in her life. That night at the cabin she did what she was taught to do: she remained quiet rather than question George or insist on sleeping in another room by herself. She climbed into bed with him despite feeling that something was not right about the arrangement. That night, he molested her.

When children are being nice they are attempting to keep themselves safe by pleasing others, in most cases the adults or older children in authority. They are doing what they have been taught to do, remaining obedient and unprotesting. When they find themselves in situations such as Lisa's, they are unable to protect themselves because the mechanisms of protection have been distorted by the message of niceness. They have lost the ability to act on the feelings they experience when something seems wrong because those feelings have been overridden by messages of propriety. Acting on their own initiative when it is in conflict with the authorities in their lives has never been encouraged. They either fear disciplinary action or, like Brad with his colouring book, are afraid they'll hurt their parents' feelings and risk their disapproval.

Children are the most vulnerable of any of us when niceness is used as a mask. When we teach children to be nice we render them incapable of trusting their sense of danger in situations where they may need to run from exploiters wearing masks. The holocaust of sexual abuse that has been exposed in recent years bears horrifying witness to this truth. Boys have been unable to tattle on the helpful and friendly coach at the hockey arena who molested them. Hundreds of children, mostly boys, have been molested by priests, whom they were taught to respect and obey. What child can protect himself or herself when the natural inclination to detect danger *and act on it* has been socialized out of them? Children are dependent on the adults in their lives for their survival. They have been taught that pleasing adults is important. They have been taught that displeasing adults brings unpleasant consequences.

Claudia Black, one of the gurus of the Adult Children of Alcoholics movement, pointed out that children who are forced to pretend all is well at home when it is not grow up to become workaholics, addicts, and eating disordered. They learn to deny their own experiences as a sort of internal conflict resolution. Children become deniers of their own experience when Mom or Dad or both are drunk and disorderly and abusive at home but insist that the children say nothing about their behaviour, when those same parents are nice to people in the community or to strangers, or when parents invalidate the experiences and feelings of their children in other ways, whether from their naivety or negligence. To deny their experiences is the only way they can make sense of the contradictions they see and hear and feel. Since people are not psychologically comfortable when they betray themselves the deep split they feel manifests in self-harmful behaviours.

Children are confused when they hear their parents lying. When they overhear Mom and Dad tell the neighbour that the new paint job on his house is lovely only to tell each other in private that the colour is hideous, they do not know what to do. How do they reconcile the information that their parents, who insist on truth from them, lie? To the parents' subsequent surprise their children learn to say what they feel others will want to hear, establishing patterns that sometimes become convenient substitutes for truth as they move into their teen years. They have learned to lie, just as they have been lied to. And the behaviour continues to cycle through generations.

Although the discussion here is limited to parents' impact on their children, they are not alone in creating the impact. As I pointed out earlier, many other players in children's lives contribute. The impact may be lesser or greater, depending on the significance of the person in a child's life and the support children get from their parents. To rise above invalidating and confusing experiences children need someone, at least one person, to free them from the grips of niceness.

IMPACT ON OTHERS

Roland's family gave him gifts that they thought he would like, but they did it from a position of having no way of knowing what he would really like because he never expressed a preference. In their company he deferred to their tastes, never suggesting he might have other preferences. Their only way of knowing what he might like was by making inferences based on his hobbies and the things they saw in his home. Since he had never voiced his preferences in the past and had not changed his surroundings after his wife's death, they assumed he liked to be surrounded by bric-a-brac. Secretly, he disliked most of the gifts he had been given but was obligated by his niceness to live with them anyway. His family had no reason to believe he did not like and appreciate the gifts.

When people are given no clues or are in doubt about others' tastes it is natural for them to choose according to their own preferences, whether the question is gift-giving, restaurant selection, how to spend a vacation day together, or something more serious. In our non-opinion-ated niceness, we mislead people about our likes and dislikes, letting them believe we share theirs. So what difference does it make if the gift-givers are led to believe their gifts are appreciated? The answer lies in the nature of the relationship.

Thinking of himself as a private person, Roland had never been one to disclose his thoughts and feelings except on a superficial level. So accustomed was he to behaving this way that he did the same with the people who loved him most. They wanted very much to please him and in trying to do so relied on the only information they had, but in a twist of irony, it meant they never could please him. By failing to be honest with them about his needs in his home, about his changing interests and the accommodations he had made for his wife all those years, he kept his loving children distant from him. They were denied the opportunity of an honest relationship. They were aware of him as a pleasant but bland and simple character. They could never get a sincere-sounding opinion from him and they noticed that he seemed to change his mind according to what they told him. Although not the intention, this kind of parenting suggests that the parent is too protective of his or her own image to give fully to the child.

The acts of gift-giving and -receiving are both real and symbolic. While it may seem that accepting a gift, whether it is desired or not, is the gracious or nice thing to do, when gifts are frequently off the mark a miscommunication is occurring. In Roland's case, he, the receiver, was using niceness as a mask to hide his true self from his children in the belief that they would think well of him. What he did in the process was hide from them, with the result that he and his children were all cheated. He felt suffocated in his home, and they never knew the joy of witnessing his sincere delight at receiving a truly appreciated gift. Often they felt disappointed by his lacklustre thank yous, though — having been raised as nice children — they never told him. The worst of it was that they were never able to skirt the barriers and get to know each other in an intimate way.

In our non-opinionated niceness we transfer responsibility for decision-making to other people. Failing to take a position on matters as insignificant as which restaurant to eat at means the other is left to make the decision. While that may be a welcome opportunity for the other person it can be frustrating if he is called upon, in this passive way, to make most decisions. It means he must choose and then may feel — or be held — responsible if something goes wrong. The implications for relationships can be great. An act of niceness meant to smooth things over becomes a hotbed of resentment when the recipient must take responsibility, time after time, and the nice person refuses to contribute to the decision-making process.

This is the routine of couples who have established a lopsided relationship in which one is submissive, the other is dominant, and both are resentful. Perhaps you have been in such a situation yourself. Maybe you have travelled with someone who has refused to voice an opinion about what to do each day. "You decide," says your companion. "I don't care which museum we visit today." You do not want the entire burden of deciding which sights will be best to see in a limited time and fear that barbs may come your way if your decision yields less than great results. Tension builds before you have even departed your hotel. And it can work in the other direction. One person who knows with certainty what she wants to do may ask the other for an idea and then be upset when one is offered. Better had she made her suggestion and stated her wishes.

Speaking up about one's choice means a discussion can take place, each person can present preferences, and a decision can be agreed upon. A valuable exchange takes place, and each person has the satisfaction of being heard and participating in a decision-making process that approximates equality rather than dominance and submission. If the choice is a good one, both share the glory of having made it, and if it is not they share the responsibility, so neither is unduly encumbered.

The daughters of Louise, the woman who requested to hear my impression of her appearance, were true to the expectations that they say nothing that might provoke even a mild confrontation. Their manner, which was in no small part a result of their upbringing in a small community where approval and acceptance were a matter of social survival, meant that their mother's appearance and condition were not discussed in honest terms. Louise became agitated because she wanted to have an honest appraisal and discussion about her condition. Her daughters lost out, too, because they were unable to connect in a way that would facilitate telling their mother goodbye. At that point in life, ill and dying, Louise was unable to repair her own contributions — her training of them as compliant members of society — to her daughters' reticence, and so the responsibility fell to them to get beyond their usual fear of honesty. They could not, and their niceness prevented real intimacy with their mother.

Susan has spent many hours in my office attempting to come to terms with her frustration with her mother. Much to Susan's dismay, her mother has always avoided any conflict with her and, in fact, has gone overboard to curry her favour. Susan wants her mother to be direct with her, to address issues and stop avoiding problems between them. Her mother's niceness frustrates and angers her. Susan wants the relationship to be real.

IMPACT ON RELATIONSHIPS

A client, Nick, mentioned in a session that his partner, Kevin, had shaved off his beard. He felt Kevin looked much more attractive with the beard and yet he complimented him on the new look. I asked why he had not been honest with Kevin. He replied that he believed his honest answer would accomplish nothing more than to hurt Kevin's feelings. When I pressed him for details he explained that one should never be too honest about such things, that people really do not want to hear less than flattering comments. I said I did not agree and that there are ways of expressing one's honest opinion with compassion, if the opinion is critical, and I made some suggestions based on Nick's own comments to me. He could say to Kevin that he still found him very attractive but that, to him, the beard flattered his face and was a better match for his personality. Nick was doubtful but agreed he would think about trying the new approach. The following week he reported that he had broached the topic with Kevin and the discussion was enlightening. It turned out that Kevin shared the same sentiments as Nick but had not said so because he thought Nick liked his beardless look.

The removal of a beard is a minor event in the life of a relationship, but the extent of our honesty with partners is not minor. Nick and Kevin were just beginning their relationship, setting the tone for, hopefully, years to come. Being able to express, with kindness, feelings and thoughts that we fear might hurt the other is an important skill to develop for the health of any relationship. It enhances and strengthens the relationship so that each partner is able to rely on the other for candour and honesty, especially when feelings of love and caring are also frequently expressed in the relationship. In contrast, the path that is set far too often is a growing pattern of dishonesty, resentment, and mis-communication, all for reasons thought to be honourable, all of which are hopelessly misguided.

Imbalances and inequality are the hallmarks of relationships in which one or both partners insist on being nice. Often, intimate relationships start out this way. Each person wants to present a winning personality to the other and tries to become the person they believe the other will want. If there is a game in love, this is it. Making oneself nice, designing a personality for the express purpose of winning love and subduing the authentic parts, is common in romantic relationships, at the beginning. The technique fails if the relationship continues, however, because it creates false expectations. A woman who encourages her partner to talk even when she is bored with his conversation will become a resentful listener. She may want to be listened to herself but find that she has partnered with someone who does not know how to hear her. A man who spends beyond his budget to impress the woman he wants may be horrified later to find that she expects he will continue to provide expensive gifts as a matter of course. Later in a relationship, if one partner always refuses to set limits for children, yielding to their wishes in order to win their love, the other partner will by default be left to become the disciplinarian. He or she will become the "heavy" in the relationship, and the family will be split because the children will understand the dynamic very well and use it to get what they want. In the short term they may enjoy their victories, but overall they do not thrive emotionally if they can manipulate their parents in this way. In order to get on with the challenging work of physical and psychological development, children need clear and fair limit-setting and parents who cooperate with each other, even if they do not always agree.

In workplace relationships a similar imbalance can occur when a manager has a strong wish to be the nice guy to his employees. If he has so disabled himself with this wish that he is unable to give balanced, critical reviews to employees, personnel may lapse into autonomous cells. Employees or colleagues might begin to make their own decisions or orchestrate a separate agenda, a situation that can spell trouble for the overall functioning of the company or institution. When someone takes too many liberties, a substitute for the manager must step in and take charge. Again, because roles are not well balanced, employees are split apart and fall into line behind one or the other of the management team. This polarization cuts into the very heart of an organization's strength, undermining morale, jeopardizing profits, and even threatening its viability and effectiveness.

Relationships steeped in such imbalances — whether personal or professional — are superficial and tenuous. Great sacrifices are made to maintain the relationship, and sometimes each participant demonizes the other while maintaining position as the martyr. Such extremes may also occur in an outright abusive relationship such as Peter and Kathryn's. In their situation, Kathryn demonized Peter and was unable to see how she contributed to the dynamic. By staying with him under the circumstances of his drinking and abuse she was sacrificing herself and she was failing to send a strong message that she would accept no abuse or disrespect. Meanwhile, Peter continued to think of himself as a nice guy and in addition thought of himself as a victim of Kathryn's criticism, denying his abuse of her to himself and to others. Through his rationalizations he was able to deny that his problem was emotional chaos that left him feeling he had no control. "I lost control" would be his explanation for hitting Kathryn. His control was brittle, rigid, and easily cracked. It covered a sense of inadequacy in dealing with the stresses and frustrations he felt. He had no idea how to soothe himself when he was feeling low. When his fragile control cracked, he lashed out. The violence had a sobering effect and rendered him contrite, which started his cycle over again, making himself nice, silencing him to his experience of Kathryn's words, never questioning or attempting to work out his feelings with her.

When people collude in the silence of niceness, as Nick and Kevin had started to do, they never truly come to know other people in their lives. Dr. William Harford in Stanley Kubrick's film *Eyes Wide Shut* wore the mask of niceness, projecting an image of the perfect young professional with the perfect family. One day, his wife, Alice, cracked the facade by revealing her fantasy of making love with a young naval officer. Harford had never entertained the notion that she could have such thoughts. His denial had prevented him from seeing her as a whole person. Her knife in the back of his delusion punctured their collusion in niceness and plunged him into foreign territory — the seamy side of New York life and his own dark side that he had masked, even from himself. Near the end of the film Harford returned home to find Alice sleeping beside a mask he had worn to an orgy the night before. He was moved to tears by the sight of the mask on the pillow beside her that symbolized what he had given to their relationship. In his state of niceness he had known neither Alice nor himself.

When people are being nice in relationships they intend to make interactions easier, to attract others to them and keep them engaged. In reality, relationships like this are based on dishonesty, and the participants may become emotional strangers, without knowing why. They may participate in the illusion of a marriage or partnership or friendship but be so isolated in thought and feeling that they barely know the person with whom they are attempting to relate. They know only their perception of and projection onto that person, only those qualities most obvious to them. Many times I have met with couples of which one partner has decided to end the relationship while the other one is shocked by the news. Discontent has been neither conveyed nor heard. The surprised person has not been listening or observing and, despite feeling frustrated at repeated attempts to let the other person know, the bearer of the news has not been persistent, clear, or open enough, or has compromised in some way, lessening the impact of previous notices of discontent.

Louise and her daughters had become emotionally estranged from each other years before the moment when Louise asked me to comment on her appearance. They had colluded in the non-communication of niceness that provided them with a convenient way of relating but kept hurt and anger and probably joy sequestered from their ongoing interactions. In the brief snapshot of time that I spent with them that day I knew this was not a one-time occurrence but a well-practiced way of relating. The daughters covered their emotions with a thin layer of psychological gauze, which insulated them from touching their mother emotionally and thwarted the growth of their relationships. They were being the obedient daughters their mother thought she wanted, many years before. Louise had not anticipated that her own frustration would be the result of enforcing her daughters' niceness.

IMPACT KNOWN AND UNKNOWN

Although there appear to be advantages to being nice, there is a high price to pay for the few benefits gained in this way. Perhaps women suffering from depression and men who dissolve quietly into addictions, hiding behind marijuana, alcohol, affairs, and work, have spent their lives being nice. Perhaps cancer, heart attacks, and strokes are, in part, the body's way of expressing the somatic effects of a lifetime of emotional denial. The effects of lifelong use of antidepressants and anxiolytics used to polish off the edges of people's reactions are still not clear. News reports about families who erupt into homicide and suicide, while neighbours tell the world what a nice family they were, point to problems festering in relationships behind closed doors. I wonder if some lawbreakers are so frustrated at being unheard that their recourse has been to find ways to shock a society steeped in niceness. Within the culture of niceness some people are silent, some act out in destructive ways, and the few who dare to speak out sometimes pay an enormous price. Thus, economics binds together in powerful and destructive collusion some people who silence themselves and others for their own purposes and others who can be silenced.

Any benefits of avoiding the risks of speaking and living authentically are not permanent and may, in fact, be short-lived. When people stray from their deepest understandings of who they are, what they need most in life, and how they impact on others, they get lost in a black emotional forest — they suffer — and often are mystified when, out of frustration, people respond to them in unexpected ways. In the long term, niceness produces suffering. Children steeped in niceness are unable to run from would-be assaulters because they have not learned to question but to be compliant. They have not been taught that disobedience is sometimes a healthy behaviour. More general is the tragedy of never knowing the other people in our lives in meaningful ways.

Silence and obedience work no better for those who believe such behaviours will save them from their fears or from the emptiness of being alone. When we are silenced and obedient in the manner of niceness we lose a sense of what we feel and think, dying emotionally, and we behave in ways that are not fulfilling or healthy. Our thoughts, feelings, and behaviour may become either conforming or reactive, deliberate not-nice states of being that are imbued in wastefulness and futility. If we have become reactive, transformation must begin with the realization that being not-nice does not mean being hurtful or rude. We must realize that there are many shades of behaviour between strict conformity and non-conformity to prove a point.

Perhaps you have wondered how your behaviour and interactions with others might change if you were simply to give up being nice. It might be tempting to think that we all could say whatever we think, to whomever and whenever, and to demonstrate to everyone that we do not fit the mould. You may know someone who does this. Perhaps they are wonderful, free spirits at their best, always ready for a conversation or some fun, always ready with an opinion and intent on doing their own thing. Often these people express an intellectual understanding of and appreciation for the higher moral ground but, in the interests of not fitting the mould, say things to others that are offensive and hurtful and belie insight into their behaviour. Sometimes they may mask their unkindness with jokes.

I caution you: making a point of being not-nice is not the answer. Making a conscious attempt to free oneself from binding social restrictions does not mean that being not-nice becomes a cause. Freeing oneself is not an excuse to be rude, mean, arrogant, overbearing, or insensitive. Impulsive, assaulting, or uncaring words are not the equivalent of releasing oneself from this particular bondage. Telling it all like it is at the moment may seem like honesty and directness, but the matter is not so simple.

CHAPTER 7
TRANSFORMATION BEGINS INSIDE

BY NOW YOU understand that being nice is a state in which people manifest qualities that may compromise their health, safety, pleasure, and relationships. It means that people submit to authority without questioning to determine the appropriateness of their obedience, or they obey people they perceive to be authority figures or judges of their character. It means silencing opinions, feelings, and thoughts in order to avoid confrontation, abandonment, or rejection, real or perceived. Being nice seems to offer protection from the things we fear, but it means we are evasive and dishonest in relationships, and the protection may be fleeting at best.

Most of us are caught up in our day-to-day living, even our very survival, and it is hard to imagine anything different than the life we have at this moment. It is hard to take a longer, more global view of the place we occupy, the relationships in which we participate, and our place in time. Our worlds become narrow and immediate, and they are driven by fear. Under such circumstances we develop little sense of our place in the universe. It is harder still to imagine how we can make our relationships any different than the way they are. In the absence of our own fresh ideas we cling to images of relationships that we see around us, in families and among friends. We rely on the media to guide our ideas about how to relate and what to expect from a relationship, rather than developing our own wisdom in such matters. Taught to trust and comply with others' views we look outside ourselves for models rather than valuing our own experiences and our own evaluations of those experiences.

As we saw earlier, we are afraid of living the "wrong" way, so we follow the messages we are given in the hope that we will do it "right" according to some monitor that is not our own. Fear, however, only keeps us riveted and narrows our views. It stunts our growth and increases the likelihood that we will become dissatisfied with our lives. The great promise of compliance is a betrayal and yields the unhappiness of emotional disconnection from ourselves and other people.

Lacking development, the central part of us that we call a "self" becomes impacted, and the energy we intuitively and spontaneously feel finds no appropriate outlet. Rather than relating in a direct manner and following our intuitive feelings, we hedge and sometimes even lie, thinking we are protecting ourselves or believing this is the painless route to getting what we want. This may be true in the short term, but in the end we pay a high price for short-term relief from fear.

Now, I am proposing ways to give up niceness and start along the path of transformation towards authentic expression of thoughts and feelings. To become authentic is to be true to yourself rather than to shape yourself into someone you believe you should be based on images or models of behaviour of which others seem to approve. The goal is to find a place of peace and settledness within you, a place that serves as a comfort, a barometer, and a guide. The process begins by opening yourself up, reigniting the energy and passion you have given up through your years of niceness. You must get to know yourself, because parts of you have been lost or are hidden by niceness. This is a building and rebuilding process, building new kinds of relationships and rebuilding the crumbled and broken aspects of yourself that were demolished before they had a chance to develop.

Authenticity may seem like a good idea, but you may find that it is far from easy even to begin, because in the process you must dispense with the protection or mask of your niceness. When being nice has become like a skin, when we embrace it as our primary way of relating to other people, attempts to shed it cast us into a state of anxiety. Even though we think authenticity as a way of relating to people is desirable, becoming authentic with others is not easy or simple. In order to change ourselves we have to give up the superficial, misleading, and self-deceiving ways of relating that are familiar to us, and that, in their familiarity, provide us with reassurance of a kind. In the first stage of giving up niceness you may stumble with words, pass up opportunities to speak or to speak in a new way, and feel embarrassed and uncertain because you are attempting to relate in an unfamiliar and uncomfortable manner. Since we always gravitate towards the familiar in times of uncertainty, becoming authentic paradoxically creates anxiety. Through the trial and error of the change process, you will learn how to tolerate your anxiety, but as you begin to make changes that anxiety may be greater than if you had continued to be nice. You may find that choosing authenticity over niceness is a hard choice to make. You may decide not to make it.

If you do choose authenticity the process will be slow. To borrow from Paulo Coehlo's descriptive metaphor, the vitriol must be released slowly or the structure will crack. This slow release is aided by courage, the courage to believe in yourself. So, as new structures, or ways of being and behaving, are put into place, you can gradually release the old inclinations towards the silence and unquestioning compliance of niceness.

Although niceness and people-pleasing behaviour has often been pathologized as an individual problem, the behaviour is actually relational in nature. If each of us were a hermit we would never have to worry about the approval of another. Keep this thought in mind as you begin your journey out of niceness, and realize that you are not alone with the problem. Others, who may resist or attempt to thwart your efforts to interact in new ways, may be fearful of letting go of their own niceness. Reminding yourself of this possibility may make the work a bit easier.

THE SEED OF TRANSFORMATION: KINDNESS

The seed of transformation is contained within the definition of *nice* itself, which incorporates the notion of kindness. To be kind can, like niceness, be agreeable, appropriate, and polite, but kindness is less passive than these adjectives suggest. Kindness, when it takes the form of pre-empting an inclination to say something sarcastic or spiteful, is a passive behaviour, but in general it requires more active engagement and may sometimes involve actions or words offensive to any who are not its beneficiaries. For example, to be kind to a friend whose character is being attacked by another friend, you may have to offend, or at least disagree with, the assailant.

Kindness is other-directed, acted out from a position of empathy in which we suspend our own feelings, however briefly, in order to experience, vicariously, the feelings of others, for their benefit. Being kind demands awareness of the other, knowing by inquiring, watching, and imagining what would be an act of kindness to that person. It demands that we come out of ourselves and focus on the other and treat that person with respect. I walked up to a bank teller one day after a long wait in line. She took the work I handed her and began going through the papers speedily. I commented on her ability to work fast, and she said, "I know what it's like to wait. I've been on that side of the counter." In the most fundamental of daily exchanges, kindness is as basic as this, to stand symbolically in the shoes of others in our lives and to relate from that position of understanding and respect.

It can be easy to not know the experiences of others, but often we forget even our own experiences. When we grow up and become parents we forget what it was like to be a child. When we learn some new skill we forget what it was like when we did not know it because now it seems so obvious. Remembering these things marks the beginnings of kindness, when we can show compassion rather than impatience for our children's childish behaviours and the unskilled person's lack of knowledge.

At the same time, kindness demands that we care for ourselves. If we do not, our own needs may interfere with our perception of others' needs. If we have not taken care of our own needs we may feel conflicted about giving to others. Acts not freely performed lead to resentment. In a resentful state we may dupe ourselves into believing we are performing an act of kindness, while in reality we are serving ourselves in some way, being nice and suppressing feelings that are crying to be resolved.

The seed of transformation lies in kindness and honest attempts at authentic connection with other people. Social relations would undergo a significant change if we were all to adopt as our new motto "Don't be nice, be kind" and to challenge ourselves to know the difference between the two. To distinguish between them means informing ourselves about our impact on other people. It is not enough to be agreeable and to speak in bland words and phrases. We must mean what we say and say what we mean in a respectful manner. To know the difference would mean caring if we hurt someone and knowing when we do, which might involve facing some demons in ourselves. It means that we worry less about being rejected, come face to face with our beliefs, risk speaking about them, and risk hearing what others have to say. Kindness demands that we take responsibility for our own judgments of ourselves and that we do not turn others into our judges.

Being true to a principle of kindness would mean taking risks with friends and family, with employers and people we meet for social reasons. But then, we can find greater honesty in relationships and enjoy more authentic connections with people who share our values. Relationships are anchored in honesty rather than left to flounder in complicit deception. From an attitude of caring and courage we may become more tolerant of diversity. A core of kindness can liberate us from the invisible tyranny of niceness. As we hear what other people really think and express our own real thoughts we may find commonalities and compassion to replace disengagement or judgment. As we listen to the words of nice others, but also take care of our own needs, we may be less easily fooled and victimized. Nick was able to be direct and not-nice with Kevin because he was kind in his approach. He showed respect by being candid and kind. His comments were a critique and yet they were acceptable and even validating. In contrast, Heather, whose relationship with Richard I mentioned in Chapter One, forfeited an opportunity to be kind when she failed to tell him what she was really thinking and feeling about their relationship. The kind act — though it would have caused Richard pain at first — would have been to be direct with him, not keep him dangling and guessing.

Kindness moves us out of ourselves to embrace community and to care about people and the environment as we let our benevolence grow to incorporate next generations. Being authentic as it manifests through genuine acts of kindness is freeing, and when people feel free they love and express themselves verbally with greater ease. As people feel free they can appreciate the good qualities of another and let them know. I am still surprised at the number of beautiful women I have had as clients who were shocked when another woman paid them a sincere compliment. Perhaps the women they encounter are not freed enough from the cultural dictates of competition to appreciate and comment on the beauty of another or to comment without envy. All women are in the grip of a culture that places greater value on physical beauty than on other qualities they possess and encourages and reinforces a competitiveness that makes mutual generosity difficult to achieve.

As people feel free they can express their pleasure and also their displeasure without fear or malice. We are accustomed to equating displeasure with anger and so still find it difficult to express displeasure with kindness. Perhaps anger has been necessary for you to express your displeasure, providing the fuel to move you out of niceness in order to speak your mind. Then, when you have said your piece, you may find it is difficult to let go of the anger. This inability to separate anger from the expression of displeasure can have devastating effects on relationships. We must be able to deal with our own anger and express displeasure in such a way that the other person is able to take it in without feeling threatened. If not, the anger tends to take over and corrode the foundations of the relationship.

Expressing your displeasure without anger is possible if you address the acts that have led to your displeasure rather than condemning the whole person. You can then let your feelings be known, with respect. When you master this, the message to others will be that you are honest and truthful, fair and kind, that you are able to articulate your thoughts and feelings clearly, taking responsibility for them without blaming others. You can disagree or agree and in both cases show respect for the person you are addressing. They may not always like what they hear but they will know they can trust you to be direct and honest with them and that even though you may not agree with something they have done, you will not perform a character assassination. They, in turn, will be challenged to respond in the same way.

KNOW YOURSELF

If you decide to give up niceness you will have to learn how to speak your own mind, how to express your own thoughts and feelings. Earlier, I outlined the influences we encounter that silence us. These influences also teach us how and what to think and even what to feel. How then can you possibly know what you really think and feel? The problem demands that you return to basics and get to know yourself in fundamental ways through your body, mind, and emotions, becoming as transparent as possible to yourself and dispensing with the states of mind and emotion that do not serve you well.

Such is the importance of "knowing yourself" that it is an implicit part of each section in this chapter, however, I separate it out here because I want to alert you to possible impediments to your progress. The crux of the transformation lies in becoming self-reflective and honest, enabling you to relate to others with forthrightness, integrity, and openness. For this, you need to know yourself as well as possible and strive to arrive at a feeling of peace within yourself. You must decide how much control you need to have *over your own life*. Since the journey into self-knowledge will turn over rocks to expose unsavoury bits, it is important that you learn to accept that you will find them.

To relate honestly to others you need to know what your beliefs are, the limits of your ability to give, and the impact that silencing yourself will have on you. This might produce a challenge to move out of denial or laziness, to explore your world and relationships in a forthright way. Most of all, it is important to enjoy the journey into self-knowledge knowing that there are always more exciting things to learn.

PSYCHOLOGICAL KNOWING

Transformation out of niceness cannot be achieved by applying Band-Aids. It can happen only when you disturb the established core that has supported the self-deception that characterizes niceness. To reach a place of real peace and self-knowing you must shake out the false stability, the one that deserts you and leaves you trembling or fleeing in anxiety when you think someone disapproves of you. This objective presents a dilemma of major proportions, because knowing yourself well enough to shake your own foundation is one of the most difficult tasks imaginable. To know yourself completely, to be an unerring observer of yourself, is impossible. You can only move yourself in the direction of such knowing.

Daniel Gilbert, a professor of psychology at Harvard University, has carried out research on happiness. Along with psychologist Tim Wilson of the University of Virginia, economist George Loewenstein of Carnegie-Mellon, and psychologist Daniel Kahneman of Princeton, he has been studying how well people are able to predict what makes them happy. The task might seem easy, but his findings show that it is not. Many people think winning the lottery, taking a trip, or buying a new car or a house in the suburbs will make them happy. Gilbert found that people who acquire such contemporary emblems of happiness soon lose interest in them and move on to pursue other prizes, but over and over, they make the same errors of prediction. Despite repeated experiences the people he studied were unable to predict what would make them happy, unable to incorporate the information that these things really do not make them happy for anything more than a moment of their lives. Gilbert, with several colleagues, also found that people tend to overpredict fear and anxiety. In another study, researchers found that people do not easily learn from experience what their emotional reactions to events will be.

How do we know ourselves, or how can we judge whether we have arrived at some degree of knowing? Anyone who has experienced the long journey through psychotherapy, ridding oneself of the many ways of distancing from authentic feelings, would say that the resulting "new" self feels familiar. It feels familiar in the sense that it is comfortable to be in one's skin. It feels like a return, as if the self that is now felt was there all along but remained inaccessible. There is debate about whether a "true" self can remain hidden and emerge fully developed when a "false" self has been dissolved or whether the same self is always there, changing over time. I believe that when we reach a particular level of understanding a shift takes place in the way we experience ourselves. Although we have never experienced ourselves in that exact way before, it feels familiar because it is authentic.

At best, then, we can help ourselves to authenticity by engaging in a lifetime course of learning about ourselves. We can achieve some reasonable measure of insight that we can apply to our behaviour, taking us to deeper levels of understanding and more conscious ways of interacting with other people. This is one of the most exciting adventures in life, but like all great adventures it is full of challenges. Facing ourselves and finding out who we are can be shocking, painful, pleasurable, and exhilarating, all at the same time.

It may be that you have already come to know yourself a bit better by reading the previous chapters. The behaviours of niceness I described are a good place to start your personal examination. Do you tell white lies, say yes when you would rather say no, say no when you feel you want to say yes, accept responsibility that doesn't belong to you, or give away responsibility that belongs to you? Do you make yourself small or give too much? Are you able to confront yourself or do you look away into denial when you recognize your own foibles or the realities of your life, including emotional pain, that you have tried to avoid? Do you mean what you say?

Maybe, as you read the preceding chapters, you were surprised at ways of thinking about niceness that seemed self-evident. You may have been vaguely aware of them even though you never articulated them. Maybe you have spoken the thoughts in phrases such as "I've got to stop being so nice," or "What will people think," or "I want your honest opinion" but have never stopped to think through what you were saying and why you were saying it. The surprise of recognition in the earlier chapters may have propelled you into understanding that the journey into self-knowledge is one of bringing what we know at an unconscious or barely conscious level to consciousness or awareness. It is a process of confronting the packed-down cores of ourselves with truths we have chosen to ignore or somehow have not been able to see. It is like unpacking a hamper of laundry, piece by piece, and dealing with the grime that has been ground in through years of use. We must listen to our own doubts about ourselves — the honest doubts, not the self-pitying or attention-seeking doubts. If we are going to run the risk of living lives of authenticity, we must look inward. We must listen to and weigh with care and honesty the complaints about us of the people in our lives, not giving them carte blanche to decide for us, but to extract the truths that are consistent with our own examined thoughts about our need for change.

PHYSICAL KNOWING

Knowing yourself is not confined to your mental existence. It is also important to know your physical body, as well as possible. The two — mind and body — function together. In fact, the three — mind, body, and emotion — function together. The greater our understanding of these processes, the better we know ourselves and the better we know our reasons for behaving in particular ways.

Knowing yourself physically means reacquainting yourself with your body and the way it functions in a thorough manner. Your body has idiosyncrasies that can be the windows into greater understanding of its workings. Your body functions in cycles — this applies to both men and women. Your body has its unique responses to pleasure, excitement, a bad meal, a good meal, disappointments, and sadness. Notice when your stomach feels full, when you get cravings, at what point in your day fatigue strikes. Notice the way your body feels when you lie down after a busy day by paying attention to the various muscles from the top of your head to the bottoms of your feet. Notice where there is tension and where there is fatigue, then try relaxing your muscles, paying full attention as you do so. You are probably already aware of the signals that tell you when you are becoming ill and that your moods can fluctuate when you are feeling physically unwell. Sometimes you may feel and act rigid about something when you might be flexible if you were feeling better. Sometimes you may feel impatient with your loved ones and even pick on them when you are feeling ill. It is common to become moodier, angrier, grumpier, or unreasonable without realizing it when we are unwell or worried about our health. The state of our health affects our ability to be kind, to choose gentle words to express displeasure, and to see those we love in the best light. When our bodies feel ill or out of sorts, or we are preoccupied with weight or idiosyncrasies, relating to others becomes difficult.

It is of special importance to begin learning how these connections work within you because knowing your body will help you develop your inner voice of wisdom. This is the voice with deep links to the spheres of mind, body, and emotion. In order to make decisions that are right for you, in order to distinguish your own thoughts and opinions from those you hear in the media or from other people in your life, it is important to become attuned to the place of settledness or peace that tells you all spheres are in agreement. If you hear a voice saying, "This isn't right for you, don't do it," and your emotional state and body are calm *in that moment*, the spheres are in harmony and you overlook the voice at your peril. You will recall the story of Max, who heard his own unmistakable inner voice of wisdom on his wedding day, telling him he should not be marrying. He ignored the voice and soon realized that he should have listened to it.

Of course, if this particular thing is something of great significance, the calm will immediately give way to anxiety. You may remain anxious and your body will feel jittery and uncomfortable until you have accepted the wisdom that you heard and felt so distinctly and acted to resolve the conflict. For this reason, becoming conscious of the state of your body, mind, and emotions when you "know" something is right for you is fundamental. In difficult times the voice you hear may be fleeting, and it is important to know and heed what it is saying and to know how your body functions in a state of knowing.

Part of knowing yourself is to understand how much freedom you want for yourself. I pointed out that restrictions on dress are one form of silencing. At the same time, walking naked through the streets may not be the freeing solution for you. More likely, you need to consider the following questions: In what kind of clothing, or which articles of clothing, do you feel comfortable? What fabrics feel good on your body? What gives you the extent of freedom of movement you desire? What do you want to express to the world through your dress? Are you over-concerned about the way you are expressing your image in the world at the expense of more important aspects such as comfort and freedom of movement? You need to know how much freedom you desire in all areas of your life in order to decide when and how to act and interact with others.

IDENTIFY YOUR FEARS

Fear lies at the bottom of the anxiety that leads to compliance and silence. Whatever your own particular fear, it is the motivator for silence and obedience. Earlier I identified the fear of other people's judgments and abandonment. Look inward and be honest with yourself: are you worried about others' feelings and opinions when you silence yourself, or are you worried what they will think of you and whether their opinion equals emotional or physical abandonment? You must give up this and other fears in order to move on, but the nature of fear is such that it can be and often is self-perpetuating. Fear fosters more fear. Despite efforts to plug it up and suppress it, it hangs on and emerges at the slightest provocation, growing larger in the process.

When you attempt to give up niceness and find yourself shrouded in anxiety, ask yourself, What am I afraid of? The question may be hard to answer. Fear is something we experience in the present about some-thing that may happen to us in the future, whether it is the immediate future or the distant future. If there is no immediate real threat, chances are the fear you experience now has origins that lie buried in the past or perhaps in a long-held suggestion that something horrible might befall you under certain circumstances. Chances are, when you begin to examine the fear you will find that it is disproportionate to the circum-stances. The fear that switches on when you attempt to give up niceness has probably been established in childhood, and that is the emotional era you return to when you find yourself in a difficult situation, or in a situation where you wish to be well thought of. Your long-embraced concern may be a fear of rejection or abandonment, a fear of being ridiculed or left alone, a fear of being punished, or a fear of being seen as inadequate. These fears arose from the reality of your childhood experience when you were unknowing and highly vulnerable.

Although you may not always be able to acknowledge and use them, as an adult you have resources that you did not have in childhood to help you deal with most situations. By identifying them, learning how to use them, and creating more of them you can move yourself out of that childhood place. If you are feeling pressured to say something, take your time, take a deep breath, and focus on what you want to say. Give yourself permission to take up space to speak at your own pace. Give yourself permission to obtain the information you require in order to make informed decisions, remembering that there are no stupid questions. Create an emotional bubble around yourself that is nurturing and stare down the fears that flit into your mind. Ask yourself if you can truly be hurt in the situation. Reassure yourself with memories of situations in which you have been successful and keep these memories in mind to recall when you need them.

If you find that your fear is beyond your understanding, that you cannot abide the anxiety that occurs when you attempt to change your behaviour or you cannot maintain new behaviours, you may need the help of a professional psychotherapist to dismantle it. Fear is like water dripping from the ceiling of your house or apartment. You can see it and hear it, but locating its source in order to do the necessary repair work can be difficult because water travels a meandering pathway before revealing itself. Many times I have found that some seemingly innocuous events in early childhood stand out and impact on adult situations. A client, Bertie, remembered standing at the door of her new classroom as a child of six and a newcomer to the country. From her brief observations of children in the playground she knew she was different than they, and waiting there, she felt afraid that they would make fun of her. As an adult, she had always known about that event — it had not been forgotten — but it had been relegated to the comic folklore of her youth and its full fear-generating impact had remained unconscious. Two decades after the event she reported to me that she had had a long struggle with irrational fear overwhelming her in situations that were manageable, from an objective standpoint. Every time certain events occurred in her life she was, symbolically, standing back at that classroom door, waiting to be rejected and mocked.

Immanuel Kant said, "Immaturity is the inability to use one's own understanding without the guidance of another." Although we all need guidance when we are young and at other times in our lives when we encounter new and difficult situations of which we have no experience, fear binds us, beyond their usefulness, to those we accept, or assign to ourselves, as guides. Finding your way through fear is an important step towards emotional maturity, and if you cling to your guides instead of challenging yourself to take that step in their presence, you may have to relinquish them so you can move on.

If you follow news stories about violent behaviour with a critical eye and ear, you will know that — wars aside — people's fear of being killed or injured by a stranger is disproportionate to the reality. In fact, most people who are killed or injured know their assailants. Nonetheless, the focus on violence in the media, whether on the news or programs designed for entertainment, has led people to believe that the world outside our personal domains is a much more dangerous place than it is in reality. Growing up in a world where we are taught not to question means we do not see opportunities to shed light on our fears. We lose the ability to explore deeply, so the fear grows. Like children who are afraid of the dark and whose parents do not turn on the light and search every corner of the room with them, we are left in the emotional dark, our fears growing while we attempt to pre-empt any activity that might set them off. But this method encourages the growth of fear.

One way through this kind of maze is to get out of your chair, away from the television set and sensational media, and become comfortable moving around in new places in the world. Similarly, your fear of rejection or abandonment may have grown to proportions unrelated to reality. Get out into your world and challenge yourself to see who is in it and what the real issues are. Take a friendly companion with you if you need to, at first, but get out there. Give up guides who keep you in the dark or misinformed. The news of lower crime rates does not make newspaper-selling headlines. What does make headlines is sensational or sensationalized crime, and yet in many cities across North America, studies indicate that crime has declined. Read widely so you are informed about the differences expressed. Believe what you see for yourself and become skeptical about fear-inducing news media. Give up the old, internalized authorities that have kept you obedient and imbued with fear.

The threat of terrorism has ruled the United States since September 11, 2001. It has been used to justify a war against Iraq that many believe was waged to gain control of the rich oil resources there. The war and the reconstruction of Iraq are costing American citizens billions of dollars and many lives. Is the threat of terrorism real, and is the Bush administration right in pursuing their war? Many are debating these questions, and the answers are far from providing outright affirmation. What is real are schools closing due to inadequate funding. What is real are tax cuts that benefit the most wealthy in the country.

What is real is that many middle-class families in the United States must pay as much as $1,000 — and some pay even more — each month for health insurance. The United States Census Bureau reported in October 2003 that 43.6 million Americans have no health insurance, an increase of 5.3 percent over the previous year. What is real are the threats to the national parks systems by people who decimate virgin forests in order to build houses that only the rich can afford.

Be sure your fears, when you have them, are appropriately placed.

TAKE CARE OF YOUR OWN NEEDS

Taking care of your own needs does not mean becoming or remaining self-centred or greedy or always putting your own interests ahead of other significant people in your life. "Put yourself first" is a message that has been distorted in recent years. Many people seem to think of it as a way of taking all they can, of justifying their greed and disregard for other people and the world they live in. This greed is damaging to all who have it and all who encounter it.

Putting yourself first means attending to your own needs for nurturance, security, and some sense of fulfillment. When you travel by plane the flight attendants play an orientation message in which they mention procedures to follow while travelling with small children. You are instructed that if oxygen masks drop down from their overhead container you must first put one on yourself, then put one on your child. Similarly, you must breathe life into yourself before you are able to give to another, before you are able to judge what you have available to give to another. Call it the paradox of self-interest — you must take care of your own needs, not to become oblivious but in order to expand, to see beyond yourself, to embrace and relate to others in meaningful ways. If you deny yourself you may not be able to understand the needs of others. On the other hand, if you overindulge yourself, taking everything you can whenever you can, you will fail to see your impact on other people or the world that supplies your needs.

If you have fallen so far out of touch with your own needs — from either denial or greed — that you do not know what they are, you may need professional help. You may be unable to say no to requests when you need to and you may find that you have little space for yourself in your own life. You may not be able to see that your schedule is packed beyond a peaceful existence or that it is packed because you are afraid of what you might feel if you stopped for a moment. You may not see that underlying some of your problems is the belief that you don't deserve any better. You may feel fearful or guilty. You may not want to know the truth about yourself because then you might need to change. Change involves decisions about what to keep and what to discard, and that seems too onerous. I am saying this knowing that many people *think* they know these things and believe they just cannot do anything about them. In most of those instances people are conscious, in part, of what is happening in their lives, but the meaningfulness of it has not been integrated, in the same manner that Bertie's fear at the door of her new classroom was not integrated. Therefore, warnings about stress, denial, doing too much, or not facing fears and their implications for well-being are either given a cursory nod or thought to be somebody else's problems. For all these reasons it may be necessary to get help in order to move towards real insight. What we cannot allow ourselves to know is sometimes better heard from a professional.

In my practice I have found that people need help learning to nurture themselves. Although the focus and point of the help is emotional nurturance, I often begin with something as fundamental as dinner, reasoning that many people, from anorexic to obese, are starving. To make the experience of nurturing concrete, I encourage them to savour meals, to notice the colours and shapes of food on the plate, to enjoy the aromas, play with the textures on their tongues — to make it a whole and sensual experience. Of necessity, this demands that people stop reading or watching television when they're eating. I encourage them to focus intently on their food and the activity of eating.

After trying this exercise people are surprised at the extent to which the experience of eating has become an unconscious act, as they mindlessly consume whatever is on their plates until the plate is empty. Sometimes they barely remember the act of eating and they have no sense of when they are satisfied — usually they feel very unsatisfied even if the sensation in their bodies is fullness. These are the people who reach for soda and chips an hour after dinner or who feel the urge to follow up every meal with a trip to the ice cream store. They have lost touch with what is nurturing to them at the most fundamental level. Hazel, a client who typified many women and men I have seen, told me about devouring large pizzas in the quiet afternoons she spent at home alone, only to be amazed that she had eaten the whole thing before she realized what she was doing. When I asked her to turn off the television and focus on the food she ate she was shocked to discover that she did not enjoy certain staples in her diet but had been consuming them out of habit. Concentrating on the act of eating led her to revolutionize both her eating patterns and the foods she ate.

In another discussion with Nick, who broached the subject of his partner's shaved beard, he revealed that he felt compelled to immediately reply "I love you" whenever Kevin said those words to him. What's more, he believed that Kevin was feeling and responding the same way to him. Nick said he did this because he was afraid of losing Kevin. Deducing that they each felt some anxiety about losing the other I suggested to Nick that they try not to repeat the love words, but to take them in when the other said them, to let the words wash over them and warm them. I encouraged him to use his creativity to enhance the experience, imagining that the words were showering his body with warmth and love.

Too often, we take the wonderful things people say to us and toss them aside either by not believing them, feeling unworthy, overestimating the value of humility, or by fearing that if we don't return them at that very moment we shall be rejected or seem rejecting. We do not let the affectionate words of our loved ones nurture us and thus we treat the gift with disrespect. Nick and Kevin tried accepting the gift, letting the words wash over them and basking in the glow of the other's love. They adopted it as their way of accepting the expressed love of the other. In doing so, they allowed each other to fulfill the need to be the giver of love, a need we all have. For both, anxiety about the relationship decreased. Each was able to give up the worry that his partner was responding to be nice: they were freed to say the words whenever they felt like doing so. Nick began to feel much better about himself and worthy of Kevin's love. Nick reported that Kevin also benefited from this change.

Self-nurturing may also take the form of making time to pursue a favourite activity, carving out periods of relaxation in the day, or bringing in help to deal with chores or projects that have become unmanageable and stress-filled. It may take the form of spending time with people who feel good about themselves — authentic people who feel comfortable with themselves. It may be finding work that is more satisfying, or making education a lifelong experience.

As the nurturing of themselves is accomplished in this and other ways, people find themselves being kinder to others and happier with them. There is a paradox, for as these people nurture themselves they appear to be "nicer." But the essence of the niceness has been transformed. No longer are they taking on the mantle of niceness to silence themselves in some way. They are not reverting to old behaviours. Although some of the new interactions and behaviours are similar to the old, there is a profound difference. In at least a part of their lives these people are making choices that break away from the deceptive selflessness of niceness. They are freed to say kind things and give up the emptiness of nice responses, but they are also freed to be direct and even respectfully confrontational, if need be.

The reinforcement for being direct can be surprising. A client, Kimberly, was upset with her former roommate for leaving behind heavy boxes full of items he no longer wanted when he moved out. Kimberly vented to me, and I encouraged her to tell him how she felt about it, to let him know that it was difficult for her to haul the boxes downstairs to the side of the road for garbage pickup. She was hesitant, but when she next saw him, she took the chance to speak her mind. As calmly and non-judgmentally as she could, she told him about her disappointment that he had left the boxes for her to deal with and that it had created difficulty for her. He apologized but then became quiet, and Kimberly thought she might not hear from him again. She was surprised and happy, then, when he telephoned a few days later to say that he was glad she spoke up, that it meant to him that she cared enough about their friendship to be honest with him.

KNOW WHAT YOU STAND FOR

We are raised with values — qualities that we hold in high regard — and the usual first agents of conveying those values are our parents. Niceness is one value you may have been taught, and in the process of acquiring niceness you would have missed out on acquiring other values that are important to you. You may be purporting to hold one set of values but acting from another set. That is, you say yes when you mean no but deliver your words without coming to terms with the sense of "no" that lurks behind them.

In the transformation process it is essential to bring to functional consciousness the values that you can live, not to which you merely give lip service while you do something else. A place to start is to identify the values with which you have been raised. What values did your parents and other people pass along? Did they live those values themselves, and if not, what does that mean to you? How do the discrepancies between what your teachers taught you and what they lived themselves affect you as you determine the course of your own life? Ask yourself if the values you were raised with make sense to you. If you have adopted other values, think about where you learned them. Ask yourself if the old and the new values fit with your idea of who you are and how you want to relate to people. Reconsider those that no longer make sense or hinder your development. Jettison them if necessary. Be brutally honest with yourself. Give up all lies. Begin to act on the values you say you hold dear, if you have not been doing so.

KNOW YOURSELF IN RELATION TO YOUR ENVIRONMENT

The environment we live in consists of many elements. I have already described some examples of human-made environments and the ways they silence us. Families, peer groups, schools, churches, hospitals, government agencies, and the workplace are all environments we may find ourselves in at some time or another in our lives. All of them are composed of human and inanimate components that affect us in our day-to-day activities and upon which we, in turn, leave our marks, in both a literal and figurative sense. There may be a temptation to think that all schools provide the same environment, as do all families, all hospitals, and such. However, they are different, even though components are similar, and the more you understand about them the easier it will be to ferret out the unique qualities of each when you need to know what they are.

KNOW YOURSELF IN RELATION TO OTHER PEOPLE

You do not live alone on this planet. I do not live alone on this planet. Neither does your partner, your children, or your parents — no one lives alone on this planet. What's more, we could not survive without each other. What other people contribute to our lives and we to theirs makes up one of the most powerful influences we feel throughout our lives. Therefore, it is important to know ourselves in relation to them.

We must develop an awareness of the world of people outside ourselves. How does it look, what is it all about, and how does it impact on us? How do we impact on it and contribute to creating it? What do other people *really* see in us that is not loaded with projections of their own difficulties or expectations? What do we project onto them or to what extent do we see them as they see themselves?

Think about your expectations of other people. Do you want them to be nice to you? Knowing, now, that niceness means silencing opinions, perhaps this wish is misguided. Ironically, a component of niceness is caring what other people think, but if you want other people to be nice to you and they are, you may never know what they think. If you and they desire a relationship of mutual withholding, unknowing, and second-guessing, you may continue to be nice. Perhaps, however, it is more to your benefit that people are honest with you, that they provide you with the kind of mirror that reflects you from a different angle, even though the honesty may be hard to hear.

The seed of transformation is kindness, and so it is important to examine your understanding of the concept of kindness and the extent to which it guides your treatment of other people. To approach this question through a back door, think about situations in which you hid behind the mask of niceness and, out of the eye of scrutiny, became impatient, intolerant, or even pushy. Think of ways that you might have responded instead with kindness. What effort would have been involved? Would you have had to give something up or speak differently? Can you envision acting with kindness in such situations in the future?

Think about fear you might have as you approach other people and its impact on the interaction. If you are concerned about their accepting you it will be difficult to focus on the interaction. Think about the ways this fear can distort exchanges between you and others both in the short and long terms.

KNOW YOURSELF IN RELATION TO THE PHYSICAL WORLD

The environment we live in also includes the physical world of animals, plants, earth, air, and water. Like human-made environments, the natural environment impacts on us and we on it. Despite the fact that people try to ignore it, distance themselves from it, use it, abuse it, or control it, the natural environment exerts its powerful force on us every day. We cannot live without breathing air, drinking water, and eating food grown from the earth. The higher the quality of these elements, the healthier we are. Many people relate changes in arthritic pain or asthma to changes of climate or weather. I am not prone to headaches, and so when I have one it is notable. Almost without fail, if I have headache pain a quick check of my wall barometer confirms that the needle has moved to "change."

The weather and climate affect us physically, and that which affects us physically affects us emotionally and in our relationships with others. We are friendlier and more secure-feeling people when we are healthy and when our needs for food, water, and shelter are satisfied. Sitting by a stream or walking along an ocean shore listening to the sound, feeling the rhythm, and smelling the water-scented or salty air tends to have a calming effect. When you walk through a tree-canopied neighbourhood in the heat of summer your body is cooled and refreshed and you feel relaxed. Sun shining on snow reflects a brilliance that warms us physically and exhilarates us emotionally. When you are exposed to cold temperatures you huddle and shiver and turn your attention inward. Walk without a hat and loose covering for your body in a desert and you risk sunstroke and mental disorientation. Jumping waves on a Caribbean beach is happily exhausting. Thus, both physical and emotional responses typify your reactions in each of these instances.

Although it is not something you think about in the course of daily life, all of these conditions, objects, and elements impact on you. Walk into a room or an outdoor space and you notice smells and colours that either invite you or repel you. A table in the middle of the room determines the traffic patterns and seating arrangements and even influences the kind of conversations that take place. Landscaping in front of a house or commercial building suggests formality or casualness. Any of these circumstances might elicit a response from you. You might feel comfortable or not, calm or tense, open or stiff. Often you are so busy that you do not notice these responses and simply carry on, vaguely aware that something has changed but too preoccupied to care. You may not notice, but you react and respond to what you encounter in any situation nonetheless.

When I wrote about the impact of education I stressed the importance of critical thinking. One reason becomes clear here. Critical thinking is important as we make contact with our environments. Examining our environments with questions that challenge our accepted knowledge helps us know them in their complexity so we can then understand what our role is in them, what is expected of us, what works for us and what does not.

To know it better, contact your world through your senses. What do you see? Hear? Smell? Taste? Feel? How does the information your senses provide agree or disagree with what you have been told by the figures in your world who act as authorities, judges, and commentators? Think about possible reasons for your emotions and reactions and then examine them so you begin to know your own sequence of emotional events. Ask yourself: Is there another way to think about this?

To know your environment better, contact it through your emotions. What do you feel when you walk into a room or a park or join a group of people? Do you become anxious, saddened, joyful, hopeful, or hopeless? To what extent does your mood depend on the others present? Ask yourself: Would you feel different in the same situation another time?

To know your environment better, contact it through your intellect. Do the things you see, read, and hear discussed make sense to you? Are there gaps in stories that require explanation? Are there commentators of integrity that have proven themselves over time? Ask yourself: Are there other ways to think about what you have heard and read and seen?

Work on heightening your awareness so that you develop greater clarity with respect to the sensations coming from outside and those coming from inside you. Although we are influenced by environment we also tend to insulate ourselves from it because of sensory overload. Take time to relearn so you know what you are ignoring and what you are retaining. Do you really want the loudest messages to be your guides? Ask yourself who is sending them and if you agree. Or do you feel you must agree because if you were honest you might have to give up some convenience, privilege, toy, treat, lifestyle, or companions?

Check your behaviour. Are you making full eye contact when you speak to others or do your eyes dart away? Do you feel uneasy when eyes meet for more than a glance? Do you feel more comfortable relating side by side rather than full face?

When you look outward with an open mind and open senses your world may appear to change. The reality is that you change when you open yourself. You begin to see shades of grey where you did not realize they existed and perhaps did not want them to exist. You are implicitly confronted and challenged to position yourself in your environment according to what you now know.

These ways of knowing yourself are both prerequisites and companions to giving up niceness. When you silence yourself you shut out awareness. As you learn to know yourself you reclaim aspects of yourself that have been forgotten or shelved just outside of awareness. They are called into service in the transformation that occurs as you let go of niceness.

CHAPTER 8
LETTING GO OF NICENESS

LETTING GO OF niceness is nothing more than embracing a state of authenticity. Sometimes joyful, sometimes scary, authenticity is the much sought after and coveted peace of mind, body, and spirit. Knowing yourself as well as possible, in the ways I pointed out in the previous chapter, assists your progress towards authenticity. Self-knowledge is both the precursor and companion to the functions I discuss in this chapter — the development of intuition, commitment to your words, choosing when to comply, saying the unsayable, releasing passion, and parenting to reduce the transmission of niceness. Since the acquisition of self-knowledge is a lifelong project, these functions are also continuous works-in-progress. It would be unrealistic to think that you will be able to change long-standing ways of interacting with other people by applying a few simple insights or suggestions. Deepening your understanding of yourself and interacting on the basis of that new understanding will take time and continued effort. At the same time, when you take the first tentative steps into authentic relating by changing your usual ways of interacting you will experience a sense of exhilaration and renewed confidence that makes the journey less intimidating.

DEVELOP YOUR INTUITION, YOUR PLACE OF PEACE, YOUR INNER VOICE OF WISDOM

How many times have you made a decision, even though you "knew" from the beginning of the decision-making process that you should have made a different choice, then found later that the choice you made was not the best one? I believe we have an intuitive sense from which we become alienated as pressure to accept the wisdom of others mounts. I call this the "inner voice of wisdom," and we ignore it at our peril.

Thoreau said, "Why should we ever go abroad, even across the way, to ask a neighbour's advice? There is a nearer neighbour within us incessantly telling us how we should behave. But we wait for the neighbour without to tell us of some false, easier way." It is when we succumb to that neighbour outside ourselves that we lose our way and behave in ways that are not good for us. Similarly, a neighbour waits for us, making us the unwitting experts on their behaviour. We become embroiled in a circularity of niceness based on the assumption that others know best what we should do. In the process, we lose touch with our original thoughts and feelings even in the face of having no real idea what the other person, whom we have made our judge, is thinking or feeling. Yet we continue to relate as if we do know, all too often heading down paths that are full of mistaken notions, all too often misleading people about our real needs and desires, in the service of being nice.

Our voice of wisdom is reduced to nothing more than a whimper when the forces of niceness decree that we pay more attention to the opinions of others than to our own and when we become overwhelmed with all the information that confronts us on a day-to-day basis. This information is dispensed to tell us what we need — vehicles, houses, trips, fast food, or whatever others are trying to sell or promote — because, they say, it has worked for them. It tells us what we must do to be happy — be thinner, put the latest faddish clothes on our bodies, drink beer, wine, or alcohol, drive vehicles, take drugs, become a relationship junkie, follow a particular career path. It tells us what to think, say, do, feel, even see, as if we cannot see for ourselves. It tells us during every waking moment of the day through print media, television, advertising on computers, radio, and the people we meet in passing who have internalized the same messages and act as reinforcers of the messages we get from the non-human sources.

All of these entities are vying for our attention, and the din is deafening us to our own thoughts and feelings. To get in touch with your inner voice, give yourself time away from the stimulation that bombards you throughout your waking hours. Give yourself time to mull what you have seen and heard, to consider what you feel about it, and to employ the methods of getting in touch with your physical body that I have already discussed. Consider your thoughts of agreement or disagreement with what you have heard, balancing these thoughts with your physical and emotional feelings. Your inner voice is not something you can summon at any time, but it is something you can hear and heed if you make emotional space for it to emerge.

You may not realize that your inner voice has worked for you in the past. There have been times in your life when you have heard it, when you "knew" the right decision for you and you made it. Remember one of those times now and try to recapture the feelings that accompanied the knowing. Recapture as well as you can the sense of knowing and what it felt like in every sense and sensation. When you recapture those elements you will have a strong sense of your own place of peace, the one that accompanies the knowing and the one that will be your guide for future decisions.

Developing your inner voice to a level that you can hear and heed it is a life's work. You can start this work by educating yourself about the world and the people in it and by learning about yourself. Start with your immediate world and notice more of it, further outside you, in ever-expanding breadth and depth. The learning includes an integration of this growing knowledge with your feelings about what you have learned. Then free yourself to allow your body, mind, and emotions to work together to process the information. The inner voice is an informed voice, an integration of thought and feeling. It is not an impulse luring you down a destructive path, but rather a knowledgeable guide. It may be saying truths to you through your own words, but you dilute its power to influence you by ignoring your own words. Take time to hear what you are saying and observe your behaviour. If you have ever said, "I've got to stop being so nice" or "No more Mr. Nice Guy," believe yourself!

HONESTY

Most people, if asked, would say they want to hear the truth from others. But many have a hard time speaking and accepting truth. So transformation begins with a close look at yourself. If you think life would be easier if people spoke the truth, look at yourself first. Do you speak honestly and openly? If you think you should spare people the reality of your opinions and feelings, ask yourself, Am I afraid of something?

If you are hiding parts of yourself and keeping them under the cover of niceness, ask yourself, Do I believe that these parts of myself are bad or harmful to others or myself? If you do, perhaps you need to change them. If you do not, your task may be to integrate them into the personality you show to other people, to narrow the gap between external presentation and internal sense of yourself. Your task is to integrate the different parts of your personality. How to do this? Begin to express the hidden parts in public. Let more people see more of you.

Dishonesty is a fundamental feature of niceness, and learning to be honest is at the core of transformation. You may consider yourself an honest person, even though your self-examination through the earlier chapters gave you cause to doubt this. *Do* doubt it. Doubt your honesty and examine your words and behaviour on a daily basis and do not be easy on yourself. Ask yourself some direct questions: Are you being honest when you tell your friend you will be glad to help her move and then beg off because of pressing commitments or some mild illness? Would it be more honest to tell her that you cannot help her move right from the start to allow her to make other arrangements? Are you being honest when you convince yourself you need something you cannot afford or want to be with someone who treats you with disrespect? Are you being honest when you promise someone you will help him find a job? Are you being honest when you make promises to your children? Are you being honest when you say it is no problem to stay late to finish work?

Are you being honest when you tell your spouse that you and the woman at the office are only friends? You may just be talking, but is it only friendship or something deeper? A client, Wanda, became intrigued with a man working in her office. At first they had snippets of conversation when they happened to meet at the coffeemaker. Soon she was taking note of the times when he was there and she began to schedule her own coffee refills around them. Then they began to continue their conversations outside the office over lunch. Wanda had told her husband about some of the conversations until she and the man began to have lunches together. Then she told her husband only that she went out with "friends" for lunch. Finally, at the company's summer picnic, she and the man walked into the woods together and kissed. But to her husband, Wanda continued to declare the man no more than a colleague who happened to be a friend. Despite her actions and despite the fantasies she had about a life with the man, she denied the truth even to herself. Her actions denied that she was carrying on with a seduction that had the potential to cause her husband and the man's wife a great deal of pain and to endanger two marriages.

Are you being honest when you ask another person a question? Do you want a simple answer to the question or are you expecting something else from them? You might need to rule out the possibility that some of your questions are thinly disguised quests for reassurance of some sort, to relieve you of guilt or assuage your anxiety. Perhaps the waiter's question to my partner, Larry — was the soup worth waiting for? — reflected his concern for Larry's pleasure, or perhaps he was seeking reassurance that he had not put off a customer. A more respectful follow-up might have been a simple question — is the soup satisfactory? — and improved service for the remainder of the meal.

We have become adept at using props to help us with our dishonesty, one of which is the ubiquitous cellphone. The *New York Times* carried a story by Kate Zernike describing the new attitudes towards lateness, in which she cites the research of James E. Katz and The Context-Based Research Group. She found that New Yorkers suggested that they have learned to delay or avoid things they would rather not do. Instead of showing up for a date with a friend or a business meeting they call on their cellphones to say they will be late. This is done when they have already missed the appointed hour by a few minutes. Zernike claims that some of these avoiders make multiple calls at intervals during the evening or meeting time, with the same message, sometimes failing to show up at all because after an evening of messages, time to meet has run out. These people do not say they would rather delay or avoid, they simply say they will be late. What are they doing instead? One person, scheduled to meet her mother, had stopped to look at pottery.

The profoundly troubling part is the collusion between the caller and the called. Callers interviewed found nothing wrong with this behaviour. In fact, they felt exonerated because they had called. Those called agreed. They accepted the behaviour. One psychoanalyst said that a client was ten minutes late for every appointment, so they started each session on the cellphone.

These examples beg the question, What does the behaviour mean, to both parties? Are those who called worried about being late, and do they believe that possibility leaves them with no options if they want to hold on to the relationship? Do they accept the behaviour from other people? Are callers ambivalent about attending the date or meeting? Are they holding on to one possibility while looking for others they might prefer? Do they want to meet the person for the pleasure of his or her company, or is there something more self-serving and disturbing about it, such as a list of phone numbers in their cellphone address book? Is there a belief that this behaviour looks important and desirable to other people? Does the person who was called need to feel wanted, so much that he or she is willing to excuse shabby treatment? Are there issues about being left, or about disappointing someone important, that are not being addressed?

There are no simple answers to these and a multitude of other questions that might arise in an exploration of the problem. Almost everyone is late from time to time. An understanding and forgiving friend, boss, or partner is a gift at those times, and a cellphone is a line of connection that can be both reassuring and caring for all concerned. But *occasional* is not a synonym for *chronic*.

We live in a culture that does not accept honesty with ease. All the messages of silence and obedience encourage lies. Friends may become distant if you tell them you do not want to spend time with them because you are not in the mood to go out, or if you have confronted them on some issue. Companies and institutions do not accept that people may need a day or two off work to hibernate, to do nothing but recover because they have been feeling stressed or harassed. People who need this must find other ways to get the time they need. They call in to work and say they are sick, extend lunches with colleagues or clients, and sign up for conferences that are meaningless to them. They rationalize that they must take a client out for a golf game in order to keep an account active when the reality is less clear. They must be dishonest to get the time off that they need in order to function as well as possible when they are at work. For people who are so nice that they cannot conceive of doing such a thing, the stress sometimes becomes unbearable and they eventually find that they really are too sick to go to work, sometimes for months at a time.

B E C O M I N G   T R U T H F U L   A N D   H O N E S T

Are you being honest when you tell your partner nothing is wrong, then launch into a silent sulk for hours? Are you being honest when, in the heat of anger, you shout out all the faults you have ever seen in your partner over the years? Silence and rage are both powerful expressions, but of what? Both of these reactions can be terrifying for both parties because they are divisive. The overall reality of the relationship gets lost when these behaviours are used to deal with issues arising in relationships. Lying, even with the best of intentions, produces the same corrosive effect.

Nick, whom I mentioned before, was afraid to talk with his partner, Kevin, about a shaved beard. Of course, he was also afraid to be direct about many other topics, but this one provides a good example of what happened when Nick decided to try to break out of the restrictions of niceness that had made him lie to his partner about this simple matter. After the session in which we discussed his feelings about being honest about the beard, Nick went home, told Kevin we had discussed the issue, and said he preferred the beard to the new clean-shaven look but that he had not wanted to hurt his feelings by saying so. He added that even though he preferred the old look, he was still just as attracted to him without it and he supported whatever choice Kevin made. To Nick's surprise, Kevin said he also preferred the beard. He was not at all offended by Nick's honest appraisal and, in fact, appreciated the honesty.

Honesty is tricky in such cases because sometimes people say what is on their minds in ways that are hurtful. Psychologically, there is a great deal more to such a situation than simple truth. Behind the comments, often defended as truth, that are expressed so often through sarcasm, mocking, or angry bluntness, there is a complicated mix of anger, disappointments, and even delusions.

Nick did not bludgeon Kevin with his critique, nor did he cloak a blunt verbal instrument in a joke so he could convey his feelings indirectly and still feel like a nice person. These approaches would have revealed problems with Nick and the relationship and produced a different result. When people are uncomfortable saying what they think — because they are not being honest or because they are holding on to feelings that interfere with direct expression — they may speak with an angry or sarcastic tone, as if anger is an integral part of directness. But it is not. Giving up the nice response means opening up and speaking from a place of peace within oneself.

Even though Nick felt anxious about being honest, he offered his comments with kindness and sensitivity. As he repeated to me what he had said to Kevin it became clear that he had been direct, with no hints of anger or condescension. He spoke the kind of words that can be spoken with full eye contact rather than uncomfortable glances. Kevin responded with appreciation and the discussion opened the door for a new way of relating, one based on honesty rather than fear.

This was a valuable lesson for both Nick and his partner. He could see that the old way of relating was creating difficulties in the relationship because he never dealt with his anxiety about being loved and lovable. The changes were enlightening, and he began to see that a relationship based on honesty was desirable even if he was not immediately able to change. Our first steps were to address the issue of his dishonesty and his fear of losing Kevin. Nick began to imagine that a world without niceness may be possible and that it would be a much more freeing world in which to live. It also meant he needed to make some tough decisions about other disclosures to Kevin.

Harriet Lerner writes about honesty versus truth in her book *The Dance of Deception*. She distinguishes between fleeting reactions and emotions from enduring principles that form values and a belief system, values such as kindness and compassion. Truth-telling on impulse may accomplish the opposite of what you would hope for if you were to take a moment to reflect on what is most important to you. For example, when you and your lover quarrel you may be tempted to blurt out all the little complaints you have been harbouring, in a moment of "truth." But when the dust settles and you two resolve your differences, you may find that truth has created a crack in your relationship that can grow to become a crevice and then an impassable canyon if there are very many other such instances. If you had stopped to consider what you were saying, you might have concluded that this did not express your honest feelings about her. Yes, you felt irritated many times over some habit or other and in that moment of disagreement it assumed proportions that seemed insurmountable. You may feel diminishing hope for your relationship. But despite that, you care about her and appreciate many of the qualities that far outweigh the irritations that seemed so important when you were angry. You care about her and do not want to hurt her feelings or risk destroying your relationship.

The honest response is to hold back the impulse to hurt through "truth" because you are feeling frustrated and hurt. Exploring your irritation further you may find that it originates not with your partner but with some other person or situation at a time when you felt power-less to do anything about it, or it may originate in some uncomfortable feelings about yourself. On the other hand, as you think about these possibilities you may conclude that there was something about the behaviour that you need to address and it is important, then, to find a way to address it with kindness and directness. These principles apply not only to intimate relationships but also to any other kind of relationship. If an intimate relationship is floundering and you believe your happiness lies elsewhere, barking cruel comments at your partner will only add to the pain of separation for you both, and it suggests you may not be happy with your assessment and decisions. You cannot be angry and happy at the same time.

Your expressions of feeling may not be honest if, in the moment, negative, or even positive, emotions are raging. Declarations of love made in the moment may not hold up for the long term if they are spoken from impulse or for any reason other than to express honest feeling. Know what your feelings are and express yourself in accordance with them. Sometimes this will mean overcoming your anger in the moment. Perhaps you will need to know more about the catalyst so you can resolve your anger or your sudden feelings of love in a non-destructive way rather than in "truths" that make up only a small part of your honest feeling.

In the self-examination of your honesty it is important to question your reactions to issues that upset you, especially where these issues involve diversity among people. If you find yourself expressing prejudice towards groups of people, whether it is because they are different from you in their country of origin, religion, language, financial position, gender, or sexual or political orientation, it will be important to get to know people in those groups on a personal level. Listen to their stories and ask them about their thoughts and hopes and experiences. You may find that your responses to them are no different than to members of your own family. You may like some, tolerate some, and dislike or at least disagree with others. You may find that you are enlightened about them enough to know that diversity can mean that people who attend your church do not all believe what you believe and people who may seem very different than you may share the same beliefs. You may realize that difference is not a good enough reason to denounce an entire group. Your honest opinion is an enlightened one, developed by educating yourself. It is not a repetition of words or clichés that you have adopted without thinking in order to attain benign acceptance.

There may be times when you lie for the sake of expediency. You may feel you need to move the situation you are in along, and an honest response will lead to more time than you can afford. If that is something you do, be sure of one thing: never believe that your lie is truth. Know it for what it is and accept that you have lied, otherwise you have also lied to yourself and closed one door into consciousness.

COMMIT TO YOUR WORDS

Earlier I pointed out that the language of niceness includes a far too frequent use of the word *nice* itself. I called this a lazy way of communicating, leaving to the listener to decide what you mean rather than expressing, with precision, what it is you think and feel. An important component of transformation out of niceness is to utter words that are expressive and honest, to challenge yourself to say what you mean with exactness. Niceness is about miscommunication, about not communicating what you think and feel. Therefore, transformation demands that you become conscious of what you say, leaving no words to habit and being clear in what you do say.

A client, Carina, related her memory of her Grade 5 teacher who gave the class an exercise to list all synonyms for the word *nice* that they could find, and to take *nice* out of their vocabularies. The teacher was coaching them away from using lazy language by focusing on the word so many of us use with great frequency. In all likelihood she knew that if you perform the exercise of eliminating the word *nice* from your conversation you will find that in your search for substitutes you will be forced to think about what you mean.

If we allow ourselves to use lazy language it means we do not think about what we are saying, that we do not *want* to think about what we are saying and doing. Our language is lush with words and modes of expression. A dearth of tools is not the reason we limit our vocabularies. At the same time, it is difficult if not impossible to express oneself with clarity and honesty and still be lazy. To express ourselves in this way means we must take charge, resolve our inner conflicts about niceness, and stop pretending. If fears about revealing too much of yourself are inhibiting you, be assured the fear is disproportionate to the reality. Most people are more concerned about themselves in these exchanges and may even learn from your handling of the situation.

An immediate result of the movement away from lazy language might, ironically, be silence. If you are reflecting on your speech, searching for appropriate words, the process may, at first, hinder your conversation. This setback is temporary. The search for expressive, accurate language becomes easier with practice.

The long-term benefits of banning lazy language from your vocabulary far outweigh any initial difficulties. As you examine your speech for lazy words and phrases and think about accurate substitutes you begin to know yourself better. Lazy language lets you hide from yourself, whereas precise expression is a conscious act. You must know your thoughts and feelings before you can turn them into language. And as you search for words to describe your thoughts and feelings you come to know them better. As you give up lazy language, speaking out becomes easier because you begin to understand what it is you can contribute to a conversation. You are forced to think before you speak,

THE TYRANNY OF NICENESS

not to silence yourself but to be certain that you are saying what you want to say and to understand how it will be heard. You invest time, thought, and effort in your communication and award it the value it deserves. Then speak with confidence.

Giving up niceness and lazy language means speaking what is true and honest for you, being emotionally and intellectually accurate, and avoiding equivocation. This does not mean that you spill your emotional concerns any time someone asks, for example, "How are you?" Only if it is relevant for you to do so would you speak about what you are feeling and what is happening in your life. And then it is important to remain true to yourself. If you wish to be private, there are ways of addressing the question with truth and honesty. Perhaps the person asking is not emotionally close to you and you feel uncomfortable because you are not feeling well but do not want to speak about it with this person. The truthful and honest answer, spoken in a polite but firm tone, may be, "I am not feeling as well as I would like but that is something I do not feel comfortable talking about." You do not need to comply with a real or perceived request from the other for more information, for then you would be denying your own real, multi-layered situation. You do not need to comply by telling what you would rather keep private, by lying, implying you might talk at another time about what is happening to you, or by pretending a closeness that does not exist for you. On the other hand, you do not need to be rude and disrespectful. What makes a response such as this one easier to say and for the other to accept is your direct and kind delivery.

CHOOSE   WHEN   TO   COMPLY

Terry had been married for fifteen years when she came to see me. She was very sad and had been diagnosed by her family physician with depression and treated with antidepressants. Her weight had increased to uncomfortable proportions and she could not motivate herself to look for work. We had been meeting in sessions for just over one year when she came to the realization I mentioned earlier: her symptoms of depression had recurred when she disobeyed her physician's orders and subsided immediately when she complied by taking an antidepressant pill — when she did what she was told. That epiphany was very important in her progress toward healing because she realized how powerful were the influences of certain authority figures in her life, but it was only the beginning. In the next few months she attempted to make changes in her life, to set a path of productivity that she had not been able to achieve for some time. She was a potter, working freelance out of her home, but before she came to see me she had let her business drain away when she became depressed. After the insight she experienced swallowing the pill she had some minor success, and with the help of a friend who found commissions for her, she began to work in her home studio again.

Terry had been working through a weekend and needed to finish a job on Monday. When her husband arrived home at four o'clock she asked if he could take care of their sons until six o'clock so she could finish the job. He refused. She was stunned. Zach had always been supportive — a sentiment she had repeated to me in sessions during the entire first year of our work together. He would encourage her to have a business at home or to take classes to enhance her health or her skills. But that moment of his rudeness and non-support jarred into focus what had actually happened in their relationship. Zach's support was mostly lip service, and when the fog cleared for Terry she could see that the reason she had crashed into depression and lethargy was burnout. She had been working at home, earning as much money as her husband, working into the night because her days were disrupted with childcare, cooking dinner, and cleaning.

Zach's refusal to help her that day shocked Terry. When she married him her mother had warned him that she did not cook or clean, yet she had taken on all the house duties as well as working full-time, and more, at her pottery business. Zach often said he was going to do things but did not. He'd go to work at seven o'clock, arrive home at four o'clock, and nap until dinner was prepared.

Terry had been a feisty young girl. Gifted artistically, she enrolled in an art college against her parents' wishes. Her talent and hard work had always brought jobs to her. She had a strong sense of fairness and had once pounded on the door of the parish priest's home and confronted him on his position against a group home in the neighbourhood. How could he claim to care for all people if he held this view? she wondered. As a young girl Terry had spoken up in support of what she believed. So how did she end up in such a stereotypical situation, unable to get what she needed for herself?

Terry related the story of her wedding. She and her husband had had a good relationship until it came time to prepare for the wedding. During the year leading up to the wedding she experienced panic attacks. She was prescribed medication by her physician, with whom she spoke on a regular basis. Three weeks before the wedding her condition deteriorated and she was sent to see a psychiatrist. Terry felt his single-minded purpose was to get her through the wedding rather than to listen to what she was really feeling. He called her symptoms bridal anxiety, told her the condition was common, and gave her even more medication. Despite all the medicine, she was so anxious that on her wedding day she had her attendant carry the pills in the event she needed more. After the wedding she shed her gown and went on an unhappy honeymoon. She continued to see the psychiatrist for five years until she was finally off medication. Fifteen years later her wedding dress was still soiled from that day and she could not bear to look at the photographs.

As she recounted her story to me about her awakening she also expressed anger with the physician and psychiatrist who had treated her at the time.

"They should have told me not to get married," she said. "My family, Zach's family — they were too close, but I was telling both doctors what I was going through and they did not advise me to call it off."

Despite Terry's strengths and ability to confront people, in the realm of her private life all the models affecting her life had pointed to compliance, to being the bride. She sensed this was not for her but could not act on her feelings. She could not imagine another way of living her life with the man she loved, but her psyche and body rebelled when she complied with the expectations of a family rooted in the traditions of their culture of origin. In the absence of support for her own deep feelings, she collapsed under the pressure of maintaining the facade.

From our first session Terry knew what she had to do. In fact, she knew before that, but she needed validation and support in order to carry through. In this intimate area of her life she had doubted her judgment because the world of her family traditions had a design for her that did not fit with her feelings. Acting against that design felt disrespectful, and so she had been paralyzed.

Years later Zach's refusal to support her request for a more equitable partnership and working situation came as a rude awakening, but it was one she experienced as "a small miracle." She thanked her husband for his rudeness because it made her see how unkind she had become to herself, how she had failed to be her own advocate. She had taken on the expectations of others, become mired in guilt for not wanting to do everything and for becoming burnt out when she tried to live up to the expectations.

Following her insight, Terry told her husband in a no-nonsense way that she needed nine hours each weekday to work, as he did. She would take nine to six as her hours, and he would watch the boys between four and six after school. Then she would prepare dinner. But she soon realized the unfairness in that arrangement and insisted they share dinner preparation. He tested her resolve, as families and friends do, because when people make changes they disrupt an entrenched, finely tuned — if unproductive, frustrating, and depressing — system, but she held firm. She changed. She tidied her workspace and brightened it with flowers, became productive in her work again, and as a bonus found she could resist overeating.

Had Terry chosen not to comply with the advice and treatment of her doctors and listened instead to her own wisdom her life might have been very different. However, she was so confused by messages from the important people in her life that her own voice could not be strong. Knowing when to comply and when not to comply and giving oneself permission to make the choice is the great challenge of transformation. People to whom we go for advice and help usually want to do their best for us. They are, however, subject to the same problems as you and I, the same lapses of awareness of themselves and the world around them. They can be helpful only to the extent that they have progressed themselves. They are not super-humans, just human. We cannot expect them to relieve us of the responsibility we must take for ourselves. We must judge whether to accept their advice and assistance by examining, with a brutal honesty, what we know about them, what we feel about them, what we know about our own needs and capacities. This requires a trust in our own judgment. If you hire a personal trainer to design an exercise program for you and you know that you will not last because the program is too time-consuming or inconvenient there is no point in accepting the advice. Better to explain your lifestyle, the time you have available, and your level of commitment so an appropriate program can be made for you. If the trainer is unable to do so you will need to find a new one.

When you inform yourself and then choose to comply with a request or advice you become active in the exchange. You take charge of the situation and its impact on your life in a way that is not possible in the darkness of not knowing. To comply in as conscious a way as possible you must know when to trust authority. It means questioning, not silencing, and it means knowing your own needs.

SAY THE UNSAYABLE

George Orwell said, "If liberty means anything at all it means the right to tell people what they do not want to hear." As you give up niceness, liberty will also come to mean being able to say those things you have found the hardest to say. Lara, who was so ready to take responsibility for the auto accident, has worked a long time in therapy to arrive at an emotional place where she is able to voice her honest thoughts and feelings, most times. Being outspoken makes her feel "bitchy" she says, but she adds that it also feels "empowering." She is feeling freer, less anxious, and less angry. When she feels angry the source is clearer and she is more able than in the past to resolve her anger or to prevent it from spilling into inter-actions where it does not belong.

Using different words, a friend, Ellen, expressed sentiments similar to Lara's. Ellen had lived with her mother for many years, taking care of her and scheduling her life around the aging woman's needs. This meant that elaborate arrangements sometimes had to be made when Ellen travelled on business or wanted to enjoy a weekend with friends, but she loved her mother, was dedicated to her, and made these preparations without resentment. For Ellen, the work was a labour of love. The time came, however, when her mother was in her late eighties and in need of more intensive care. She required medication at frequent intervals and could not be counted on to remember to take it. She was becoming feeble, and her safety while at home alone during the day was a concern. After a great deal of soul-searching, agonizing over the mere thought of finding residential care for her mother, Ellen faced reality: she could no longer continue to care for her. With deep sadness and worry about the risk of upsetting her mother and causing further deterioration to her condition, she said the unsayable. She told her mother that she was looking for a place for her to live where she would have around-the-clock care. As she imagined, her mother was upset. However, the upset was temporary, and, in hindsight, Ellen believed her mother must have known the move was necessary.

As in Lara's situation, the result of speaking difficult words meant liberation for Ellen. Her mother was situated in a comfortable setting, the care was attentive, she was eating three hot meals each day, and she had people around her to talk with all day, if she wanted. Ellen had taken care to ensure that her mother's new home was an appropriate and nurturing setting. When she realized that her mother was well situated, her relief at knowing her mother was safe, well fed, and happy evolved into a sense of freedom. She purchased a new home, based on her own needs, ate when and what she felt like, took up opportunities to socialize with friends after work, and began to live her own life. She visited her mother twice each week and was able to enjoy her when she did.

The hub of transformation is kindness. Being kind to others on a small scale, on a day-to-day basis, is important. Although she would never have guessed it, Ellen's candour with her mother was an act of kindness. She liberated herself but also her mother, who had been spending a great deal of time alone, dependent wholly on Ellen and on occasional visits from other relatives and friends. In her new home, she had the attention and company she needed.

Although Terry felt anything but kind when she said the unsayable to her husband, Zach, her words, too, were an act of kindness. After years of struggling with her unhappiness she finally told Zach that when they married she'd had strong feelings that she should not do it. To her surprise, this revelation did not destroy him. Although he felt hurt, he was able to accept her admission. Perhaps her words validated something he had always understood but had never heard articulated. To Terry's surprise, her words did not destroy her marriage. Having spoken the thought that lingered unsaid all those years, Terry felt relieved and empowered in her honesty. She moved out of passivity, became more accepting of her own needs, and asked for more help and consideration from Zach. He responded, sometimes with resistance, but generally with co-operation. Together with their children they developed a new lifestyle that served them all better.

MOBILIZE INDIGNATION

Learning to say the unsayable to family and friends is the hardest step for some people but a first step for others. For some, speaking with candour to their families presents the greatest emotional hurdles. Others struggle to be direct with their friends. Speaking in public causes near-universal angst. There are times, however, when, to be true to oneself rather than be silenced, it is important to speak out.

From the beginning of our training we learn in different ways not to be whistle-blowers, not to stand up and protest in the face of opposition. With our intensive training in obedience it takes courage to break out of the patterns we are encouraged to adopt — to look away, not hear, tell white lies, and lie by omission. Betty Krawczyk spends time in jail because she refuses to stop her protests against logging policies. She is more concerned about the future of all species that depend on the forest to live than her own comfort. Learning to stand alone when necessary, in order to be true to ourselves, is an important part of transforming ourselves out of niceness.

Kindness on a larger scale means pursuing some who are doing damage in the world, to other people, or to the environment. Sometimes it means raising your voice in protest when social injustices occur. Sometimes it means criticizing leaders on both local and global levels when they are not living up to their charge. Sometimes it means taking a stand and risking criticism, joining community projects for the betterment of yourself and your neighbours.

If you wonder whether it is worth the risk and effort, ask yourself, What better legacy can we leave our children and succeeding generations than to create a better world for them — to *leave a world* for them? Let us see beyond our own front doors, for ourselves but also for our children. They are important and need jobs and we want them to have a good life. But think, as well, about the need for a sense of purpose, a sense of doing something meaningful in their lives, something beyond acquiring material goods. Let us not assist them in languishing in apathy. Let us show them a way to be significant human beings by raising our own voices and being actively kind and respectful of ourselves, other people, and the world we all share, even if that means stepping on some toes and saying things we were always too afraid to say. With this good example, our children may find the way out of niceness, too.

Freeing ourselves from niceness means being authentic. Sometimes that means taking risks, and sometimes it means taking the filler out of our lives. Sometimes it means seeing beyond our own front doors, looking hard and mobilizing the indignation we feel when we see people hurting each other or the world we inhabit. It means confronting oneself — on the premise that it is simply not acceptable to not know yourself, to not know the damage you are inflicting on others. It means confronting others, with respect, when they say or do something hurtful to you.

RELEASE PASSION

After years of dishonesty and layering niceness upon niceness, passion fizzles. It is not possible to please everyone and remain a passionate person, because by its very nature passion is an individual expression. What arouses your passion may appeal to some but not to others. Passion requires expression to stay alive. Even though passionate self-expression is exciting for those who witness it, its sustained appeal is limited to those who share the views expressed. Niceness and passion are uneasy bedfellows, but it is passionate expression that makes us feel alive and vital, so if limiting one's appeal is the price, it seems worthwhile. For Marcus, it was.

Marcus was living a fairly typical city-dweller's life when he came to see me. He was married but did not feel fulfilled by the marriage and was uncertain of its future. The son of a school principal, whose school he attended, Marcus had grown up feeling the pressure of image maintenance. He always heard the messages from his father that he had to set a standard for the other students, and that he was never to embarrass his father with disobedience. In adulthood, Marcus had conservative, passive-behaving friends whom he enjoyed well enough at dinners and evenings out. He suffered from low-grade, chronic unhappiness and anxiety and was apathetic about work. "Out of the blue" his wife left him for a much younger man. Marcus was shocked and hurt, but he survived, succeeded in maintaining a friendship with his wife, and began to put his life back together, adjusting to being single and alone.

Then he fell hard for a passionate woman. He began to feel more alive with her than he had ever felt before. With her, he felt opened to possibilities, both in his career and personal life. He took up distance running and fitness and confronted himself in areas of his professional life where he had felt lacking and began to make changes there. The romance that began with intensity seemed to hold promise for a future. Marcus was hoping for that. The woman he loved was a roller coaster of feelings and actions, just what he thought he needed in order to unleash the outrageous in him, but ultimately she was unable to commit to him. For more than a year he vacillated between tears and a feeling of being on top of the world.

The relationship did not survive, though Marcus learned a lot about his own contributions to his relationships before it ended. He also made an important connection. He accessed the part of himself that had been missing for years before, the passion he felt inside but had suppressed in his lifestyle and relationships, maintaining an image, as he had been taught to do. In his past his only outlet for "living out loud" was to lose his inhibitions, on occasion, through alcohol. Marcus knew, after this revealing relationship, that he needed to keep accessing the passion he now understood and felt so distinctly and continue letting it help him move through his life in a fulfilling way. He believed it would be the key to his success in relationships and business, and indeed, as he internalized this lesson, he found himself passionate about work, more expressive of his opinions without the assistance of alcohol, and standing on firmer emotional ground.

When we silence self-expression we suppress our passion. Passion is fuel that helps us fulfill our potential, and by suppressing it we place limitations on our possibilities. To keep them alive and to develop them we must keep the flame of passion burning.

The most fundamental expression of passion is through your voice. This is also the most obvious victim of niceness. Raising your voice is basic to letting go of niceness and releasing passion. Be another Monica Seles. She kept on grunting despite the name-calling she endured and the knife in her back. She would not be silenced, and she kept on competing. Release your own voice. Find a comfortable venue and work on your yell. Become familiar with the full extent of the power of your voice. Take risks by exercising your voice in public places by contributing to discussions in public forums.

Your body is also integral to this part — releasing the passion — of your transformation. Your body supports your voice by providing the musculature and lubricants required to create sound. Your body is the house for all your functions, and if it is unhealthy and weak it demands attention. In its best state, it frees you up to think, feel, and express yourself to the best of your potential. Therefore, you must feed your body, but feed it well. Quality food in adequate amounts is the required fuel. Insufficient nourishment, poor-quality food in excess, or even excellent food in excess is anathema to the body and all it houses. If you are to experience and express your passion you must free up your body to assist that experience.

You will find that as you release your passion through your voice your range of expression will become much more satisfying. Whether you are a person of ideas or manual skills, you will begin to express the possibilities you could only intuit before. Ideas are generated when we share, not when we work in insular competition. To share means not to give something up as you were expected to do as a child, but to open up, to trust and to speak. It means releasing, not suppressing, the passion that fuels creativity. In speaking of creativity I am not limiting my meaning to the visual arts, although painting, drawing, or sculpting may be wonderful products of your passion. We can be creative in a multitude of ways, every day. Once you decide not to silence yourself, many shackles fall away and your creativity can be called into service to forge direct and honest interactions with other people.

If you feel limited by your friends or surroundings or workplace, you may try expressing yourself to them, in them, in different ways. If the sense of limitation remains or increases, you may have to move on to people and places that support your passion, who are willing to hear you and who will be open to your creative approaches. For some people, creativity may be nothing less than reconfiguring their lifestyle, perhaps with a move from the city to the country, a change of occupation, or a reconceptualization of their life's work. It may mean reorganizing the priorities in their life to include more time for love and pleasure. Others may find their passion leads them to critiquing the world and its leaders, or contributing time to their community.

Releasing passion may lead some into a deeper sense of their own spirituality. Although many people desire a connection with something greater than themselves, they may feel they must be loyal to the traditions of their parents and their past. Or they may simply not know how to search out something more satisfying for themselves. As they mitigate their angst about being disobedient by staying on the path they have always known, they also mute their spirits.

Releasing passion enables you to see and act on possibilities that you may have felt but ignored in the past because you were too nice to risk failure and the judgment of others.

NOT-NICE PARENTING

You who are parents are presented with a golden opportunity to begin breaking the cycle of niceness in your families by raising your children to be heard, to value their own opinions while taking the opinions of others into consideration, and to make their own judgments and decisions, free of blind obedience to authority. This opportunity means you must critically examine the models of parenting with which you were raised, think about the effects you feel, and determine which approaches can be followed and which must be discarded. You will need to be creative in searching out new ways of raising your children and you will need to decide that no other job is so important as parenting your children and then live by that belief.

There can be a significant discrepancy between what parents think they are telling their children and what they are actually conveying to them, a point I made in an earlier chapter. Children often interpret as criticism suggestions that parents make in attempts to spare their children effort and tough learning. Sometimes parents wishing to tell their children difficult information may neglect to tell them enough, with disastrous results.

Simon, a long-term client in psychotherapy, felt guilty about almost everything, and a story he told about an event that occurred when he was ten years old sheds light on some of the reasons. At that time, Simon was attending cub scouts and playing on sports teams. One day, when he was playing in a baseball game, his father took him aside between innings and told him that he could no longer attend the scout group. His father gave no reason nor opportunity for discussion and the news came as a complete surprise to Simon. What was he to think? With no information and no invitation to ask questions about the decision, Simon did what most children would do under the circumstances: he blamed himself. Automatically assuming he was being punished for doing something wrong he wracked his young brain to make sense of the situation, wondering whether he had neglected schoolwork or some duties at home.

These thoughts did not disappear over time. Although he did not think about the event on a daily basis, as he grew into adulthood he would frequently remember the situation and wonder what he had done wrong. The matter lingered as unfinished psychological business. It was two decades later when the truth was revealed to him. The scoutmaster had been caught molesting some of the boys in the troop, the real reason his parents had taken him out of it. His parents had been right in protecting him, but their inability to talk about the reason left him with a sense of guilt, of having done something very wrong. No other reason for such an abrupt end to a privilege came to mind. Since he did not know what it was he had done wrong he could not correct his error. Instead, he lived for decades believing he had been responsible in some unknown way for being deprived of something he loved to do.

The process was both shaming and guilt-inducing. Perhaps even worse, Simon realized that his father had inadvertently deprived him of the opportunity to disclose an incident of sexual abuse that had taken place just two months prior to his father's news. Simon had been playing with some children his age and one older boy in a park near home. The older boy had led him away from the others under the guise of play and had then molested him in a nearby garage. When the boy finally let him go, Simon headed for home but kept the terrible news to himself. One didn't talk about such things in his family. Simon was unable to tell anyone of this event for decades, but the shame, humiliation, and guilt did not leave him, and we worked for many months together before he was able to mitigate some of the long-term effects of the abuse and the secrecy surrounding it.

A difficult aspect of parenting is to overcome the inhibitions we bring to the task. Simon's story illustrates one unfortunate effect of parents' inability to discuss sexual functioning, and perversity, with their children. They can be so concerned with their own embarrassment that they cannot imagine what it might be like for their children to be deprived of the information. In Simon's case the effect was devastating and resistant to the passage of time.

PARENTS: MODEL AND LISTEN

Your own transformation out of niceness is your goal, but your children will benefit from your efforts as well. One of the most effective ways of training your children away from niceness is to let them see you interact in a direct manner with other people and to allow them to experience you as an honest, authentic person who also happens to be a parent. Although parents mean well with their good advice to their children, parents' own actions say much more to their children. Children watch their parents and feel the sting of broken promises and dishonesty. But we live in a culture that places value on shortcuts. We have little time to spare, and so shortcut parenting is a temptation, and being direct and honest all the time will seem time-consuming and tedious. We are accustomed to telling children what we think will be time-saving, labour-saving, and will move our agendas along. Those agendas often include lessons and commitments that we believe will make our children's lives easier or richer when they grow up. Maybe they will, but on the other hand, maybe they create stress for the children and sway them from their own intuitive sense of what is right and meaningful for them. Parents who help them explore the activities that excite and engage them are assisting the child away from niceness that could otherwise stand in the way of his or her fulfillment in adulthood.

We need to give up giving good advice to our children. At least, we must give up this habit until we get to know them in such a way that we can understand what they need from us. We often become so wrapped up in our agendas for our children and in our good intentions for them that we fail to listen well to them. We think we know who they are because we birthed them and have cared for them all their lives, but often we see them more as extensions of ourselves or as fulfillers of our own unfulfilled dreams. Beyond the margins of safety, we need to give up advice-giving and instructing and instead listen to them and get to know who they are. Their words are the windows through which we can really see them, if we take the time. If we fail to hear them accurately, we silence them because we cannot respond in a fitting manner and they will eventually stop talking to us.

You may believe that you already do listen to your children. Just to be sure, test yourself with the following: When your children start talking to you, do you stop what you are doing and make eye contact with them? Do you let them say what they have to say without interruption? Do you listen for words of distress, pleasure, anger, sadness, hope? Do you validate these feelings and open the children to themselves by naming the feelings and not trying to extinguish them? Do you encourage them to say more? Or do you attempt to remove any so-called negative feelings by telling your children everything will be "okay," or some variation on that theme? When we reassure too much, chances are we may miss a chance to simply validate children's feelings. Our attempts to mitigate the feelings are often more about our own discomfort than the children's discomfort.

If you are one of the fortunate parents or other adults in whom children confide, you may already realize that what they tell you is a sacred trust. When a child pours his or her heart out to you the best thing you can do is cherish the communication, the worst is to betray their trust by repeating what they have told you. A friend recounted the story of his relationship with an aunt who became his favourite because she was an attentive listener and seemed sympathetic to his struggles with his parents. One day he became involved in a dispute with his mother about his wish to go to Florida with friends during a school break. Backing up her position against the trip, his mother said, "Aunt Blanche says you hate going to Florida." When he learned that his aunt had repeated to his parents what he had told her about his dislike of visiting relatives in Florida he was appalled. Adding insult to injury, his mother used this to her advantage by twisting the essence of the betrayed confidence. It is no surprise that he stopped confiding in his aunt after that exchange. Even worse, stinging from her betrayal, it was many years before he felt comfortable revealing much of his inner world to anyone again.

Listening well and validating children's feelings may well be one of the most difficult tasks of parenting or being a friend to children in our lives. We want what we believe is best for our children. We want them to have lives free of physical and emotional pain. We want them to have success and reach their maximum potential. But our attempts to supply these things often lead us down a path that does not meet the children's deepest needs. What children require most for healthy emotional development is to be heard and to have their feelings validated. They need to be heard as we might hear some esteemed orator, with our full, rapt attention. They need to be believed when they are afraid or angry and defended in the face of authority figures who have been unfair or misunderstanding. They need to be encouraged with direct questions to make their own analyses of the situations they talk about. They need to be drawn out rather than stopped up with advice, no matter how good it may seem, with suggestions, no matter how relevant they may be, or even with praise, if it does not reflect what the children think is praiseworthy. As Alice Miller said, and D. W. Winnicott before her, children need one person in early childhood who will not abandon them if they express their feelings. Children who are taken seriously in this way will be able to meet the world on their own terms.

Parents have many opportunities to validate their children's real feelings and thoughts. Rather than abandoning them emotionally by not listening and taking the children seriously, they can stay with their children by listening and reflecting back so children know they have been heard. Children have an amazing capacity to move themselves along if their feelings are validated. If they are heard instead of being taught to be nice, they have a chance of becoming honest, kind, fulfilled adults. If their parents are attempting to move themselves along to a better way of communicating, that, too, will have a supportive and modelling effect on the children. This means that parents are honest with children when they disagree with them and state, with respect, their reasons to the children. It also means that parents refuse to confirm other people's lies to their children, and they will confront the offenders on behalf of their children. Through these communications children will learn that they can express their thoughts and feelings to their parents, no matter how outrageous they may seem.

For parents to do this for their children may require some retraining. To begin, parents must be honest with themselves about their expectations for their children and assess the reality of them. Parents must also be honest with each other and agree on the limits of their support for each other. Young Brad was devastated when his reaction to his mother's gift of a colour-by-number book seemed to hurt his mother's feelings. To make matters worse, his father scolded him for his honest reaction. How different that event might have been for Brad if his father had reassured him that although his mother was upset she would recover and still love him, even though he did not like her gift. Another client, Gerry, was full of guilt that she believed could easily have been resolved if only her mother had admitted that marriage to Gerry's father was a mistake. In the absence of such an admission, Gerry carried the weight of her father's pain as if it were her own. Parents need to be brave and know that it may be their own niceness that is getting in the way if they are unable to advocate for their children with authority figures. The parents' failure to do so may result in the unintended message that children should always be silent and obedient to authority.

Parents will find that if one slips into a white lie or a broken promise the other may still validate the child's reality, rather than attempting to cover up by agreeing with the lie or justifying the broken promise. They can enhance trust and a sense of security when they are consistent in the things their children hear them say outside the home and inside the home. If there are great differences, parents must address their own blind spots and issues about image making. Children need parents who provide them with a strong, united environment, but it must be one that validates the children's reality. Parents who are united in their lies to their children, no matter how well intentioned, will leave them feeling unsupported and invalidated.

Parents can act as effective advocates for their children, paving the way for them to speak and express their thoughts and feelings. The encouragement they offer after understanding what the children's foci are, the listening they do, and the support for their children's own ideas and accomplishments are all inducements for the children to speak and act authentically. Children will learn that they can trust their home environment. That trust is something they can hold inside them so they have no need to succumb to niceness in the external world. They will know that if someone approaches them in a way that feels uncomfortable, their parents will hear their concern. They will learn that if someone — including a teacher — is bullying them at school their parents will listen to their fears and hurt and believe the seriousness of the problem. They will learn that their parents will share their joy in what they believe to be their accomplishments.

This is a tall order for parents. It amounts to striving to live an exemplary life and suppressing some of the responses to your children that have seemed appropriate in the past. Expressed in another, perhaps less formidable way, it amounts to becoming as honest, direct, and authentic as possible and encouraging, with your example and respect, your children to be the same way. The wonderful thing about being a parent is that new ways of parenting can be applied no matter how old the child.

GIVE UP NICENESS AND MOVE ON

There are many stories of transformation among the clients I have mentioned throughout this book. Brad, who as a child was so distressed by his mother's reaction to his outspoken dislike of the colouring book she gave him, grew up to be the quintessential "nice guy." He struggled to find his own path in his relationships, his sexual orientation, and his work but was able to learn to be an authentic intimate partner and to succeed in his chosen field. Andrew, who had been unable to form his opinions without first observing what others thought, had been depressed and ready to leave his marriage, believing that separation might be the only way to pull himself out of the mire of his inauthenticity. As he grew stronger he renewed his commitment to his marriage and gained confidence in his own capabilities as a husband, father, employee, and friend. Terry created a remarkable change in herself and her relationship with her husband. She eventually found a new variation on her career, one in which she moved out of the isolating work of her studio. She developed a more satisfying relationship with a friend whose lead she had always followed. She learned to understand the differences between them and to value her own points of view and ideas rather than assuming her friend's were superior.

Olivia was a client whose story satisfies the challenge that a life without niceness is not only possible, but rewarding as well. She was forty years old when she came to me for help. She indicated that the problems she was experiencing included stress at work that was pushing her towards burnout, uncertainty about the direction of her career, and personal issues related to these. A psychologist who had never married or had children, Olivia had moved to Toronto several years earlier from the west to pursue a career with a school board, believing that the work would offer greater security than any she could find in her home city. Her desire to escape from the long arm of parental involvement was also a motivating factor.

Although she enjoyed the children she worked with and felt she was competent in her assessments of them, she had discovered that the pace of work and the bureaucratic impediments to providing the kind of service she wanted to give were taking their toll. Her health was suffering and she was embroiled in emotional conflict about her future. In relation to these workplace problems and other issues in her life, she was always weighing the advantages and disadvantages of staying in Toronto versus returning to her home city.

Adding to her conflict was the man, Jamie, with whom Olivia had carried on a long-distance relationship since she made the move. Jamie was a former military chaplain who was working as a counsellor in a community agency in her home city. He was an alcoholic whose binges continued despite all of Olivia's efforts to help him stop drinking. They had never lived together or discussed marriage, but it had been Olivia's hope that, in time, Jamie would join her in Toronto. To this end, she made frequent trips to see him and took most of the responsibility for nurturing the relationship. She believed in him, she said, and his potential to be a good partner, if only he would stop drinking. On occasion, he fed her hope for a happy future together by sobering up and making the trip to Toronto to spend a weekend with her.

Olivia was the younger of two children of a criminal lawyer who was well known in his community. Her mother had stayed home with her and her older brother, and appearances would suggest that theirs was an ideal family. They lived in a lovely home in one of the best neighbourhoods, Olivia and her brother were sent to good schools, and the parents had important social connections and were respected in the community. They were a "nice" family. Behind the facade lay her father's alcoholism, her mother's passivity, and her brother's inclination to bully his younger sister.

In a material sense, Olivia's childhood was privileged, but other aspects of it were disturbing. Her father was not often home except to sleep, and when he was home, the family was forced to tiptoe through the house because he would be working in his study. No one spoke more than a rare word or inference about her father's drinking or even hinted that it might be a problem. Her mother was not responsive to Olivia's complaints about either the silence that was expected in the house or her brother's bullying. Rather than discipline her brother, her mother and sometimes her father would berate her for being a whiner. She became the identified problem in the family and was sent for counselling. Olivia felt she had no allies. Her mother, who had never been a source of support, was, in Olivia's mind, "null and void."

In her teen years and adulthood, Olivia's frustration expressed itself in self-destructive ways. She began to experiment with drugs and alcohol at an early age. Feeling that the important relationships in her life were beyond her control, she resorted to controlling herself instead, through her eating habits, and she became anorexic. In hindsight, the only beacon of hope during that period was school. Olivia always attended her classes, achieved top grades, and was selected to be valedictorian for her secondary school graduating class. She went on to university and majored in psychology. She continued to achieve, remarkably so, because as hard as she worked during the week, so did she party on the weekends. Almost anything was possible in the interest of giving herself relief from the restrictions and pressures she felt during the week — alcohol, hallucinogenic drugs, wild dancing, and compromising sexual practices. Control snapped into place during the school week when she became a serious student once again. She carried on two different lives, one for public viewing and one for private binges with a tough group of people whom she befriended.

When Olivia became a psychologist she changed her lifestyle. Feeling duty-bound to be respectable she gave up drugs, drinking, and dancing and settled for a restricted personal schedule. She worked long hours, lunched on occasion with friends, went shopping or to movies, and clung to the relationship with Jamie. She was conscious of maintaining appearances, mimicking her family's way of presenting its face to the public. She left herself with no outlets for expression of the passion or relief from her anger because she feared encountering clients in public venues. The life she created was one fashioned on the family model and it left her feeling empty, much as life within her family had. Work became her primary focus but it was not satisfying, and there were holdovers from her past. She still felt like the errant child to her parents, who, with increasing frequency, would telephone to let her know what they thought she should be doing with her life. Nor was her relationship with her brother resolved. A corporate lawyer, he had moved to Toronto to study and remained there to develop his career. He was married with two children. In adulthood, Olivia attempted to develop the relationship into one that would be satisfying for them both, and this was one of the reasons she had chosen to move to Toronto. However, tensions remained, and the brother was no source of comfort for her as she attempted to make choices about her life. On the contrary, his bullying assumed an adult form. She would arrange meetings with him to attempt to further the relationship but these would turn into opportunities for him to criticize her lifestyle and choices. Still, she clung to the hope that they could have a loving relationship and that he would understand her and support her attempts to become more independent.

Olivia's adoption of the restrictions of niceness were evident in her appearance. She dressed meticulously and carried herself with a degree of caution that belied the passion and energy that lay inside her. Her demeanour was controlled, and she was careful in her choice of words. She was not a stranger to counselling and psychotherapy as a client, having been in treatment in her late teens and early twenties for substance abuse and her eating disorder. But even though she came to see me and was willing to engage in psychotherapy she was skeptical of the process. Her ongoing questioning resembled her approach during the time she spent in drug rehabilitation earlier in her life when she was always critiquing the therapy. Yet she did engage in the process for over a year and during that time made remarkable progress.

Olivia's life had been driven by fear. As a student she had always been supported financially by her father. Although she held part-time jobs she was reliant — and encouraged to be reliant — on his largesse for funding her tuition and all other expenses. After graduating she worked in her profession, but her fear of being unable to take care of herself prevented her from taking professional risks or taking time for additional training that might have improved her financial prospects. The position she held with the school board provided a steady but modest income and her parents provided extras. In part, her fear was that she would never be free of this pattern of dependence. Her parents did nothing to encourage her to take risks. They offered her money even when she did not ask for it and encouraged her to stay with her job. Both they and her brother faulted her for the restlessness that had led her to move from job to job in her home-town before heading to Toronto.

A focus in her therapy was to address the issue of a possible move back to her home city. She had never felt comfortable in Toronto and missed the culture in which she had grown up. At the same time, whenever she floated the possibility to her parents or brother they accused her of following old patterns and making a move for the sake of moving. They wanted her to hold on to the security she had in her job.

Her first behavioural breakthrough came in a somewhat paradoxical way. She told me in a session that the previous weekend she had broken one of her taboos and gone dancing in a club and flirted with a man she met there. She said that nothing else had happened, that the experience was innocent, but it did allow her to get in touch with the passion she had always felt when she went dancing in her wild and uninhibited fashion. This event was significant because she went to the club fearing recognition from someone connected to her work and because she allowed herself to flirt with a man other than Jamie. It was a challenge to her way of presenting herself in public, which was to be nice. As we worked through some of her fears and other feelings related to family matters and Jamie, Olivia began to speak her mind. She told her mother to stop giving her advice about how to live her life. She told her father that she would not visit with them when she next visited the city unless he remained sober. She told Jamie that she would not stay with him on her next visit if he was drinking. And she became a less frequent caller to her brother, granting herself some distance from him in order to save herself from his criticism.

Throughout her psychotherapy I encouraged her to talk about her passions, her doubts about the work we were doing, and her struggles to find her strength in her relationships with family and Jamie. She needed to be able to say the unsayable, to be able to critique me, the symbolic parent, to receive support and encouragement to make difficult decisions, and to be validated for arriving at her own solutions. She stood firm on her position with respect to Jamie's drinking, and as she found that he was unable to meet her requirements she lessened her contact with him and eventually announced the end of their relationship.

Within a year of beginning our work together, Olivia made the decision to return to her home city and to pursue work she had long wished to do, play therapy with children, in private practice. She set about arranging for additional training in her home city to prepare herself and expected that within a year from the time she moved she would be ready to open a private practice. Anticipating that she might be lured back into a relationship with Jamie, as she had been several times in past years, she felt cautious but remained determined to hold firm in her decision. Her parents were hesitant to support the decision because they believed she was repeating a pattern, but they were also pleased to have her near them.

Olivia has kept in touch from time to time. She has reported that her return to home was the right decision and she felt she had been revitalized and surrounded by loved ones. She has managed to stay away from Jamie and forged a much more positive relationship with her parents, relating for the first time with them as adult to adult rather than as child to parent. Her studies progressed well, and she set up her private practice. She reported success and contentment with the quality of her work. In her last note she added that she had fallen in love with a man who she believed was good for her.

In any story of transformation there are many small victories and incremental changes. So it was for Olivia, whose progress was based on them. They allowed her to gain a foothold on her courage for the larger challenges: setting limits with her parents, letting go of a relationship and taking the risk of being single for life, giving up a job and moving to a new city without the promise of employment. The overarching aspect of her growth was the newfound ability to make decisions based on her own needs rather than the expectations of family, to allow herself to loosen the stranglehold she had placed on her own life. By breaking the barrier of her niceness, by insisting on taking the path she felt was right for her rather than the one determined for her by her family, Olivia transformed herself from a fearful, compliant, and conflicted individual to someone whose life was renewed and whose confidence in herself became consistent with the great potential she held within her. She had no promises of a better life when she challenged herself to follow a path that felt right to her. As it is when we make any change, we have no way of knowing what the exact impact of the change will be. Olivia took the risk to be authentic and act from her deepest needs and feelings without knowing what lay ahead. For her, the risk was worthwhile.

FROM NICE TO NOT-NICE

To be nice is to silence yourself in some way, whether it be in word or deed. It means obedience to authority without questioning the wisdom of the authority and whether being obedient is in your own best interests. Encouraging niceness — silence and obedience — in others means you will be unable to have an open and authentic relationship with them. The inclination to adopt niceness as a way of relating to other people is instilled in our psyches from infancy, and as we grow older it becomes an accepted part of us. Some of us become nicer than others in ways that our culture encourages and supports. Sometimes niceness is used as protection and sometimes to mask silenced agendas. For those who use it as protection, it is a self-perpetuating phenomenon in that its continuation depends on fear, especially the fear of non-acceptance. For those who use it as a mask, it is self-perpetuating to the extent that it works, or seems to work, to further our own agendas. Those who use it as protection cannot give up fear long enough to test other ways of being. Those who use it as a mask cannot give up their successes long enough to try other ways of meeting their own needs. Thus, people motivated by both reasons are caught in the tyranny of niceness, unable to free themselves and move on to more authentic ways of relating.

The impact of niceness on us as individuals and people in relationships is great, threatening the vitality of body and spirit. For most nice people, however, the impact amounts to a quiet alienation from one's self and other people and an inability to make decisions based on one's inner convictions. Letting go of niceness means giving up a particular way of relating, one that is based on inauthenticity. It means creating, instead, relationships that are based on direct, honest ways of relating. It means being scrupulously honest with oneself, even when facing uncomfortable confrontations with familiar ways of being, even when faced with guilt and self-loathing.

It is possible that anyone who attempts to leave niceness behind and move on to authentic relating will move through periods of emotional angst, as they look back with regret at past modes of behaviour. This is a necessary phase, one that signals progress, painful though it may be. Giving up niceness means becoming conscious of one's own thoughts and actions. This is not an easy task, but it is a necessary one if psychological growth is the desired outcome.

Letting go of niceness does not mean hurting people with unnecessary and attacking "truths." Although such outspokenness might be mistaken for authenticity in the early stages of transformation, it is not the goal. Attacking truths, when submitted to scrutiny, rarely exist on their own. More often, they are part of a larger phenomenon in which the speaker has not worked out the complete extent of his or her feelings about a person or matter. On their own, these truths are not completely honest.

I have suggested that niceness is a way of maintaining social order, and so a question emerges: Can a nation function without niceness and maintain social order? Will people keep peace, or will they create anarchy? In fact, the answer may be that the social order would improve and relationships of all kinds might improve if people acted from a place of authenticity, holding kindness as its core relational motivator.

If, in niceness, we feel coerced to do what we believe others want us to do — everyone from the agencies of social order to our families — anger, self-loathing, or apathy builds up because we cannot possibly meet everyone's expectations. If we learn what we truly require to live satisfying lives, give ourselves that much and let go of the rest, we have no reason to be violent or abusive or resentful. If we learn, for example, that we need to rest and take time with family and friends rather than get another job to carry the mortgage on a larger house, we may feel less stressed. If we take steps to release ourselves from obligation and focus on giving ourselves what we really need — rest and a social life, albeit in a more affordable home — we may find our lives becoming easier and more satisfying.

As we mature, we add layers to our personalities, layers of complexity that make us unique and add to our character. Giving up niceness means dispensing with a particular part of that complexity, a part that interferes with honest, direct relationships and makes us appear bland. We do not need to hide behind white lies or euphemisms to make ourselves acceptable. As thinking, feeling individuals we generate plenty of individual differences and complexity, yet remain similar enough to others to engage many people in satisfying relationships. We must trust ourselves that this is enough, that we do not need to place a wall of niceness between us and others to ensure acceptance. Giving up niceness means integrating the layers of personality and giving them expression, showing ourselves to the world in all our glorious uniqueness.

BIBLIOGRAPHY

Armstrong, Alison J. "When things fall apart: The rise and fall of electronic learning." *This*, November/December 2003.

Atwood, Margaret. "If You Can't Say Anything Nice, Don't Say Anything At All." In *Dropped Threads: What We Aren't Told*, edited by Carol Shields and Marjorie Anderson. Toronto: Vintage Canada, 2001.

Atwood, Margaret. *Cat's Eye*. Toronto: McClelland & Stewart, 1989.

Berry, Jason. *Lead Us Not Into Temptation: Catholic Priests and the Sexual Abuse of Children*. Urbana: University of Illinois Press, 2000.

Braiker, Harriet. *The Disease to Please: Curing the People-Pleasing Syndrome*. New York: McGraw-Hill, 2001.

Breggin, Peter. *The Ritalin Fact Book: What Your Doctor Won't Tell You About ADHD and Stimulant Drugs*. Cambridge, MA: Perseus Books, 2002.

Caplan, Paula. *They Say You're Crazy: How the World's Most Powerful Psychiatrists Decide Who's Normal*. Reading, MA: Perseus Books, 1995.

Cloutier-Steele, Lise. *Misinformed Consent: 13 Women Share Their Stories About Unnecessary Hysterectomy*. Toronto, ON: Stoddart Publishing Company, 2002.

Coelho, Paulo. *Veronika Decides to Die*. New York: HarperCollins Publishers, 1999.

Damasio, Antonio. *The Feeling of What Happens: Body and Emotion in the Making of Consciousness*. New York: Harcourt, Inc., 1999.

Gershon, Michael. *The Second Brain*. New York: Harper Collins, 1998.

Gertner, John. "The Futile Pursuit of Happiness." *The New York Times Magazine*, 7 September 2003.

Gilbert, Daniel, Elizabeth Pinel, Timothy Wilson, Stephen Blumberg, and Thalia Wheatley. "Immune Neglect: A source of durability bias in affective forecasting." *Journal of Personality and Social Psychology* 75, no. 3 (1998): 617-638.

Hancock, Jeffrey T., Jennifer Thom-Santelli, and Thompson Ritchie. "Deception and Design: The Impact of Communication Technologies on Lying Behaviour." In *Conference on Computer Human Interaction*, 130-136. New York: ACM, 2004.

Healy, David. *Let Them Eat Prozac*. Toronto: James Lorimer and Company Ltd., 2003.

Healy, David. *Psychiatric Drugs Explained*. London: Harcourt Publishers, 2002.

Healy, David. "When Psychopharmacology Goes Wrong." Toronto: Leading Edge Seminars, 2002.

Ivins, Molly, and Lou Dubose. *Bushwhacked: Life in George W. Bush's America*. New York: Random House, 2003.

Jacobs, Jane. *Systems of Survival: A Dialogue on the Moral Foundations of Commerce and Politics*. New York: Vintage Books, 1992.

Janis, Irving. *Groupthink*. 2nd ed. Boston: Houghton Mifflin, 1982.

Kirsch, Irving, and Guy Sapirstein. "Listening to Prozac but Hearing Placebo: A Meta-Analysis of Antidepressant Medication." American Psychological Association: *Prevention and Treatment Volume 1, Article 0002a*, 1998.

Lerner, Harriet. *The Dance of Deception: Pretending and Truth-telling in Women's Lives*. New York: Harper Collins, 1993.

Lippman, Paul. *Nocturnes: On Listening to Dreams*. New Jersey: The Analytic Press, 2000.

Mate, Gabor. *When the Body Says No: The Cost of Hidden Stress*. Toronto: Vintage Canada, 2003.

Meaney, Michael. "Stress and Disease: Who Gets Sick★Who Stays Well." Toronto: Cortext Educational Seminars, 2001.

Miller, Alice. *The Drama of the Gifted Child: The Search for the True Self*. New York: Harper Collins, 1997. Originally published in German as *Das Drama des begabten Kindes*, 1979, by Suhrkamp Verlag, Frankfurt am Main.

Morton, J. Bruce, and Sandra E. Trehub. "Children's Understanding of Emotion in Speech." *Child Development* 72, no. 3 (June 2001): 834-843.

Nova: Secret of Photo 51, first broadcast on 22 April 2003 by PBS. Directed and written by Gary Glassman.

Oppenheimer, Todd. *The Flickering Mind: The False Promise of Technology in the Classroom and How Learning Can Be Saved*. New York: Random House, 2003.

Perlow, Leslie, and Stephanie Williams. "Is Silence Killing Your Company?" *Harvard Business Review* 81, no. 5 (May 2003): 52-58.

Perlow, Leslie. *When You Say Yes But Mean No: How Silencing Conflict Wrecks Relationships and Companies.* New York: Crown Business, 2003.

Petrie, Anne. *Gone to an Aunt's: Remembering Canada's Homes for Unwed Mothers.* Toronto: McClelland & Stewart, 1998.

Petty, R.E., K.D. Williams, S.G. Harkins, and B. Latané. "Social inhibition of helping yourself: Bystander response to a cheeseburger." *Personality and Social Psychology Bulletin* 3, (1977): 571-574.

Postman, Neil. *Building a Bridge to the 18th Century: How the Past Can Improve Our Future.* New York: Alfred A. Knopf, 1999.

Ravitch, Diane. *The Language Police.* New York: Alfred A. Knopf, 2003.

Sternberg, Esther. *The Balance Within: The Science Connecting Health and Emotions.* New York: W.H. Freeman and Company, 2000.

Valenstein, Elliot. *Blaming the Brain: The Truth about Drugs and Mental Health.* New York: The Free Press, 1998.

Walker, Barbara. *Dancing Devil: My Twenty Years with Albert Walker.* Ayr, ON: MAC Publishing, 2002.

Wilson, Timothy, Jan Meyers, and Daniel Gilbert. "Lessons from the past: Do people learn from experience that emotional reactions are short-lived?" *Personality and Social Psychology Bulletin,* 27 (2001): 1648-1661.

Workforce data. Source: *The Contrarian: News & Comments on Women's Issues.*

Youngson, Robert, and Ian Schott. *Medical Blunders.* London, U.K.: Constable and Robinson, 1996.